RETHINK
YOUR WAY OF
THINKING

WISDOM FROM AN INVISIBLE
FATHER – THE SHEPHERD'S WAY

CAN QUANTUM SCIENCE TEACH US
ABOUT CONSCIOUSNESS AND HUMANITY?

SHAJAN K. NINAN

RETHINK YOUR WAY OF THINKING

**WISDOM FROM AN INVISIBLE
FATHER**—THE SHEPHERD'S WAY

SHAJAN K. NINAN

Library of Congress Cataloguing-in-Publication Data is available upon request.

ISBN
978-1-963539-01-1
978-1-963539-02-8

eBook - 978-1-963539-00-4

Dedication

To **Preeya S. Ninan**—my birthday gift for my child.

"Why Invisible Father?" may be a question that arises when reading my book. My unwavering belief in my child's potential helped make that potential a reality, giving her a degree of freedom in a patriarchal society. This book is like my child—I have invested my blood, sweat, and tears into it. Perhaps it will be the best thing I've ever created. I can now put my hands on my hips and say, *"I created it,"* and watch as this beautiful manifestation of myself takes on a life of its own and inspires people to **'rethink'—to reconsider or revise their opinions or beliefs**. This is the proudest moment in my life—a feeling of pride and accomplishment in creating the book. I remain invisible, not looking to be recognized.

Why Invisible Father?

The expression "invisible father" exudes a certain allure that captures people's curiosity. It's intriguing to observe how often we hear people lauding and venerating their mothers while their fathers seem to fade into obscurity, often unseen and unacknowledged.

It is the "*mother*" nature: our mothers bring us into this world. There is no life on this planet without our mothers. Their unconditional and selfless love, sacrifice, and care for their children make them unique, beautiful, and the most invaluable creation of God. As pivotal as a father's role is in raising a child, I am still bound to say that mothers deserve all the credit. Hence the subtitle *"invisible father."*

Contents

RETHINK
YOUR WAY OF
THINKING

Preface

"The problem is within, not outside" is a powerful expression that urges us to take a deeper look within ourselves for solutions to our mental and emotional struggles. This notion drives us to take accountability for our thoughts and actions and to engage in introspection. By acknowledging that the root of the problem lies within, we can seize control of our lives and make strides toward enhancing our mental well-being.

Through this debut, 'Rethink Your Way of Thinking,' Shajan Ninan provides a holistic view of life from his journey as a father, a husband, and an educator. *This book takes you on an emotional rollercoaster—evoking laughter, tears, and deep contemplation as you read.*

The book centers around a central theme: the perils of not loving ourselves first—the danger of giving away the power of our minds to external validation or external freedom and becoming victims of our environment. The author's insightful analysis of the destructive nature of human emotions and their manifestation in various settings such as classrooms, workplaces, families, and religious institutions inspires individuals to recognize and harness emotions for positivity and growth. He draws upon his life experiences and theories from sociology, psychology, quantum science, and neuroscience to instill a desire to seek our internal freedom and find a sense of purpose in life.

What makes us unique? We are all unique. There are no weak, dumb, bad, or evil people. We become vulnerable, dumb, or bad when we don't recognize our God-given value and succumb to the dark forces that pray and thrive on our insecurities. Humanity's gravest danger today is our inability to control our thoughts and emotions. The smart minority—the elites in our society—through news media, social media, and religious institutions exacerbate our feeling of deficiency within us and capitalize on our sufferings. He expounds on the power of being self-aware and conscious of our present in our pursuit of attenuating our sufferings and attaining happiness.

Instead of asking ourselves, "why me?" and resorting to destructive behavior in a spur-of-the-moment decision, we should ask ourselves what we can do to improve our lives. The beautiful version of ourselves is within us, but it's not the best version because the "best is yet to come." Creating that growth mindset is vital to finding peace within ourselves. For that, we need a vital group of people who can not only spot our "blind spots" but also help us fight the battles of life and build a better version of ourselves. That is the essence of oneness —we are all connected as one. *There are no self-made people on this planet.* He inspires you to ask yourself: "*What causes what and why?*" This powerful inquiry offers invaluable insights into our thought processes. Our way of thinking causes our suffering since we resist rethinking. This book persuades you to find the space and time to challenge your way of thinking, cultivate self-acceptance, and foster self-love.

Don't miss out on this life-changing journey! Transform yourself and make a difference in a child's life with this book. Your purchase supports a child's growth and sense of worth, creating a win-win opportunity to cultivate compassion. By scaling your self-compassion, you can make a meaningful difference in the lives of those who need it most.

Part One

We Are Being Conditioned

"We are brainwashed, conditioned, curated, indoctrinated, and photoshopped to fit in. These toxic mindsets distort our sense of reality. Nonetheless, our minds have the power to shape our own realities and embrace our true selves."

Introduction

Don't Retreat:
Face Life and Learn from It

"To write about life, first you must live it."
– Ernest Hemingway

The question of why I suffer has consumed me for years, driving me to explore the depths of human conditions. If I am an instrument of God, I have little control over my environment. My curiosity ultimately culminated in a book that delves into how my experience has shaped my thoughts and made me consciously aware of my emotions.

So, there is a spiritual dimension to breaking free from suffering. As the biblical verse says, we can find joy even in the midst of suffering by linking our passions with Christ. To me, spirituality is getting closer to my mind—*seeking happiness from within*. It is an undeniable fact that life presents us with a multitude of challenges and issues. However, our minds possess the power to navigate our emotions, build mental fortitude, and discover a sense of tranquility within ourselves. It is about cultivating love, empathy, and compassion for ourselves and others, regardless of our religious or philosophical beliefs—*the secular approach to my spirituality.*

I can breathe, walk, run, smile, laugh, and earn a living, while many struggle with these fundamental aspects of life. But behind this seemingly perfect facade lies a story of unyielding perseverance, unwavering determination, and relentless hard work. This book encapsulates that story. **"Rethink Your Way of Thinking"** is a holistic approach to understanding ourselves and the world around us, with the best of what I've learned throughout my life documented for everyone to benefit from. I thought sharing my stories and insights could empower others to embrace *"the beauty of life."*

As a Christian, I explain Christianity and my life experience in three words: *suffering, lesson, and blessing.*

Jesus refused to take help when he was faltering while carrying the Cross. He wanted to bear his own Cross and experience every single moment appointed to him by the Father. Personally, there is no escape from my *suffering.* None can bear the Cross for me. Cross is a valuable lesson in my life. I *learned* to accept the realities of life and build compassion—both self-compassion and compassion for others. That is my *blessing.*

On the morning of June 30, 2022, while I was looking at my emails, I saw an email with the subject line: **Final message from Fr. McShane**. Fr. Joseph Michael McShane, the President of Fordham University, wrote to members of the Fordham family:

Peace of Christ,

"At 5 o'clock this afternoon, I will leave the keys on the desk, turn off the lights, and walk out the door of my office in Cunniffe House. As the door closes behind me, my service as the President of our beloved Fordham will come to an end."

As soon as I read the email, I couldn't wait to start writing this book and capturing the profound insights of such an accomplished individual.

Embrace all life offers—trials, tribulations, excitement, success, compassion, love, kindness, frustrations—life moves on.

This book is about the most impactful life lessons I have learned over the years—my wisdom to my younger self. It took me years to understand what drives my emotions, how those emotions shape my behavior, and its impact on the collective well-being of everyone around me. I want to take you to my world—*the journey I started decades ago.*

My retreat is experiencing the realities of life and transitioning it into mindful moments: my struggles to succeed academically and find a job, the responsibility to support my family, the hardships I endured along the way (both emotional and financial), and the peace I found within me. There are no best practices. My life evolves daily, and the best is yet to come—*I learn and grow.* Like writing this book, each day unveils new insights and fresher perspectives.

I asked myself,

"Should I give up or persevere through hardships and misfortune?"

Instead of running away from the realities of life, I embraced them. My decision to confront my impulsive behavior and challenges head-on strengthened me emotionally. As long as I keep the right perspectives and emotional maturity, each of these hardships is a learning opportunity. Although those moments were excruciatingly painful, they were the best experiences in molding and positively shaping my thoughts and emotions.

How do I think about my life?

It is a journey of self-awareness and self-acceptance. I believe in the ancient wisdom of "Know Thyself." I consciously look inward, understand how I react to different situations, and try to be at the wheel of my thoughts and emotions. It is my rational approach to living a happy life in an insane world. Happiness is about changing the relationships with my thoughts—a state of being less tormented and at peace with who I am.

I find it empowering to spend time in nature, engage in self-talk, and laugh at my insanity.

A little about me:

I am an ambitious introvert from a humble upbringing in a remote village in India. While growing up, I was confined to my own world with very little interaction with society. Needless to say, I have poor social intelligence—a fancy way of saying I am socially abrasive, socially awkward, or socially inept. Often, I was vulnerable to criticism, obsessed with my problems, and downplayed every positive part of my life. It was emotionally draining and self-destructive. Overcoming my angry and egotistical tendencies has been an arduous task, especially since they are at odds with my compassionate nature.

I struggle with my listening skills as I'm often too eager to jump in with my own stories and insights. Common wisdom suggests leveraging the power of our silence. It's natural to want to share our own thoughts and experiences, but there can be much value in simply being present and listening to others. When I listen to others, I learn more about others and their perspectives, which only helps me expand my worldview. After all, God gave us two ears and one mouth for a reason.

I refuse to succumb to unattainable optimism and remain a skeptic in an uncertain world. I believe in being kind, empathetic, and compassionate towards others. I try to avoid conflicts and always aim to keep things peaceful and cordial. But that doesn't mean I'm a pushover who will blindly follow others. I prioritize maintaining harmony and fostering positive relationships, even if it means going along with their wishes at times.

To navigate this world, I set clear goals and ambitiously explore various paths to achieve them. My unwavering dedication ensures that I have done everything possible to succeed. Regardless of the outcome, I move forward confidently, secure in the knowledge that I have given it my all.

Nothing has prepared me for dealing with the life I lived for 26 years in the US as an immigrant from India. A common expression is,

"When you hit the rock bottom, the only way is up."
I hit twice.

Luckily, I was able to persevere through every adversity. The chapter "Embrace the Beauty of Life and All of Its Struggles" covers my struggle and survival, while "Four Pillars of Happiness" explains where I failed and how I finally found peace within. Life is a beautiful journey, and I'm grateful for every step. Every hurdle I surmount brings me one step closer to the person I am destined to be. This book is that destination.

As I begin exploring the first chapter of my book, I hope to provide a foundation for us to understand our emotions better. One of the most crucial aspects of this process is learning to recognize and acknowledge our feelings. By becoming emotionally literate and correctly naming our emotions, we can begin to tame them and healthily process them. Personally, my emotions range from feelings of rejection, regret, sadness, anger, envy, and jealousy to joy and gratitude.

We all have flaws and shortcomings that we tend to keep hidden from others. Due to the stigma attached to our emotional issues, we suppress them even more. This often leads us to fall into behavioral patterns that we may be unable to control.

My vulnerabilities are not my weaknesses but rather my experiences, which I use to connect with people meaningfully. I am drawn to those who have gone through similar experiences, thoughts, emotions, and behavior. I have realized that the first step in finding meaning in my life is taking responsibility for my behavior—bearing the burden of life and going through personal growth to deal with my emotional distress. I meditate on it: I let those emotions surface and observe them fully rather than suppressing them. It bloomed me and made my life easier to bear.

Throughout the early chapters of this book, I delved into my personal experiences that have shaped me as a child, an adult, a parent, a husband, a failed entrepreneur, and an educator—the cues and clues I missed throughout my life. I cannot picture the world with specificity as to how the world should be. However, I reflect on my experiences and express how I see the world: It is not only experiencing and overcoming challenges but also constructing a historical narrative that can inspire people to think positively, which is central to this book.

I am not trying to take away the ownership of your beliefs or to alter your belief system. Instead, I intend to motivate you to reflect on your behavior; otherwise, I am afraid this book would be a futile exercise. I invite you to critically examine my stories, views, wisdom, and the quality of my thought process. *"Rethinking my way of thinking"* is about my courage to reflect on my beliefs, humility to accept how little I know, and curiosity to learn more. When I consciously observe my thoughts, I take control of my thinking and engage in a highly metacognitive process (see Chapter 1). I am consciously aware of thinking about my thinking, which empowers me to gain deeper insights into myself and my thought patterns. When I resist rethinking, I fundamentally give up my cognitive prowess. Sadly, rethinking is somewhat controversial or politically incorrect— conforming to the crowd or majority is the norm.

Our perception—how sensory information is organized, interpreted, and consciously experienced—is shaped by our surroundings. We are being conditioned. We are a bit of everything from our environment. Our identity or sense of self is rooted in everything we absorb from our surroundings. It is astounding to see how little awareness there is about the impact of a toxic environment on our perceptions and emotions. I have noticed that even people with great success, solid education, and indisputable intelligence display a complete lack of self-awareness—how we experience and understand our character, feelings, motives, and desires and whether these hurt or help us.

We often judge others quickly, not knowing we have limited knowledge about others. When someone is angry, they are projecting their suffering or fear. It is not a reflection of 'who they are.' It may seem that way.

We often ask,

"Are you happy with your spouse or children?"

The question should be,

"Are you happy and content with yourself?"

Take a moment to reflect.

People who are happy within don't hurt others[1].

I was angry but not cruel. I have not caused harm to anyone. However, I have struggled with my own emotions, and at times, I have hurt myself with my inner turmoil.

---

[1] "The surprising finding is that our relationships and how happy we are in our relationships have a powerful influence on our health," Robert Waldinger, director of "The Harvard Study of Adult Development" and the co-author of "The Good Life."

Despite the fact that I endured cruelty far worse than what I have shared in this book, I strive to find positivity in my experiences and use it to bring positivity to those around me.

I asked myself,

"How can I free myself from my destructive emotions?"

The answer lies in forgiving myself and having compassion for those who hurt me. Whenever anger begins to stir inside me, it serves as a call to action to take command of my emotions. Instead of succumbing to its overwhelming force, I redirect that energy to strengthen myself; I swallow the negative emotions without reacting. This mindset builds my mental resiliency and empowers me to confront obstacles with clarity and determination, which resonates positively around me. Otherwise, it will be emotionally draining and unhealthy—like drinking poison.

I have this coffee mug with this carving: 'Love yourself first.'

My negative thoughts or narratives about someone only fuel my pain, creating a vicious cycle. I transform my relationship with others by letting go of my resentment or sense of betrayal. I often tell myself I must learn to love myself first, in all my glory and imperfections. Or else I cannot fully develop my ability to love others.

I rethink and evaluate how I view the world and reflect on events that trigger negative thoughts leading to destructive emotions. I create a positive mindset for sustaining happiness, which is a buffer against all odds in life—*my reference point or true self*: my courage to accept the realities of life, challenge the status quo—not being subservient—

and still move forward fully unscathed. I take ownership of that success because "I did it."

It took decades to shape me from "what I was" to "who I am." The chapter on "Marriage Made in Hell" reveals the destructive nature of our thoughts, feelings, and emotions. The lessons of life are valuable opportunities to learn and grow. None gave me these perspectives while I was growing up.

I have devoted many chapters to addressing my emotional illiteracy and its consequences. Looking back on my life and career, everything I have accomplished stems from my insatiable desire to succeed—I value education and see it as a means to achieve success.

Later in the book, I discussed my crusade to educate my child. I have learned that parents' basic emotional intelligence is more important than their academic achievement, social status, and money. This means actively listening and fully comprehending a child's innermost thoughts and feelings to create a safe and nurturing environment where they can freely express themselves without fearing judgment. As a parent, I recognize that I failed to make my presence count as a role model when my child needed me the most. Being present is a potent tool that enables us to concentrate and be conscious of our experiences in the current moment. I am not guilty of my parenting. Instead, it is the time for introspection. This book is part of that healing process.

Children must be trained to believe in themselves, experience the rough and tumble of their environment, and resist the impulse to respond to triggers around them. I am alarmed by the pernicious effect of the dark forces on our mental (thoughts) and emotional (emotions) well-being, especially on children—a poor internal sense of self-esteem, depression, anxiety, panic attacks, suicide, and other emotional issues are just the starters to what may end up being a dire catastrophe.

This book offers a broader framework for how we look at the *forces of destruction*. The most pressing issue is that people are so gullible—easily carried away by the propaganda of *social media, news media, and religious institutions*, which are primarily controlled and funded by the *elites* in our society. Consolidating media ownership into the hands of a few powerful elites threatens the integrity of the press and, ultimately, the viability of our democracy. It's frightening to see these elites wield their power and influence to manipulate public opinion and undermine independent media. I wonder what these elites are accomplishing besides displaying their deep insecurity despite their great wealth, name, and fame. They invest their heart and soul into conditioning people and building affiliations with certain political and religious ideologies. We often see politicians pander to those sentiments. Sadly, they become puppets of the elites, being bought and sold by them. Those politicians create a semblance of serving the public interest, but their interest is self-serving—motivated by material well-being.

Social media has become an integral part of our lives, and when used correctly, it can be incredibly beneficial. As I see it, social media is a platform to savor my experience and maximize the benefits. Of course, I can travel virtually worldwide and facilitate the mutual sharing of ideas with anyone with an internet connection. I can share some good deeds I am doing for the community, share some inspiring ideas or thoughts, and connect with the public. Utilizing social media to spread the impact of our benevolence through the beneficiaries can

13

be an effective approach. In his work, Adam Grant emphasizes the notion of being a "giver," but often, people may question our intentions when we give. Instead of promoting our giving mission, it can be more impactful to let the recipients of our kindness be the ones to spread the message. This way, their voices become the centerpiece of the campaign, making it even more compelling. Social media is indeed a powerful tool to amplify such voices and build a strong brand. In that sense, the use of social media is virtuous.

However, we must also acknowledge the negative impact social media can have on our mental health. Cyberbullying and harassment are all too familiar, and constantly comparing ourselves to others can leave us feeling insecure and anxious, leading to feelings of inadequacy, jealousy, and depression. Companies tap into our feelings of deficiency within us—we are not good enough, rich enough, or beautiful enough unless we buy their products—and thrive on them (discussed in Chapter 13). Moreover, social media has taken over our lives, displacing essential activities like sleep, exercise, and face-to-face interactions. While digital communication has made it easier for us to stay in touch with people, it cannot replace the warmth and intimacy of face-to-face conversations that come with the feeling of being more connected and less lonely. Human beings are social creatures, and we thrive on social connections.

Rather than adopting an identity based on external factors, recognizing our inherent worthiness brings enormous joy and contentment.

Our resistance to rethinking the forces that shape our thinking has a powerful destructive effect on our everyday lives.

As an educator, I value the importance of a device-free classroom, as it allows students to be fully present and engage in the learning experience.

So, why do we think social media makes the younger generation fragile?

Because we don't often take personal responsibility for our behavior. Government intervention to make social media safe and responsible is often ineffective, as politicians are in cahoots with the elites—" get rich too." But we can choose not to misuse the platform. Moreover, parental responsibility is also essential in ensuring children use social media safely and responsibly. Sometimes, we blame someone or something for our problems instead of taking personal responsibility for our behavior.

Every time I walk into my classroom, I am reminded of my parenting style. Demanding; at the same time, I instill in them the importance of believing in themselves and dreaming big. As an educator, I bring a few vital finance concepts critical to building an open mind in the classroom. To name a few, questions like whether capitalism is working given the alarming income inequality and racial inequality in the US or the truth behind stakeholder capitalism. These are considered more sensitive discussions on college campuses—a place where ideas are supposed to be freely debated and tested. As a consequence, open-mindedness has been reduced to a taboo on college campuses where extreme political correctness is rapidly strengthening its roots. This conformity of thoughts—the lack of introspection—destroys the freedom of thoughts and ideas in classrooms. It is important to remember the wise words of the Bible, "Do not conform to the pattern of this world, but be transformed by the renewing of your mind."

Einstein once said,
"A ship is always safe ashore, but that is not what it is built for."

Universities are meant to cultivate the spirit of openness, build a sense of compassion, and create opportunities to open up our vulnerabilities. That is how we connect with people—our social capital.

We are witnessing a consumer-driven culture in universities: education is for fun. However, at its core, education is a financial, physical, and psychological investment in ourselves. It is a period of self-development, and it pays enormous dividends. Universities are not just another stop on our journey through life. It is our life. It is not a place to infantilize students and turn them into victims.

We live in a world where we are afraid to speak our minds for fear of negative consequences. Our feelings or voices are often quashed under the echoes of political correctness. It's the culture of silencing those who tell the truth and following the crowd, the masses, or the majority.

For the first time as an educator, I faced real-world emotions in my classroom.

Wokeness is another trigger word getting more attention in academia and among politicians. I have devoted a chapter in this book to Woke and Anti-Woke culture on college campuses. Case in point, when I discussed the concept of stakeholder capitalism in my undergraduate corporate finance class, I brought my perspectives on wokeness. Wokeness refers to our heightened sensitivity to injustice or discrimination in society.

I told the students that just being 'woke' is not enough. Each one of us needs to take responsibility for contributing to positive social changes. That evening, I received an email asking me to schedule a meeting with the department chair. It never occurred to me that students were so offended by comments on wokeness. My compassion towards students often resulted in a "no good deed goes unpunished" feeling. Since then, I have changed my teaching style for fear of retaliation and my safety. I no longer bring my life stories and practical world experience into the classroom.

Recognizing that students are so sensitive to certain ideologies is not comforting. Discussing such doctrines creates a hostile climate on college campuses as it riles students' emotions. I am not convinced whether mental health concerns were the reason for such hostility or whether it was used as a cover-up—an anti-free speech movement. Move our students, not movements, to face challenges in life and blossom. That inspiration is vital to building a fruitful life. Creating a nurturing environment that fosters independent thinking is crucial for the growth and achievement of students. I discussed the same incident with my graduate students taking the same corporate finance course. After the session, a young lady in my class came to me and said, "We have a WhatsApp group, professor; we will support you."

That was a heartwarming experience. Plenty of students are keen to learn and benefit from my life experiences. However, they have been deprived of an opportunity to share their thoughts and learn from others in the classroom by a few who are *persistent in their resistance to rethinking.*

Conversing without inadvertently offending someone can be challenging in today's sensitive society. The cancel culture we practice promotes and celebrates the censorship of those who use certain trigger words. We don't take the time to think critically about the information and misinformation we gather from our environment.

That requires a *growth mindset.* With a growth mindset, we can maintain the belief that our abilities and talents can be developed over time through hard work, dedication, and perseverance. This mindset allows us to embrace challenges and view failures as opportunities to learn and improve. It's essential to be mindful of our triggers and control our impulses for our overall mental and emotional well-being. Exposing students to triggers that create anxiety makes them courageous, not more anxious and depressed.

Throughout Chapter 1, I discussed neuroplasticity—the idea that the brain can adapt and change based on our experience. I delve into both the positive and negative implications of this phenomenon, highlighting the potential benefits and drawbacks of having a malleable brain. Our feelings and behaviors shape our neural pathways and ultimately impact our cognitive functioning.

Persuading students to rethink their thought process requires patience, forceful and rational arguments, and compassion. Engaging respectfully with different perspectives, freely expressing our thoughts and feelings, and creating a condition for open debate is the bedrock of any educational institution. Succumbing to the sensitivities of a few brainwashed and green-washed students, adopting trigger warnings in the syllabus, and opposing 'no-platforms' for speakers with perceived controversial views only infringe on academic freedom. This *monoculturalism*—judging people based on the values of one's own culture, is rendering college campuses devoid of curiosity and intellectual diversity. We are mainly ignoring the ideological bias in universities and its potential impact on the quality of education.

Part Two of this book discusses my academic journey and how I strive to motivate my students to believe in their abilities and potential while visualizing a brighter future for themselves beyond what they have currently envisioned. I advise my students to take a holistic approach to life—a big-picture view of life and career—and focus less on their grades. Experience the gratifying process of realizing our true potential, not accumulating wealth. Wealth is often regarded as a visible signal of accomplishment. The sole focus on securing a job and becoming wealthy is very costly as it can push people farther away from actualizing their abilities. The challenges we face often help us grow and develop as individuals.

In Part Three of this book, I provide a new perspective for the younger generation and a roadmap for discovering inner peace through my *four pillars of happiness*. Learning is a social, emotional, and collaborative process. Our emotions are contagious. I have learned rather painfully that my immediate reaction to what people said or did to me—*the classic fight, flight, or flee reaction*—only made me emotionally weak and distressed. These days, I pause for a moment and reflect before I react. It works beautifully for me, especially in my classrooms. Also, I have introduced mindfulness meditation in my classrooms. When I hear my students feel stressed out, I always remind them that setbacks and challenges are a natural part of the journey toward success. It's essential to maintain a positive mindset and equip ourselves with the right tools to overcome adversity and emerge even stronger. Mindfulness meditation is one such tool I highly recommend, as it has been scientifically proven to profoundly impact the brain, improve emotional intelligence, and ultimately lead to greater emotional well-being.

In Part Four, my focus shifts to the hypocrisy I observed in my Christian tradition and our hardships.

How often do we question our way of thinking?

I always hear, "You cannot change me." However, the reality is that our brains have the power of neuroplasticity, allowing us to grow and evolve continually. We're often taught what to think instead of how to think, leading to a conditioned or indoctrinated mindset. By acknowledging our biased perceptions, we can work towards a more open and critical approach to our beliefs. I intend to persuade others on their terms with this book because I don't think I am right in assessing a person or situation. Every time I think about life, I am astounded by how little I know about human conditions and how little control I have over the forces in the universe, regardless of my education or wealth. But we have the power of our mind. I was struck by a powerful realization that my own perceptions, just like everyone else's, are naturally biased. It's a humbling thought, but it also reminds me to have compassion for myself and others. The book draws connections between principles in quantum science and human consciousness, ultimately conveying the powerful message that only the Higher power can claim to possess an unbiased perspective.

My thoughts on spirituality, which are not affiliated with any particular religion, conclude the book. I outline some steps for a brief mindfulness meditation practice to help anyone find inner peace and calm.

Our time on this planet is precious. And yet we—whether it is media, religious institutions, or politicians—spend our valuable time ripping apart those with different views, looks, and shapes instead of lifting them. We find our joy in bringing people down.

I have learned to look at human conditions from a deeper perspective and see them through the prism of love, compassion, and forgiveness. I love them for who they are as human beings. I want to instill the same desire for change and a sense of self-awareness in humanity.

So, what is my motivation?

Lead a "Meaningful Life" that can profoundly impact humanity: bring hope to people who need our help and be part of that powerful and transformative experience.

"Value yourself, trust your gut, and develop decision-making skills. Seek advice but avoid relying too heavily on others' opinions because people are conditioned, and their advice is biased. The key is to practice and engage in self-reflection to make confident and informed decisions."

I hope I can convince you to rethink!

Chapter 1

Emotional Intelligence and Success in Life

Developing emotional intelligence enables us to manage emotions effectively and avoid being derailed by a flash of anger. Think of your emotions as bumps on the road while you're driving. Without emotional intelligence, it's like losing control when you hit a big bump with no seatbelt on. Developing emotional intelligence is like becoming a skilled driver who can handle those bumps smoothly. It helps us manage emotions so that sudden anger doesn't make us lose control. It's like staying on track instead of crashing. Emotional intelligence keeps us in control, just like a good driver on a rough road.

In the book "Getting There: A Book of Mentors," Warren Buffett shares a valuable lesson taught by Media Executive Tom Murphy. The lesson is all about emotional intelligence and is one that Buffett considers indispensable. Murphy said,

"You can always tell someone to go to hell tomorrow."

This advice may seem harsh initially, but it highlights the importance of taking a step back and not acting impulsively.

Let me translate: taking a moment to pause and reflect before reacting impulsively can prevent us from making decisions we might regret later.

By creating a space between the trigger and reaction, we can gain greater awareness of our emotions and develop a deeper understanding of our feelings to regulate them effectively—embrace the power of metacognition.

Create a breathing space before acting impulsively. However, what must be noted here is that this approach may not always work; I tried this approach. It did not work very well for me. Why? Well, while it's crucial to distance yourself from triggers before reacting or responding, it's equally important to anticipate how others will react or respond. Unfortunately, no matter how long we wait, not everyone will react positively. So, it is crucial to maintain a sense of calm and patience. Anticipate, process, and accept the outcome, be it positive or negative, before lurching. We only have control over our emotions.

When it comes to emotional intelligence, most people fail to regulate their emotions, let alone control them, often due to a lack of awareness. I was no different. While I may have known the *triggers* of my reactions, I lacked awareness of what *caused* my reaction.

If something pulls the trigger, what mechanism causes the motion?

I have no authority in the field of neuroscience. However, I was curious to understand the impact of our environment on our perception, thoughts, and emotions, so I delved into neuroplasticity and epigenetics. The areas of epigenetics and neuroplasticity are fascinating and offer valuable insights into the workings of the human brain. Epigenetics, which involves studying heritable changes in gene expression without changes to the DNA sequence or our genetic makeup, sheds light on the complex interplay between *nature* and *nurture*. Meanwhile, neuroplasticity highlights the brain's remarkable ability to adapt and change throughout a person's lifetime. Together, these fields provide crucial knowledge on how our environment shapes our perception and affects our mental well-being.

We have the power to shape our lives through epigenetic changes by altering our environment and designing a fulfilling life without being held captive by our genetic makeup.

I realized that our perception of the world is shaped by our brain and how it processes information. We form our thoughts based on our perceptions. Our brain constantly adapts to our surroundings, making our perception biased and ever-changing. So, testing what we feed into our brains is critical, including filtering others' opinions, ideas, or expertise. This is my way of saying *"rethink."*

By carefully evaluating the information we expose our minds to, essentially rethinking our perspectives, we can better nurture our mental well-being. Just as our mental health isn't biased against any specific group, it's our own interpretations, uncertainties, and pessimistic thoughts that contribute to discrimination in all its manifestations.

Our mental health condition does not discriminate against humanity. It affects people at every level of education, age, or wealth. Breaking free from negative self-talk and self-doubt by nurturing self-love creates a healthy sense of self-worth. Focusing on the things I am grateful for, however small, helps the brain flourish with *oxytocin*, a hormone that promotes happiness and well-being. Recognizing the root cause of our distress is crucial to overcoming it. Our destructive thoughts influence our emotions and behavior, creating a vicious cycle.

Rethink. Suddenly, problems that once seemed impossible become more manageable, our perceptions of ourselves and the world around us shift positively, and we can think more clearly and make better decisions. Knowing that we can improve our lives by developing our emotional intelligence is empowering.

Peter Salovey and John D. Mayer formulated the theory of emotional intelligence. I genuinely believe that building emotional intelligence from a young age is incredibly powerful. It's something that I didn't fully understand until recently, but it's clear to me now how crucial emotional well-being is when it comes to making wise decisions and thinking clearly.

According to Salovey and Mayer:

Emotional intelligence is a set of skills associated with monitoring one's and others' emotions and using emotions to guide one's thinking and actions. Emotions impact our attention, memory, learning, ability to build relationships with others, and physical and mental health (Salovey and Mayer, 1990).

Understanding the basics of emotional intelligence is vital for developing emotional literacy. By achieving emotional literacy, we can better comprehend our emotions and those of others, leading to improved relationships and increased self-awareness. It's a skill that can be developed and honed over time. When we understand our emotions, we can identify what triggers them and learn how to manage them better.

In 1970, Claude Steiner coined the term *"Emotional Literacy."* It encompasses a range of skills and capacities we acquire as we mature into responsible, capable, and emotionally healthy adults who can effectively track, feel, manage, process, express, and work with our emotions. Developing emotional intelligence and literacy is crucial for successfully navigating life's complexities and establishing robust, positive relationships with ourselves and others.

As humans, we tend to fall into habits and routines. Our brains are wired to conserve energy and make quick decisions based on past experiences and assumptions. Even though we have evolved, our primitive instincts are still present. Our brains perceive change as a threat, triggering the release of *cortisol*, the stress hormone, and activating the fight-flight or flee response. These triggers cloud our thinking and hinder our ability to think critically and creatively. Emotions are a crucial response to our thoughts, feelings, and actions. They allow us to react to our environment, whether real or perceived. For example, being chased by a wild animal or being rejected by a friend can trigger emotional and cognitive consequences. We may experience fear, depression, anger, jealousy, or sadness, which can propel us into action. The negative thoughts we hold onto harm our immune system and hinder our brain's potential.

As I reflect on my personal experiences, I realize that I was not always aware of the underlying emotions fueling my reactions. Feelings such as anger, shame, sadness, and fear would make me overwhelmed and powerless. My brain's response was usually fight or flight, and I struggled to maintain control of my reactions and keep calm. I found myself constantly behaving almost automatically without really understanding why. It was as if I was on autopilot, just going through the motions without any real awareness of what was driving my emotions or how to regulate them. I was emotionally illiterate and emotional.

But if we can transcend the negative emotions by having the emotional intelligence to acknowledge our emotions, we can comprehend our situation correctly. Instead of being in the rut of fight or flight, we can make better-informed decisions regarding saving ourselves from the wild animal and accepting the rejection as redirection toward something else.

Emotional intelligence is more than just a tool; it is an instinctive trait that has to be instilled and nurtured. It is not a prompt that we can feed and expect to work consistently. To help you understand this, let's look at Daniel Goleman's theory. In his book on emotional intelligence, Daniel Goleman explains the concept of '*Working Memory*' used by neuroscientists—the capacity of our mind to hold facts essential for completing a given task.

Have you ever become anxious or angry, only to notice that it becomes increasingly difficult to think clearly and make rational decisions?

It's no coincidence that intense emotions like these can create a kind of neural static that can interfere with the *prefrontal cortex's* ability to maintain working memory. This means we struggle to focus, learn, and remember important information. The prefrontal cortex is responsible for attention, memory, and learning, highlighting how crucial it is to manage our emotions effectively to perform at our best.

Our brains process and store everything we expose ourselves to, so we must filter out the negative and harmful content. It's incredible how much our perspectives can be influenced by the people we interact with, our experiences, and the media we consume.

In this book, I aim to shed light on our surroundings' profound impact on our mental health. One crucial aspect I emphasize is the concept of conditioning, or brainwashing, which refers to how our environment shapes our thoughts, emotions, and behaviors. By acknowledging this fact and becoming more mindful of our surroundings, we can take proactive steps towards taking control of our mental well-being and making choices that positively impact our lives.

So, did I understand either the theoretical or the practical aspects of my perception?

I did not. We see things differently from others based on our experience, knowledge, and beliefs. Even when two people observe the same thing, they can interpret it differently.

Our mind is made up of various mental states that are generated by the neurons. These mental states include our beliefs, ideas, opinions, and emotions. Neurons, called nerve cells, send and receive signals from our brain. These signals travel along *neural pathways*, essentially the connections between neurons in our brain. The brain is the hardware that allows us to experience these mental states and process them accordingly. The human brain and mind collaborate seamlessly to influence our experiences and shape our perceptions of the world. Every thought we have ever had is encoded in a unique pattern of neural pathways, which work together to create the complex tapestry of our consciousness. This is where neuroplasticity comes in.

When you have a new thought, it starts as a weaker neural pathway, like a baby taking its first steps. But with repetition, the neural pathway becomes stronger and more dominant until it eventually becomes second nature. Neuroscience has revealed that *neurons that wire together fire together,* which means that our habitual thought patterns become more firmly ingrained over time. Learning creates neural networks—learning ignites the activation of neurons that connect with each other, forming a potent neural web. This web is the foundation of our ability to learn and remember new information. The more we think a certain way, the stronger that pattern becomes.

It's like walking on a muddy path—the more we tread the same path, the deeper the grooves become. This is particularly true when it comes to our religious beliefs.

Negative thought patterns can be especially damaging, as they can make it easier for future negative patterns to take hold. However, the good news is that positive thought patterns can also become stronger over time. So, next time you're learning something new, remember that with enough repetition, you can create a strong neural pathway in your brain.

Whenever we think about something or remember a memory, we're strengthening the connections in our brains. Our brains truly have incredible power to evolve and grow! The stronger our emotions, like shame or sadness, are attached to a thought or experience, the stronger those neural pathways become. It's important to be mindful of what we expose our brains to and work on managing negative thoughts and emotions.

According to neuroscientists, we cannot undo the neural pathways in our brain, but we can replace negative thoughts with positive ones and create new neural pathways. If you find yourself constantly experiencing negative recurring thoughts, it could be due to deeply held beliefs built up over time. Recognizing that our thoughts directly impact our emotions, finding ways to overwrite those negative thought patterns with positive affirmations is vital to our mental and emotional well-being.

Understanding the impact of negative thoughts is a powerful motivator for *rethinking our way of thinking*. Our limbic system and hippocampus, responsible for emotions and memory, often influence our thoughts before they reach our prefrontal cortex, where we process logic and reason. This can lead to biased thinking. Nevertheless, with emotional intelligence, we can challenge these biases and make more objective decisions with conscious awareness and effort—*give the space and time before the limbic system takes control and reacts.* However, it is hard work. Therefore, we are less likely to question our way of thinking and more likely to follow the masses or majority and familiar patterns. In other words, it leaves our brain on autopilot. Mindfulness meditation is one practice I use to overwrite my existing neural pathways and regulate my emotions (see conclusion). It is an excellent exercise to help us better comprehend our thoughts and emotions, leading to a more profound sense of inner peace and well-being. We can learn to live in the present moment with persistence and commitment.

Now, while being smart does not equate to emotional intelligence, it is possible to excel in both aspects simultaneously. Of course, it is not easy, but it is not impossible, so I think mindfulness meditation should be practiced from a young age. Mindfulness meditation helps children build confidence, cope with stress, and develop resilience. Once we start learning and life starts adding experiences to our mindset, we develop a form of neural stubbornness to relearn our thinking patterns (bias vs. logic; comfort vs. new territory). It is human nature to resist newness and changes if they do not align with our existing values, even if the rethinking could lead to our betterment.

We often ignore the power of emotions and focus more on our intelligence or IQ. The truth is that intelligence can do no good but lead to dangerous outcomes if we fail to understand and control our emotions.

We all have choices in life: the choice to love yourself, to pursue a major in school, to work for someone or start your own business, to select a life partner, to live in a particular place, and so on. I often find myself questioning the decisions I make in life. It's easy to think I must have made the right choices if things had turned out well. Not so fast. It's not always that straightforward. Our career paths, educational pursuits, and business ventures can often feel ambiguous. Ultimately, success is more about mastering our thoughts and emotions than anything else. I impart these same words of wisdom to my students. I remind them that while they may not have complete control over the grades they receive, they can control their effort, manage their emotions, stay engaged in class, and complete assignments to the best of their ability.

"What do you want to be when you grow up?"

This is a question we often ask children. But how often do we teach ourselves and our kids to be kind and compassionate, to do what they love, and to find fulfillment in that journey? Seldom. Often, we evaluate children based on a narrow standard of success, such as test scores or graduation rates. This approach to education seems to be based on a factory model, where the primary goal is to prepare children for a job that impresses others. While preparing for a living is essential, narrowing the gap between our talents and what we do is also vital to building our passion. It is self-sabotaging to live someone's dream. Focusing too much on getting straight A's and striving for perfection can lead to stress, anxiety, and depression in children. This can make them terrified of getting anything less than a straight A and even make them pursue a job that matches their academic achievement. Anything short of that will be depressing for them. Here, we do end up doing the exact opposite of instilling a sense of emotional intelligence; we cultivate young minds to be result-oriented against being better at judgment.

In a podcast, Sir Ken Robinson[2] shared a story about a child completely absorbed in drawing during class. The teacher asked the child what she was drawing, and the child confidently replied that she was drawing a picture of God. The teacher said nobody knows what God looks like, but the child remained undeterred and said, "They

---

[2] Sir Ken Robinson was an authority on creativity, education, and human potential.

would know in a minute." This story is an excellent reminder of the incredible imaginative abilities of children and why it's essential to encourage them to explore their creativity rather than just focusing on their grades or comparing them to their peers. Ultimately, their unique efforts and talents matter much more than their grades (discussed in Chapter 14, Pillar #3: Career Well-being). As someone who followed a traditional Asian parenting style, I learned the hard way that pushing for academic success at the expense of creativity can stifle a child's creativity and hinder the personal growth of that child.

In Daniel Goldman's[3] book, there is a story of a sophomore student who was determined to get into Harvard Medical School. This student, Jason, received a B grade on a physics quiz, which he believed would ruin his chances of getting into Harvard. Unfortunately, he reacted by attacking his physics teacher. Luckily, the judge found that Jason was not responsible for his actions because a psychiatric assessment revealed he was psychotic. Jason claimed he was planning to commit suicide due to his test score. Despite this setback, Jason persevered and took advanced courses, ultimately graduating with an impressive average of 4.614, surpassing the perfect 4.0 norm.

It's difficult to understand why Jason reacted so strongly to his low score on the quiz. Still, it is crucial to remember that academic success doesn't necessarily translate to emotional intelligence. His behavior was likely influenced by the rigid structures imposed on him at home, school, and religious institutions.

---

[3] Emotional Intelligence by Daniel Goldman

It's interesting to note that a study by Goldman revealed a group of primary school boys who performed exceptionally well on IQ tests but struggled in school due to issues with their prefrontal cortex. Despite their high intelligence, these boys often exhibited impulsive, anxious, and disruptive behavior, frequently leading to trouble. These children were at the highest risk of developing problems like academic failure, addiction, and criminal behavior. The study suggested that these boys' emotional circuits were shaped by their childhood experiences, which could have potentially impaired their ability to control their emotional life.

Academic intelligence is commonly known to be a vital aspect of our lives. However, it is not the only factor contributing to a fulfilling and happy life. Despite having exceptional academic accomplishments, many individuals find navigating the complexities of their personal and professional lives challenging. This is where emotional intelligence plays a significant role. By enhancing our capacity to comprehend and manage our emotions and those of others, we can establish stronger relationships, make better choices, and achieve greater happiness and satisfaction in all aspects of our lives. Therefore, while academic intelligence is undoubtedly critical, it is only one piece of the puzzle of leading a successful and gratifying life.

One of the most important things we can do to manage our thoughts is to be self-aware.

In a recent article published in the Harvard Business Review, Tasha Eurich highlighted the importance of self-awareness in developing emotional intelligence. The author shared some interesting findings and statistics that resonated with me. The following passages *(in italics)* are the summary of the article. I have incorporated my personal stories wherever appropriate.

In a scientific study conducted by Tasha Eurich and her team, they discovered that only 10% to 15% of the nearly 5,000 participants fit the criteria for self-awareness. The study revealed that self-awareness can be divided into two broad categories: internal and external. Internal self-awareness pertains to how we see our values, passions, and aspirations fit with our environment, reactions, strengths, weaknesses, and impact on others. On the other hand, external self-awareness refers to understanding how others view us regarding the same factors. People who focus on building internal and external self-awareness can reap the rewards of increased self-knowledge, such as making sounder decisions, building stronger relationships, and communicating more effectively.

The article goes on to explain four self-awareness archetypes. One is **introspection***, which refers to examining the reasons behind our thoughts, feelings, and behaviors. While introspection can be an effective tool in enhancing self-awareness, it is crucial to approach it correctly. Their research has shown that those who introspect are less self-aware and report lower job satisfaction and overall well-being. One of the most commonly used introspective questions is 'Why?' This question helps us better understand our emotions, behavior, and attitudes. For instance, we may ask ourselves why we dislike certain individuals, act in a particular manner, or why are we against certain ideas. It turns out that asking 'why' may not always be the most* *effective approach. Research shows that many thoughts, feelings, and motives are outside our conscious awareness. This means that we tend to invent answers that feel true but are often wrong.*

For example, my anger with my child sometimes had nothing to do with her behavior. After some reflection, I realized that the root cause of my outburst was my own emotional struggle.

Moreover, asking 'why' can be problematic because we may be wrong and tend to be overly confident in our answers. Our minds don't always operate rationally, and biases often influence our judgments. We may latch onto insights without questioning their validity, ignore evidence contradicting our beliefs, and try forcing our explanations to fit our preconceived notions.

So, the question 'why' is effective as long we search for our blind spots (areas we need improvement), seek feedback from others, and be emotionally literate: grease the wheels of cognition. In other words, create a meta-awareness. We can tame it if we are consciously aware of our feelings and emotions. I tried to understand what caused my emotional outburst in the earlier example.

Reflecting on my own life, I sometimes feel depressed and hopeless. I feel stressed and overwhelmed at other times, but I'm unsure why. It's important to name our feelings, but it's equally important to take action to improve our negative thoughts. Meditation and looking within helps me be grateful for the things I have and find peace within myself.

Therefore, ask "what" questions to increase productive self-insight and decrease unproductive rumination. 'What' questions help us stay objective, future-focused, and empowered to act on our new insights, *"What steps can I take to deal with my destructive emotions?" This way, we can focus on solutions and move forward positively.*

According to psychologists J. Gregory Hixon and William Swann, people react differently to negative feedback depending on how they approach it. In a study involving a group of undergraduates, feedback was given on their sociability, likability, and interestingness. Some were prompted to consider the reasons (or why) for their behavior, while others were urged to consider the nature of their character. Interestingly, the students who focused on the 'why' or 'why me' spent their energy rationalizing and denying the feedback, while the students who focused on the 'what' were more open to the new information and how they could learn from it.

The article (by Tasha Eurich and her team) further highlights that experience doesn't always lead to learning, and expertise doesn't necessarily help identify false information. Sometimes, being too confident in our abilities can lead to a lack of thoroughness in whatever we do and prevent us from questioning our assumptions. An interesting finding from a particular study was that managers with more experience tended to be less accurate when assessing their own leadership effectiveness. This phenomenon is further explained in Chapter 11(Optimism: The Perils of Ignorance), which sheds light on our limitations and the potential risks of overestimating our predictive abilities.

Additionally, the more power someone holds, the more likely they will overestimate their skills and abilities. This is supported by research that showed higher-level leaders tended to overvalue their skills compared to others' perceptions. This was true for almost all competencies measured, including emotional self-awareness, accurate self-assessment, empathy, trustworthiness, and leadership performance.

According to researchers, there are two main reasons why this phenomenon occurs. The first reason, in the context of an organization (organizations are people), is that senior leaders have fewer individuals above them who are willing to give them honest feedback.

This can also be observed in the context of questioning the hypocrisies of religious leaders, as we often refrain from questioning them due to the belief that it is a sin to do so, resulting in a lack of authentic feedback for their actions (Discussed in Part Four, Seek the Truth, Find Jesus—Walk the Talk).

The second reason is that the more power a leader has, the less likely people are to provide constructive feedback, as they fear it could negatively impact their careers. But this doesn't have to be the case always. The article further states how the most successful leaders actively seek critical feedback from various sources. By doing so, they become more self-aware and can improve their leadership skills. At the same time, their research indicated that people who have improved their external self-awareness had done so by seeking honest feedback from loving critics; I call it 'the vital group.' These 'loving critics' always have our best interests in mind and are willing to tell us the truth, even if it's not what you want to hear.

I strongly agree with Adam Grant, an organizational psychologist, that criticism or feedback is of utmost value when it comes from individuals who genuinely know us, can assess our situation, and have our best interests at heart. I believe receiving this kind of support and guidance from people who play significant roles in my life, such as friends, family, or bosses, is crucial for my personal and professional growth.

I did not have a loving critic. I struggled with my destructive emotions and found that my emotions often got the better of me. It wasn't until recently, through introspection, that I realized how poorly I behaved and how it impacted those around me. I had no idea how others perceived my behavior and often acted without considering the consequences of my emotional outbursts.

In my personal experience and to concur with the study, I'm not entirely convinced that discussing our situations with our friends, relatives, colleagues, or even religious practitioners always yields the best solution. Sometimes, confiding in others may result in our brain being involuntarily conditioned by a biased opinion, thereby overshadowing our truth. A listening ear works wonders to calm us; however, we should mindfully filter the support we receive.

The study highlights the importance of being mindful of the company we keep. Chapter 17, A Marriage Made in Hell, elaborates on this. It's critical to recognize that those we turn to for support may also be struggling with their mental health challenges, which they may not be consciously aware of—not always effective to ask 'why' or introspect without asking "what." (I find it quite amusing every time I read this paragraph)

Experience is not enough; instead, the question of 'what' can we do to improve our mental well-being makes a positive difference in our lives. We hear stories of emotional struggles daily, where even mental health professionals or doctors treating critically ill patients struggle with their mental health issues. Seeking their help can sometimes exacerbate our problems rather than alleviate them. The same applies to religious practitioners. They rarely get authentic feedback, and society considers it taboo to question their actions. Relying on their advice intensifies our emotional reactions to the situation. In my chapter on 'My Christian Faith,' I have discussed the hardships religion can inflict unless we rethink our approach.

Ultimately, the solution lies within us. While getting professional help is crucial, it's also important to take the time to reflect on our thoughts and emotions and be self-aware. We must understand that our thoughts about a situation create emotional issues, not the situation itself (see "Conclusion" for a solution to seeking our inner peace).

The research of Tasha Eurich and her team concluded that those who prioritize both internal and external self-awareness, actively seek feedback from those who care about their growth, and ask 'what' rather than 'why' questions are best positioned to gain a clearer understanding of themselves and enjoy the many benefits that come with self-awareness.

I have noticed in my own life that reflecting on my feelings and how others perceive me is crucial for creating a positive life experience. If I am feeling down, I know I must step back and journal my thoughts and emotions. Once I have taken the time to process my feelings, I can then take action to improve my mood before connecting with others, whether it is a family member or someone outside. It's like flipping a coin—my negative experiences can catalyze a spiritual revolution through introspection and taking action.

I've cultivated greater mental resiliency and emotional regulation by turning inward and reflecting on my thoughts and actions.

I genuinely believe in the power of neuroplasticity when it comes to cultivating a positive or abundant mindset[4]. By understanding and harnessing this power, we can truly take control of our internal voice and turn it into a positive force that propels us towards our goals. With practice and persistence, I have seen firsthand how we can manifest our desired outcomes and create a life of abundance and positivity.

So, I want to hammer home that understanding oneself is crucial to developing self-awareness. By practicing introspection, we can identify our strengths and weaknesses, learn from our mistakes, and make positive life changes.

---

[4] First coined by Stephen R Covey in 1989 in his book The Seven Habits of Highly Effective People. An abundant mindset sees the world as full of opportunities. You can unlock positivity, gratitude, and generosity by believing in abundant resources, opportunities, and successes.

Chapter 2

Memories of My Early Childhood

Often, parents are not equipped to understand their children's feelings or the source of their emotional and mental struggles. It is important to note here that parenting never comes with a guidebook. There is no roadmap to raising another soul, being responsible for their well-being while upholstering values, instilling goodness, and creating a life for them. These responsibilities are enormous and also take a toll on the parent, irrespective of their status or background. In our society, there's often a prevalent expectation that having children is the natural progression of life. This expectation can put immense pressure on individuals and couples to become parents, sometimes without considering the emotional impact it may have on them. This societal norm doesn't always consider parents' emotional wellness.

I firmly believe that it's essential to recognize the emotional challenges that come with parenthood and provide adequate support. One way to do this is by creating more parenting support groups. These groups could serve as safe and welcoming spaces where parents can come together to share their experiences, concerns, and triumphs without the fear of judgment.

All too often, parents may internalize feelings of inadequacy or doubt their abilities when faced with the challenges of parenting. This can be isolating and detrimental to their emotional well-being. By fostering a culture of open dialogue and support through parenting groups, we can help parents realize they are not alone in their struggles. They can learn from each other's experiences, gain valuable insights, and feel more confident in their nurturing roles.

Such groups can also help break down the misconception that there is a one-size-fits-all approach to parenting. Every child is unique, and so are the challenges parents face. By sharing diverse experiences, parents can appreciate the wide range of available parenting styles and solutions, reducing societal pressure to conform to a specific standard. However, this is not a norm, and children grow up lacking emotional well-being. I was no different.

I would not blame my parents for my lack of emotional well-being. They were overwhelmed by everything they needed to care for us and survive. In hopes of grappling with life's circumstances, the focus would be on grades rather than emotional well-being, which is the case for almost all parents.

As parents, we can liberate children emotionally by allowing them to express their feelings, asking the right questions, and listening to them without judgment. Those are powerful ways to validate their feelings. When it comes to parenting, validation doesn't equate to affirmation. I failed to understand these concepts as a parent. I used both interchangeably. Believing in my child's potential, telling my child that she is so intelligent, and creating a 'can-do attitude' were ways to get my child to do well in school. But I never took the time to validate 'how my child was feeling.' For example, why was she nervous about exams, tests, public speaking, or afraid of her father?

It never occurred to me that I had not emphasized validation quite as much until I introspected.

Do you see the drift now?

Breaking the cycle of generational curses, such as the notion of 'tough love' in upbringing, requires a significant shift in our approach to parenting. To do this successfully, we must prioritize emotional awareness and intelligence.

Traditionally, tough love has often been seen as an effective way to instill discipline and resilience in children. However, this approach can unintentionally perpetuate damaging emotional repression and detachment patterns. It may make children feel unheard, misunderstood, or even emotionally neglected.

To break this cycle, we need to redefine the concept of empathy and discipline. Proper discipline isn't about punishment and control but teaching and guiding children to understand their actions and consequences. On the other hand, empathy goes beyond mere sympathy; it's about actively listening to and understanding a child's emotions and experiences.

Ignoring or brushing aside a child's emotions can be damaging in the long run. Children, like adults, have complex feelings and experiences. When their emotions are dismissed or invalidated, it can lead to a lack of emotional intelligence and self-awareness (see Chapter 1). They might struggle to express their feelings in healthy ways or have difficulty understanding and empathizing with others' emotions.

Addressing children's emotions respectfully and early on is

crucial for their emotional development. It means creating an environment where they feel safe to express their feelings, whether positive or negative, without fear of judgment or punishment. It involves active listening, validation of their emotions, and helping them learn to navigate and understand their feelings.

By doing so, we equip children with essential emotional intelligence skills. They learn to recognize and manage their emotions, develop empathy for others, and build healthier relationships. This approach not only benefits the child but also contributes to breaking the cycle of tough love and emotional neglect that may have been passed down through generations.

EARLY CHILDHOOD

I was born in a remote village in Kerala, India. I am the middle child of three siblings. I cannot move forward without describing my humble upbringing—a life close to nature. I grew up in a beautiful land of coconut trees, combining breathtaking beauty and peaceful ambiance. I lived in an eco-friendly house by the side of a river—a fancy way of saying a thatched mud house—made of earth and other natural materials. I enjoyed swimming in the river. Today, I dream of living in a similar mud house I grew up in.

Reflecting on my upbringing, I realize that the seed of emotional and status consciousness was planted in me at a very young age. I often reflect on my relationship with my grandfather, who played a significant role in my early years. I lived a typical life of a child growing up in a mud house with little to eat and no proper clothes.

One day, my parents left the house to visit a relative, and we were left with our grandfather. We were starving, and later that day, my grandfather went to a shop and bought some food. I noticed he was hiding the food in his clothes when he came home. He felt ashamed of buying food for us because he did not want others to know we had no food at home. I realized his love and concern for his grandchildren. At the same time, I noticed his sense of shame.

When I reflect on my childhood, I can't help but acknowledge the impact that my grandfather's obsession with social status had on me. From a young age, I felt a strong need to impress others and seek validation from society. This attitude became deeply ingrained in my personality and influenced my thoughts and actions. I've realized that much of my life has been shaped by the opinions and expectations of others. Such is the impact of our environment, where society easily influences our decisions, often without us even realizing it.

I recall my grandfather's strong sense of stubbornness as a defining personality trait. I could not comprehend this quality as a child. I merely observed it. Children have an uncanny ability to observe things around them. They can easily spot others' moods and emotions since survival depends on their ability to observe things around them.

One day, my father took my grandfather to a photo studio to have his picture taken. Taking your picture back then was considered a luxury, so it was a big deal. The photographer tried to get my grandfather to pose a certain way. But my grandfather was the kind of person who didn't like being told what to do and had a powerful personality. His picture reflected the stubbornness and mental fortitude he was known for.

Let me end my grandfather's story with the lasting impact of his name on my way of thinking. Out of love and as a tradition, my father chose my grandfather's name as my official name for the school record. We are often asked, 'What is in a name?' Growing up in my local school, I felt humiliated whenever I had to introduce myself. My name was the source of constant ridicule, and I couldn't help but feel self-conscious about it. It was an old-fashioned name that made me stick out like a sore thumb, and I was always worried about how others perceived me. I learned from my grandfather that status was important, which only added to my anxiety. And at the end of it, I always struggled with social situations.

My name had a significant impact on my life when I was younger. It hindered my ability to connect with others and caused me to avoid social situations, ultimately leading to a decline in my social intelligence. I struggled with self-awareness, finding it challenging to understand my emotions and comprehend others' emotions. This negatively affected my relationships in and outside of work.

The quality of relationship experiences during the first few years of life can directly impact children's early development. This underscores the importance of providing children with a nurturing and supportive environment during their formative years to ensure their social and academic competence in the long run.

Children start shaping their behavior and forming opinions at a young age. I can attest to it rather painfully in my then three-year-old child. Albert Bandura, a professor of psychology at Stanford University, in his social cognitive theory (social learning theory), considered how both environmental and cognitive factors interact to influence human learning and behavior:

Children observe the people around them behaving in various

ways. He conducted experiments on observational learning and investigated if social behaviors can be acquired by observation and imitation. His Bobo doll experiment demonstrated that children can learn social behavior through observation learning and watching another person's behavior.

I fondly remember my early childhood when I first started learning the letters in my local dialect. I can still picture myself sitting on the ground outside my house, drawing the first alphabet with my index finger. My father was there to help me, holding my finger and guiding it along to form the letter in the sand. I could observe the occasional moments of frustration from my father when I didn't learn as quickly as he wanted.

Later, I went to a local teacher and learned the letters. It was a formal education, and I sat with other children, learning how to write letters. The teacher would hold my finger and guide me through writing the letters in the sand. It was a fun and engaging experience. My teacher had all the alphabet carved on a palm leaf, which I took home to practice.

My environment and teachers slowly conditioned me. Growing up, I exhibited the same anger and impatience as my parents. My parenting style reflected the same rage and impatience.

I started attending a nearby primary school as a first-grader when I was six. My dad would always drop me off at school in the morning, and after classes were over, I walked back home with some of my classmates. I remember walking barefoot since I didn't have any shoes then. Lunchtime was always the highlight of my day since the school provided free meals for all students. They would cook wheat grain and serve it on a banana leaf that I brought daily.

As I went through my schooling, I slowly developed a sense of insecurity. I couldn't help but compare myself to other students who came from wealthy families and had all the advantages that came with it. I was jealous of those students—their clothes, confidence, and cozy relationship with teachers. It seemed like they were always treated far more favorably than me by my teachers, which only made my jealousy worse. Despite my efforts to push these feelings aside, they lingered in my mind.

My school environment started impacting my thoughts and emotions. The concept of neuroplasticity highlights how repetitive experiences can mold our brains. It's fascinating to think about how our brains are wired to focus on negative things. It is human nature that we have a negative bias, and our brain is built with greater sensitivity to unpleasant and harmful things in life. This negative bias could be detected at the brain's earliest information processing stage. So, children are more susceptible to their surroundings around them. Looking back, I realize I spent too much time focusing on what I didn't have instead of being grateful for what I did. This negative emotion only reinforced negative neural pathways and caused a stronger emotional response. Neuroscience has found a way to counteract this. By cultivating positive emotions through meditation, we can overwrite the recurring negative ones I explained in the book.

I often felt overwhelmed and unable to control my reactions to situations. If I had known then what I know now, I would have been able to handle things much differently and avoid some of the negative consequences, such as anger, shame, and regret, that came from my lack of emotional regulation.

I was a skinny kid with deep insecurity. I was emotionally weak as well. I suppressed those feelings. I've learned that mental and emotional well-being can significantly affect physical health. My skin becomes more sensitive when I feel anxious or stressed, triggering itching. This occurs because emotions can activate the stress response and release hormones and chemicals that can cause inflammation. My skin problems lead to emotional distress like shame, guilt, or low self-esteem, making it a vicious cycle. I had developed severe skin rashes, deterring students from sitting close to me or making friends. My classmates made fun of me for my skin condition. I felt hopeless, socially isolated, rejected, and lonely. I always sought sympathy and affirmation from others as a way to cope with my sense of insecurity within me. I was emotionally dependent.

During my school days, I always struggled with my grades. Although I managed to do well in certain subjects, I always felt ashamed whenever I scored lower than my classmates. Looking back, I realize that my performance reflected my lack of emotional intelligence. I was so afraid of failing that I avoided participating in extracurricular activities, sports, and games. I only now understand that my mistakes and failures were opportunities for growth and learning.

The day I finished 4th grade is still fresh in my memory. I was excited to move on to the next phase of my education. My father accompanied me to the new school where I was enrolled in the 'upper primary school.' My father handed over my transfer certificate to the headmaster, who then looked at my name and commented on it, which only intensified the shame I had felt about it all along. He said that it was an old name for a child. I felt embarrassed and wished to change my name to something more modern and acceptable.

The school was a few miles from my house. I walked to school, as always, barefoot. One day, I was walking to school, and it started raining. I took shelter under a tree. By the time the rain subsided, I was late for the school. I ran. I tripped and fell. My lunch was scattered around. My shirt was muddied up. Even worse, when I reached school, my teacher did not let me in the classroom until I got my shirt cleaned up.

SCHOOL UNIFORM

It was a tradition for us to wear new clothes on the first day of the school year. Since it was a public school, there was no formal uniform. My parents couldn't afford to buy me new clothes, so my mother cut up her old sarees and sewed some shirts for me. These moments were filled with anxiety as I sat in class, wondering what my classmates thought of me. Whenever I wore those shirts, my classmates would ridicule me, further amplifying my insecurities. Focusing on what was being taught in class became increasingly challenging as I was consumed with thoughts of how others perceived me. It was a difficult time, and I could feel my self-esteem fading.

Although I didn't take part in the school festival program, I was intrigued by the idea of acting. Sadly, my interest in it didn't last very long. However, I did create a short film that showcased my hidden talent a few years ago. The idea of learning from my failures was foreign to me until recently. There was no guidance or encouragement from my parents either.

I've always been interested in reading books about successful people. When I was younger, and I had the opportunity to order some books through my school, I preferred biographies of scientists. My teacher ordered books on Albert Einstein and Sir Isaac Newton for me. While reading Einstein's biography, one thing Einstein said caught my attention:

"It is not that I am so smart; I stay with the problem longer."

That phrase has stuck with me to this day. I realized that to be a successful student, I needed to adopt this mindset of perseverance. Whenever I face a challenge, I remind myself to "stay with the problem longer." Thanks to Einstein's wise words.

ALUMINUM BOX VS. IRON BOX

I always stacked my books, bound them with a rubber band, and carried them on my shoulder when I went to school. I had this one student in my class with an aluminum box to keep all his textbooks and lunch at school. It was a symbol of wealth and pride in those days. I wanted a similar one and asked my father for one, so I could carry all my books while I was walking and keep my books safe during the rain. My father could not afford to buy one for me at that time. So, I decided to save money by stealing and selling a few coconuts from my farm. I saved 20 rupees and gave it to my father, and finally, my father bought a small iron box in red. That was the cheapest available. I wanted an aluminum box!

Many fellow students faced financial difficulties just like me. However, it is unfortunate that society often stigmatizes less fortunate individuals. This can be disheartening and intensifies the desire for validation even further. Instead of seeking validation, I wished I had sought ways to earn money at a young age—going door-to-door, delivering morning newspapers, and facing the slam on my face. Those experiences would have prepared me to face rejections early on. But our culture prohibited that kind of initiative for a child. It only added more shame to the family that a child had to earn a living for the family.

In my case, I struggled with self-esteem and felt I had to be someone else to fit in.

It's a common problem, especially with social media, where we constantly compare ourselves to others. I never realized how much my childhood experiences shaped my perception of the world and humanity. Indeed, the environment we grow up in can significantly impact how we see things. Society tends to treat those born into lower-income families differently than those born into wealthier families, which can dramatically affect our outlook on life.

Growing up, I often held back my emotions due to societal expectations. Expressing feelings was not something that boys were supposed to do. But as I got older, I realized that bottling up emotions can seriously affect our mental and physical health. The weight of childhood trauma and emotional wounds can make even the simplest tasks feel overwhelming and strain personal relationships. I have experienced this firsthand.

Additionally, it's not just IQ that sets one child apart from another. Building emotional intelligence is vital to one's success: the ability to observe one's thoughts, feelings, sensations, and impulses without judgment as they occur. Growing up, however, I struggled with my poor emotional intelligence, which led me to assume I was not as talented as others.

Labeling someone as talented or not at a young age can lead to patterns of achievement or underachievement that can last for years. Some children are overlooked, discouraged, and pushed out of the pool, while others are given special attention and opportunities due to their family's wealth. This is what sociologists call 'accumulative advantage.'

In his book "Outliers," Malcolm Gladwell calls this situation 'the Mathew Effect,' where external factors and opportunities determine whether someone can reach their full potential or face obstacles.

I don't discount luck in our lives. But success in any field is not just about blaming or relying on luck. It's about having the inner drive to achieve your goals and thinking independently. Parents, schools, society, and religious institutions all play a significant role in cultivating a positive attitude in children. Like the famous expression,

"It takes a village to raise a child."

But how can adults or parents cultivate this if they are unaware of their emotional intelligence?

Raising a child is a collective effort. Every child deserves attention and care; it takes a community to provide that. However, cultivating this environment can be challenging if the adults or parents involved are not emotionally intelligent."

Based on my childhood experiences, it is clear that I have always had a strong drive to discover and cultivate emotional intelligence. This has been a guiding force throughout my life, helping me to cope with challenges and strive for a better future. Without this inner drive, I can only speculate as to whether I would have been able to achieve anything I had set out to focus on.

Chapter 3

Insatiable Desire to Succeed

Establishing a nurturing and positive atmosphere for children to thrive in is essential. When I say the right environment, I mean a healthy and supportive environment that can instill an internal sense of self-esteem in children.

Let's pick it up from the previous chapter, where I shared my early childhood life. Take that and suppose we internalize a poor image of ourselves. In that case, that 'poor self-image' becomes a self-fulfilling prophecy, where our negative beliefs fuel our negative actions, creating a cycle of negativity that is hard to break. Mental well-being implies the 'feeling of positivity' and 'functioning well.' Children's bodies require nourishment to function well, which can positively affect their psychological well-being. I was emotionally impaired and insecure. Nonetheless, my desire to succeed intensified as I grew up.

The famous quote by Roy T. Bennett will inspire you:
"Don't be pushed around by the fears in your mind. Be led by the dreams in your heart."

I completed my middle school education, and my father transferred me to a new school for my high school education (8th grade to 10th grade). On the first day of my class, when my teacher took attendance, he did not call my name. I was concerned. I mustered some courage and asked him why my name was not on the list. He started making fun of me. Jokingly, he asked me to go to each class and ask if they wanted me in their class. Whenever I see my classmates, they still remind me of that hilarious situation.

Despite being a mediocre student, I developed a keen interest in speaking English fluently. Unfortunately, my school did not prioritize building English communication skills.

As usual, I walked a few miles to get to school every day, rain or shine. It was a bit of a challenge, but I was determined to make it to school no matter what. Seeing some of my old classmates from lower primary school, especially the girls, was lovely. I was always shy and introverted, with poor self-confidence and self-esteem.

During my school days, I seldom had lunch. Watching my classmates relish their meals from afar constantly reminded me that I couldn't afford to buy food. Instead, I headed to the nearby lake in the afternoon and drank water. That was my lunch. It was tough. Sometimes, my classmates generously shared their lunch with me, which made me feel grateful.

From a young age, I developed empathy for those struggling to get by, just like me. This sparked a deep interest in helping others in need and has become integral to my life's purpose today.

As I grew older, I began to focus on my studies. I saw an opportunity to improve my profile in society through public speaking. In the 10th grade, I took the opportunity to speak in front of the class. I wrote everything I had to say and read it. I was very much nervous. But it gave me the impetus to get better.

My academic performance continued to improve. I passed all of my subjects with flying colors and even excelled in a few of them, particularly history and science. Then came a miracle—I completed my 10th grade with a 'First Class,' which surprised many, including my teachers. It was a significant accomplishment for me, although my performance was no way near the 'usual smart ones' in my class. My headmaster congratulated me. He was a priest who also used to make fun of my name and looked down upon me for my lackluster performance in class. However, my willingness to surpass all odds grew intense when I received his appreciation that day.

I started believing in myself and my abilities. I realized that I am capable of achieving my goals. It's incredible how much our mindset can impact our lives. Once I shifted my perspective and started focusing on my strengths, I saw positive changes in my life.

An American sociologist, Robert King Merton, developed a notable concept called "self-fulfilling prophecy":

"The concept of self-fulfilling prophecy is one type of process through which a belief or expectation affects the outcome of a situation or the way a person or group will behave."

This suggests that people's beliefs influence their actions.

A belief is an attitude that a particular condition exists or that some proposition about the universe is true. The principle behind this phenomenon is that people create consequences regarding people or events based on previous knowledge of the subject or experience.

By harnessing the power of neuroplasticity (see pages 24-25), we can take control of the voice in our head and turn it into a positive force that helps us achieve our goals.

We can manifest our desired outcome through unwavering persistence and unshakable self-belief. The ultimate path to success is through our journey of self-discovery and internalizing the belief that our mind has the power to do wonders.

VIRTUES OF FAILURES

George Bernard Shaw said,
"A life spent making mistakes is more honorable and useful than a life spent doing nothing."

My college life (11th-12th grade) was an extension of high school life—filled with many mistakes, obstacles, and struggles to fit in. I was accepted into a local college. I took science subjects, intending to go to medical school. Interestingly enough, all my classmates from my high school were enrolled in the same college. I was a dreamer. My goal in college was to do better than my friends.

Attending college lectures was secondary for many students, partly because there was little we could learn from the lectures. Professors were not that motivated to teach. They would instead earn some extra money by tutoring students from their homes rather than come to the college and teach. Consequently, I took extra help from a tuition center near my college.

This story is worth mentioning as a college student:

I took a local bus to get to my college. One day, I was running late for college and didn't have enough money for the bus fare. I decided to pay only for a few stops before my destination, hoping to avoid getting caught by the bus conductor. Unfortunately, my plan failed, and the conductor caught me red-handed. I was forced to get off the bus a few stops early, leaving me with a long walk ahead. While walking, I encountered an unexpected problem. The strap on one of my slippers broke, and I had to continue walking barefoot while holding the broken slipper. It was an embarrassing moment for me, especially since other students were around to witness it. Trust me, it was not a pleasant experience. If you're curious, you can check out my short film about the ordeal on my YouTube channel, "Shajan Ninan." I did not understand then that our hardships and struggles were valuable life lessons. I was angry over my life situations, compared myself to others, and developed a lack of self-esteem. I asked myself why I couldn't dress like others, wear decent footwear, or have lunch. My destructive thoughts and emotions sabotaged my self-confidence. I did not understand human nature and often judged people based on appearance and expression. I misread people's motives and overlooked the dark side of humanity.

But I decided to channel my anger, frustration, and bitterness into something good for myself. I had this insatiable desire to succeed. Subconsciously, my experience made me a more determined person. I focused more on my education.

I completed 12th grade in college and graduated with a 'First Class' again. I continue to gain some confidence in my ability to learn. I enrolled for my three-year undergraduate program (BSc), majoring in Physics and minoring in Chemistry and Math. I was weak in Math in high school, but I took that as a challenge and did well in Math at college.

When I was in college, English was always a difficult subject for me. I had no opportunities to practice speaking it, so I was clueless about conversing in English. This became especially apparent when I traveled by train to another city for an interview, and a fellow passenger asked me if I spoke English. I said, "No." That moment made me realize I needed to improve my English skills quickly. So, I bought an English dictionary and started memorizing new words and phrases whenever I had free time. It was a slow process, but eventually, I started feeling more confident speaking in English.

I graduated with a 'First Class' in Physics, one of my life's most satisfying experiences: All my hard work and dedication had paid off, and I was excited to see what opportunities would come my way. After my undergraduate degree, I thought about attending an elite institute like IIT (Indian Institute of Technology), but I knew deep down that it wasn't the right fit. I didn't have the intellectual horsepower to comprehend complex concepts and equations. I wanted to avoid setting myself up for failure. It hurt to let go of that dream, but I knew it was the right decision.

I chose physics as my major because cosmology and the origins of the universe fascinated me. Religion always seemed like an abstract concept to me. As I delved deeper into physics, I was struck by the undeniable connection between the universe and the Higher power. In my book, I explore how this connection manifests and how the divine hand guides us all. It's a fascinating look at the intersection of science and spirituality, and I can't wait for you to read it (discussed in chapter 14). I remember reading Einstein's quotes in middle school and how they came in handy during college: "I stayed with the problem longer." As a physics graduate, I learned that tenacity and perseverance are part of my persona. I can perform better if I stay with the problems a little longer. This principle has stayed with me throughout my life, and I always strive to work hard and stay long enough to solve any problem that comes my way.

After graduating from college, I took a year off to explore my options. I even secured admission to a local college for an advanced degree in physics. However, I put my interest in physics on the side for a while. Instead, I focused more on my lifelong dream of coming to the United States. This dream started at a young age, and I had always wanted to experience everything America offered. Unfortunately, my first attempt to obtain a visitor visa to the US did not go as planned. I went to the consulate with all the necessary documents, but the Consular Officer asked me some questions I didn't understand. She even called in a translator, but the interview remained unsuccessful.

Alternatively, my community recognized my academic accomplishments. I was able to have some good interactions with society and even built a small circle of friends. Yet, I was naïve and unfamiliar with the dynamics of society. But I envisioned a successful life—I kept my dream of going to the US and getting an education.

In the meantime, a relative of mine advised me to pursue a Master's in business. I liked that idea. With some financial assistance from my aunt, I went to college outside of my state. My decision to go outside the state was to learn to speak English. I was not entirely convinced that MBA was the right career path. My interest was still in getting an advanced degree in Physics. It has nothing to do with my ability to learn Physics but rather to impress others that I am capable. I had no idea how a degree in Physics would have ever helped me build a career unless I graduated from a top school like IIT.

I was self-motivated and aimed for highs, but my emotional outbursts disguised those qualities. My parents called me a bookworm. I took everything in a literal sense. Mostly, my career ambition was tied to what society thought highly of. Seeking that social validation was ingrained in my mind. But life is not linear. The challenges we face early on in life can be crucial for our success if we learn from them and embrace them. Sometimes, I find myself projecting my insecurities or fears onto others, especially when I encounter situations that trigger memories from my childhood. For instance, I tend to gravitate toward friendly people and avoid those I think don't like me.

I was socially abrasive and awkward, often missing social cues and struggling to understand others. It's something that has caused me intense insecurity over the years. However, I've realized we all have our blind spots: anger, envy, fear, resentment, or even hatred.

Our anger only begets more anger, becoming a vicious cycle. Children must have supportive systems around to get through that. Instead of letting these negative emotions consume us, we can learn to harness them and turn them into something productive. In my case, I did not have any supportive system around me.

Chapter 4

A Foggy Future

I want to take you on my journey of learning English, my interest in physics and romance, and my struggle for success. I decided to enroll in an MBA program. I journeyed to Pune, a city located in Maharashtra, India. I had a relative accompany me to the college. Everything was a novel experience for me. Prior to this, I had never lived in a city other than my hometown. Being an introvert only heightened my anxiety. The initial day was filled with a whirlwind of emotions, and I grappled with intense homesickness.

A combination of poor language skills, a new environment, poor self-esteem, and lack of self-confidence gradually diminished my academic performance.

Let me be clear: I did not engage in self-handicapping to avoid making efforts that could lead to further failures and damage my self-esteem. Nor was it due to any intellectual insecurity on my part, as the study materials were not challenging to comprehend. However, I did face difficulties with maintaining focus. My relationship with a beautiful girl on campus worsened the situation—it consumed most of my time and was emotionally draining.

Reflecting on my past experiences, I noticed that my shortcomings mainly stem from my lack of emotional intelligence. Looking back, I realize that my lack of experience in dealing with my emotions had led me down a few misguided paths—I had struggled with impatience and insecurity. I regretted the time I had wasted worrying about the future and being upset about my present circumstances. As time went on, I gradually overcame my anxiety. The campus boasted a diverse student body hailing from various states and even African countries. This created an intriguing dynamic. I had the opportunity to immerse myself in different cultures and languages, which was an enriching experience.

On my first day on campus, I tasted the breakfast from the college cafeteria. We grabbed a plate and stood in line. There was little choice when it came to food. Every day we had bread and dal curry. Nonetheless, it was the most delicious food.

When I walked onto campus, I noticed everyone was wearing shoes except for me. My cousin had given me his old shoes, which were too big for me. But I didn't want to go barefoot, so I wore it anyway. It didn't go unnoticed by other students and was a bit embarrassing.

During my first few weeks on campus, I made a few friends from my community. I was grateful for their kindness since my friends spared me from a hazing ritual involving being dropped into a dirty concrete rainwater tank. Thanks to my quiet, simple, humble nature. I was relieved I didn't have to go through that experience.

As course registration approached, I sought advice from a senior student and decided to enroll in a combination of prerequisite courses and a core course, specifically Industrial Psychology.

I remember feeling very nervous on my first day of Industrial Psychology class. The lectures were all in English, and as I looked at myself, I realized I could hardly speak the language. All the other students in the class had previous backgrounds in psychology and were fluent in English, which made me feel even more intimidated.

Even though I had been doing well academically until then, I felt incredibly dumb sitting in a classroom full of such smart students. It was a challenging experience and further eroded my self-confidence. In the chapter "My Crusade to Educate My Child," I have explained my child's experience at her high school.

I had a young female professor who introduced us to the concept of "Group vs. Mob." I remember feeling completely lost when she asked us to find the difference between the two. However, as she explained that a group has a goal and a mob doesn't, it started to make sense. But then things got even more challenging when she introduced role-playing in the class. We had to read mini-cases and take on different roles every week. I was assigned the manager role in a case about employee behavior, and I was paired with a classmate who was much more fluent in English than I was. I was so embarrassed and couldn't even speak a word. Another day, the professor asked me to explain a concept in front of everyone, and I was so nervous that I turned to the blackboard and stood with my back to the class. She made a joke to lighten the mood: "No one wants to see your back," but I felt so embarrassed.

I did poorly on the course, and the professor gave me a D. This was the beginning of a downfall; I started with a GPA of 1.00. I realized that I had made a mistake by taking the course based solely on the fact that my roommate, a senior student from my community, was also enrolled. Irrespective of all the challenges, my interest was still in getting a degree in astronomy and astrophysics. Next to my College was the University of Pune. The University had a program on

Astronomy. Consequently, I spent more time in the library reading physics books than studying for my MBA class.

I think many of us have been there, feeling that knot of anxiety when faced with a daunting task. In my 'History of Management Thoughts' course, the professor assigned me a topic for a class presentation. When it was my turn, I didn't show up. I was too nervous and unsure of myself, and I let my fears get the best of me. It was a wake-up call that I needed to refocus and figure out what I wanted to do.

It's okay to stumble and feel unsure sometimes. What's important is finding a way to push past those doubts and forge ahead. It's all part of the journey toward self-discovery and growth. So, to any student out there feeling held back by their own uncertainties, remember that you're not alone. It's never too late to refocus and take that next step forward.

COLLEGE CAMPUS ROMANCE

During my first few months on campus, I received several anonymous letters from girls inviting me to meet them at a particular place. As a shy person with weak English language skills, I only bothered to meet a few. It turned out that some of those letters were just pranks. Years later, one of my classmates admitted to pranking me. However, some girls were genuinely interested in meeting me, but I wasn't interested in them. I often wondered what it was about me that they found appealing.

One day, I noticed a beautiful young girl sitting beside me at a coffee shop. It turned out that she was a model and a rising star on campus. When I went to a nearby photo studio, I saw her pictures all over the wall. I was immediately drawn to her charm.

I attended a community-based seminar on campus every Friday night after church. I was surprised to see her there. I then realized she was from my community.

While I was in the cafeteria one day, I couldn't help but notice her sitting across from me. As she got up to leave, she turned around and waved her hand at me. I thought she was waving at me, so I waved back. That was the moment I decided to talk to her. I waited for her outside her class and finally found the confidence to say, "Hello." She responded positively, and we hit it off. We went to a coffee shop and talked for hours. She said she wasn't waving at me that day in the cafeteria, but that was all the motivation I needed to pursue her. And now, here we are, sitting together.

We both soon fell in love. I had something to focus on now. It was hilarious, to say the least, when I was struggling with my GPA. The relationship consumed so much of our time. The students on the campus noticed our romance, especially 'my' relationship with a beautiful girl. Some of her friends told her, "Shajan is so simple and humble."

Every Friday evening, we had a prayer meeting. After that, I walked her to her hostel. Often, we stayed outside the hostel and talked for a few minutes. The lady in charge of the hostel always got very upset with me. She happened to be from my community as well. Our relationship solidified as the days went by. I would visit her at her hostel whenever I wanted to see her.

My friends introduced me to something they called "5-6." At first, I had no idea what it meant. They explained that it was the only designated time for couples to meet. Typically, couples would get together for just one hour, from 5 p.m. to 6 p.m., near the lady's hostel, next to the cafeteria. It was a tight timeframe, considering our dinner hour stretched from 5 p.m. to 7 p.m. Nevertheless, I made it a point to stop by the lady's hostel on my way; she would be there waiting for me. This gave me the impression that our campus was liberal and accommodating towards dating and courtship, but not as much when it came to career-building. Our relationship was no secret on campus; practically everyone knew about us. However, there were certain restrictions in place, particularly for my girlfriend, who was an undergraduate student. Her teachers often cautioned her about these rules, emphasizing that she could face expulsion if violated, which added an extra layer of complexity to our relationship. As a graduate student, I didn't encounter such issues.

Months later, during a chilly December Saturday morning, I braved the cold weather and asked one of her friends to let her know I was waiting for her. I reluctantly left after waiting a few minutes.

Later that day, when I met her, she was angry over my emotional outburst to her friend. I still remember those few moments of rage unleashed over trivial things. Psychologist calls this "neural hijacking" (amygdala hijack).

Understanding how our brain processes emotions is critical to managing our reactions. The amygdala, known for processing primal emotions, hijacks our thought processes, triggering subconscious reactions before our rational brain (prefrontal cortex) fully comprehends the situation. This neural hijacking can lead to a loss of control and destructive emotions. By learning to regulate these responses, we can improve our emotional intelligence and make more informed decisions. However, I was unaware of how to control my emotions, let alone assess their impact on my mental and emotional well-being.

The relationship took up most of my time, leaving little time to focus on my studies. Then something happened. Her parents decided to take her to a new school, and that shattered everything we'd built with each other.

She decided to leave the campus and visited me a few times. One day, I told her we could not continue this as it badly impacted my studies. That was the end of that relationship.

The experience taught me a valuable lesson about the irresistible beauty of women, which can make men feel powerless and vulnerable. Unfortunately, as someone who is emotionally sensitive, this dynamic negatively impacted my mental well-being. Despite this, I was undeterred. I kept moving forward.

I made it my mission to improve my English language skills and become a confident public speaker. I was determined to progress. I approached my dean and asked to join the graduation club prayer meeting. To my surprise, I was allowed to lead the team in prayer. Standing before my classmates, I recited a prayer that I had memorized, feeling proud of myself for taking on this challenge and continuing to work on my public speaking skills.

WHAT I WANT TO ACHIEVE IN MY CAREER

I spent much time considering my career options. I realized that my introverted nature, intellectual curiosity, and analytical and quantitative skills would make me a good fit for research-related jobs.

I discovered my passions when I was 23. I'm not one to procrastinate because I know that when I panic, I can't perform at my best and build up cortisol in my body. I tend to experience a sense of panic days or even weeks before a deadline.

I am particularly interested in human behavior, especially what motivates people to act in certain ways within a work environment. My fascination with this subject led me to an engaging course on organizational behavior. While reading a book, I stumbled upon a Japanese concept known as Quality Circle, which focuses on "*continuous improvement.*" Intrigued by this idea, I decided to delve deeper and discovered that a few companies near my college were actively practicing Quality Circle principles. I reached out to one of my professors. He introduced me to someone responsible for overseeing Quality Circle initiatives through his connections. And so, my journey into this field began.

As a part of the MBA program, we had to complete a dissertation. It was a more rigorous part of our program, where we had a Mini-PhD thesis with the defense team and a final thesis presentation. For my thesis, I researched the intangible impact of the Quality Circle at work. I had a few professors on my defense team. One of them was Col. Rodrigues. Given my poor presentation skills and lack of attention to his lecture, he often teased me in class. He commented that I could have been more spontaneous during one of my presentations. Although I promised to do better next time, he said, "It is meaningless," reminding me that it was my last class under him.

While writing this book, I remembered a story about Col. Rodrigues that I'd like to share. Writing has been a passion of mine since my college days. Despite my lack of confidence in my writing abilities, I forged ahead. I wrote an article on Quality Circle for our Business School magazine. Col. Rodrigues was the editor. He read my piece and didn't mince words. He called it the worst he'd ever edited.

It was disheartening to hear that from my professor. Also, referring to my article, he said, "The road to hell is paved with good intention." It's a saying that hits close to home for many of us, as our sincere efforts to help others can sometimes result in unintended and even disastrous consequences. This truth has become more apparent later in my life.

I often find myself thinking of this in a slightly different way:

"No good deeds go unpunished."

It's a reminder that despite our best intentions, we may encounter challenges and setbacks. But it's essential to remember that even in the face of adversity, our good deeds can still positively impact and contribute to a better world. So, while it may seem like a tough road at times, our intentions to do good should never waver.

After many months of reading and researching, I submitted my proposal for the dissertation. That was as far as my research dissertation on Quality Circle went.

In retrospect, my graduate program was a valuable learning experience that taught me a lot about myself and the importance of emotional management. I realized that ignoring our emotions is not an effective solution (discussed in Chapter 14). When I encountered setbacks and failed to meet my academic expectations, I struggled with fear and anxiety, which had a negative impact on my mental and emotional well-being. However, I was determined to find constructive ways to cope with these emotions and work towards my goals.

Science proves why we are susceptible to our emotions. Emerging research has shown that our brain development starts in adolescence and continues into the early 20s: the prefrontal cortex—responsible for weighing consequences vs. instant gratification, making thoughtful decisions, and managing emotions—doesn't fully mature until the mid-20s and possibly even later.

Therefore, it is imperative to instill a sense of worth and value in ourselves from an early age. We must challenge our beliefs and adopt a "rethink" approach to life. Creating an academic environment that focuses on building critical thinking skills ("how to think") is crucial. By doing so, we can overcome our emotional impulses and make informed, rational decisions that lead to academic success and fulfillment (see Part Two, "My Academic Career")

I remember feeling so helpless to deal with my anger and emotional outbursts. No one taught me how to handle my emotions, so I developed this attention-seeking behavior to cope. It wasn't until I became a young adult that I realized I needed to find a better way to address my feelings.

Looking back, I wish I had known about emotional intelligence earlier. When I read Daniel Goleman's book, I understood the importance of understanding our emotions and why we act the way we do. It's not something we're born with but a skill we can learn and develop. Now, I see the power of positive emotions (positive neural pathways) and how they can help us navigate life's challenges.

Here is a situation in a shop:

We call it a corner shop since it is at the corner of our college campus. It was on a Saturday night. I was drinking Kala Paani (black tea) with my friends. A mutual friend of ours came to me. He became upset over my comment about him, and his frustration escalated to the point where he began physically pushing me around. I embarrassed myself in front of others. It was unthinkable for a simple, humble young man to fight with someone twice his size. I could have easily avoided that confrontation if I had managed my ego and apologized to him for saying something that offended him.

Speaking of ego, I remember lying to my friends. I had a few close friends who knew me well, but I always felt insecure about my humble upbringing. I went to great lengths to hide it, even telling them I had a home telephone connection when I didn't. I even gave them a fake phone number to reinforce the lie. Looking back, I realize how silly and unnecessary it was to lie about something so trivial, but my ego got the best of me there, too. It reminds us how our egos can sometimes cloud our judgment and lead us down dangerous paths. Moments like these teach us the importance of humility and honesty in our interactions with others.

MY FIRST JOB

"Life is like riding a bicycle. To keep your balance, you must keep moving."

— Albert Einstein

I applied for a few jobs and finally landed a job in a small

75

company. They offered me a salary of 1500 rupees, and my job was to start a small tea company. The first few months were spent doing a feasibility study, and we decided to begin the business. I struggled with the job's marketing aspect and was not very good at handling the company's internal politics. My primary responsibility was procuring tea, packaging it under the company's brand name, and selling it to local stores. However, this was a resale business, and we were competing with major brands. Although my first job experience was challenging, it taught me a great deal about the challenges of building a company. It was a valuable lesson that helped shape my future career path.

I recognized my poor sales skills and decided to focus on my strengths. This realization led me to pursue a research and investment banking career when I moved to the US.

I often share my early life experiences with my students, hoping to inspire them to take on internships and discover their strengths. I remind them that failure is not the end of the road but rather an opportunity for growth. Many successful people have faced significant setbacks and challenges. However, what sets them apart is their willingness to learn from those obstacles and use them as motivation to keep moving forward. The distinguishing factor is their ability to glean valuable lessons from those hurdles and transform them into fuel that drives their progress. This is the essence of resilience and determination.

As an educator, I strongly encourage my students to embrace their failures and use them as a driving force to achieve their goals. I have personally experienced the benefits of this mindset in my own life. The first third of my life was filled with valuable lessons I learned from my failures. These lessons have helped me reap the fruits of my labor in the following third of my life. In Chapter 5, "Embrace the Beauty of Life and Its Struggles," I share the struggles I endured and the success I achieved by embracing my failures.

A NEW CHAPTER IN MY PERSONAL LIFE

"A great marriage is not when the 'perfect couple' comes together. It is when an imperfect couple learns to enjoy their differences."
— Dave Meurer

Translation: "Shared interests foster *unity,* while differences ensure *Cohesion in a marriage.*"

It is the differences that bring diversity and excitement to a relationship, and being able to embrace them can strengthen the bond between partners. However, marriage is treated mainly as a social and legal contract. The way I think, marriage is the union of two individuals that brings greater commitment, intimacy, and emotional connection, but not necessarily financial security (see Chapter 17, "A Marriage Made in Hell"). I was undeterred and determined to maintain the "sacred union" within this definition of marriage. For me, it meant cherishing the deeper connection that transcends societal norms and legalities, emphasizing the profound emotional and spiritual ties that bind two people together.

One relationship ended, and another began to blossom.

Two individuals raised in distinct cultures came together with such profound feelings for each other that they sensed an instant connection as if they had known each other their entire lives.

In June 1994, my parents sent me a letter informing me that they had found a girl they wanted me to meet. They showed her a picture of me that I had taken with my ex-girlfriend's camera, which was a very flattering shot.

I was around 25 years of age, very thin, and confused. I was nowhere like what I was in the picture. But it was a great marketing tool. I decided to meet the young lady. Accompanied by my sister, younger brother, and a relative, we set out for our rendezvous. I can't deny feeling a mix of nervousness and shyness as the moment approached. It's a sentiment many of us who have traversed the path of matchmaking can certainly relate to. The anticipation and uncertainty of such encounters are palpable, yet they often lead to valuable experiences and new connections.

Everyone's eyes were on me as I sat at the table. A young lady approached and offered each of us a glass of tea. I couldn't help but notice her beauty—her wide-broad eyes, beautiful teeth, and stunning smile. Nevertheless, I was drawn to think that she could benefit from losing a few pounds. Without thinking, I asked her if she had ever considered visiting an obesity clinic in the US. Looking back, I realize how insensitive and socially awkward I was. However, she didn't seem offended by my comments, or perhaps she didn't understand my English very well. Either way, I regret my behavior and wish I had been more thoughtful in my choice of words. After that short rendezvous, a family member asked me if I liked her. Instead of answering, I asked for his opinion. He thought she was beautiful. Although I wanted to share our thoughts with her, my relative was mature enough to suggest otherwise: it wasn't the right time to express our opinion. Reflecting on that moment, I realized I was petulant, socially abrasive, and self-absorbed.

While on my way back home, it was a challenging feat. It was a bit jarring at first, but I kept an open mind. After returning to Pune, I took some time to think about the situation. Eventually, I decided to ask my father for his opinion. He and my family encouraged me to pursue the relationship since she was beautiful and around 22. I spent several days pondering the matter, and eventually, I had an epiphany that I should go ahead with the arranged marriage. The decision felt right, and I was confident it would be life-changing for me, even though I had only chatted with her for a few minutes.

During my first meeting with my future mother-in-law, I noticed a hint of uncertainty in her demeanor as she had not yet formed her own opinion of me as her daughter's future partner. She was a straightforward and humble lady. She asked me a few questions and smiled at me. However, I couldn't help but notice a reflective mood in her, which made me wonder about her views and dreams for her daughter's future. The engagement went smoothly, and we married in a church a few weeks later. Now that I think of it, I am grateful for my mother-in-law's kind and accepting nature, which made our transition into married life much easier.

My wedding day was quite an unexpected experience from the very start. During the ceremony, the priest supposed to officiate the wedding became upset with us over some payments we had overlooked—*count the money, not the blessing* (see pages 325-328, "The Envelope—Does God Need Our Money"). Despite all the challenges, I married her on July 25, 1994, at around 11.45 a.m. That moment was a turning point in my life, as I realized I had taken on the responsibility of supporting a family at a young age. I've always followed my passion with unwavering determination, regardless of the challenges that may arise. This trait still defines who I am today.

After the wedding, we walked out of the church and were greeted by two angry dogs barking and attacking each other. It was a chaotic scene, and I couldn't refrain from feeling uneasy about it. It seemed like a bad omen to me.

After her parents left for the US, she stayed with me for a few weeks. We decided to travel by train to Pune and then to Mumbai for her flight to the US. In Pune, we met a few of my close friends. I dropped her off at the airport the next day.

Now, I needed to be more responsible. I asked myself how I could make a living. After a few days of soul-searching, I got some sense as to what I should pursue. I still could not map out my career path and felt I should stay focused on my strengths: a rational and analytical mindset.

Throughout my life, I've found that success is primarily determined by the degree to which one deploys their talents—create an *abundant mindset*.

As discussed in Chapter 1, the term *"abundant mindset"* is a belief that there are enough resources in the world for everyone and that if you work hard and stay positive, you can achieve your goals. This mindset is the opposite of a *scarcity mindset*, which is the belief that there is never enough and that you must compete with others to get what you want. By cultivating an abundant mindset, you can start seeing opportunities where you once saw obstacles, and it can help you feel more confident about your future. Neuroscience backs this idea, and I've found it true. Staying focused and motivated has been easier for me since adopting this mindset. While I had no idea what the future held, I felt my dedication to this principle would serve me well. Recalling those days, it's clear that none of us can predict with certainty how our lives will unfold (see pages 245-254, "Pure Consciousness: The Intersection of Quantum Science and Humanity). It's often a journey marked with uncertainty, surprises, and unexpected opportunities. Yet, by wholeheartedly investing in our talents and continuously striving for improvement, we equip ourselves to navigate this uncertain path with resilience and the potential for remarkable achievements.

Chapter 5

Embrace the Beauty of Life and Its Struggles

"If you want to live a happy life, tie it to a goal, not to people or things."

—Albert Einstein

The scripture says, "As you sow, so shall you reap."

Life is a beautiful journey as long as we have a positive mindset. I have encountered obstacles and challenges, but I was determined. I have learned to adapt and overcome struggles. I am grateful for the lessons I have learned and the experiences that have shaped me. As I continue my journey, I am excited to see what the future holds and where this path will lead me.

Create goals and strive towards accomplishing them. That is the secret to success. A goal in life keeps your life moving, and of course, you can enjoy a sense of accomplishment, regardless of how small those accomplishments are.

I moved from a failed insurance salesman and stockbroker to an analyst to an investment banker. My career took a giant leap forward.

I never focused on money. I always believed in the process, not the outcome. That principle worked very well for me throughout my life and career. So, I wrote this great line,

"Follow your passion, money will follow."

Later, I modified it into *"follow your passion, get better at it, money will follow."*

On November 6, 1995, I was interviewed at the Mumbai US consulate for my visa. I appeared before the consular officer, and she asked me if I could speak English. I said, "I can." She reviewed all the papers and said,

"Welcome to the United States."

Well, this was my fourth interview at a US consulate before coming to the US. I sat at the consulate for a few more minutes before I made a phone call to share the good news with my wife. Looking back, I'm proud to say that I achieved two significant goals I set for myself early on: *learning to speak English and immigrating to the United States*.

On November 22, I landed in the United States of America. It was brutally cold. I reunited with my wife, and she looked beautiful as ever. However, life was far from footloose and fancy-free.

PURSUIT OF FINDING MY DREAM JOB

My father-in-law took me to a few places and introduced me to his friends and a few of his relatives. My wife drove me to my cousin's home for dinner. It was my first time witnessing a woman drive a car, and I was truly impressed by her driving skills. The next day, she took me to her friends at her college. Some of her friends told me, "I sounded like a kid on the phone." I had a taste of Chinese curry chicken at a Chinese restaurant nearby.

She took me for a train ride from Liberty Avenue in Queens to Manhattan. I experienced the New York City train service and subway system. On our way back to Queens, the train was nearly empty, and it was then that my wife attempted to kiss me. I hesitated and declined, as public displays of intimacy were considered taboo in India. Nevertheless, I couldn't help but admire her audacity in such a public setting.

After receiving my social security card, I was eager to begin my job search in the US. Despite the challenge of heavy snowfall during my interview period in January, I persisted and made it to interviews. During one interview, I was offered a position of selling products door-to-door. My colleague and I braved the brutal cold to reach potential customers. He acquainted me with "impulse buying" and elaborated on how individuals buy products spontaneously without prior planning.

I realized I wasn't interested when I observed him pitching the product to potential customers. The following day, I had an interview and took the subway to Franklin Square, only to realize I had gotten off at the wrong stop. Feeling lost and unsure of what to do next, I eventually decided to head back home.

I distinctly recall a period when I felt quite adrift in my life. I was in the midst of a job search, actively seeking employment opportunities. During this uncertain time, I came across an advertisement for a financial advisor position at an insurance company. They promised to pay $2,000 for the first six months of training, which caught my attention. I applied and was excited when I got invited in for an interview. The manager I met with was of Indian descent, and he brought in another person to explain the job responsibilities and how to achieve the million-dollar roundtable. I knew I had a lot to learn and a few licensing exams to take before becoming a fully functioning agent and financial advisor.

While studying for the exam, I had the opportunity to travel with an agent knowledgeable about the business. During my travels, I met a few of his clients who asked me if I enjoyed the work. This made me realize how competitive the industry is and how difficult it can be to advance one's career, particularly for someone with an introverted personality and limited sales skills.

I felt good about myself and my abilities, so I wasn't prepared enough when it was time to take the insurance exam. I assumed that I could pass it easily. Nonetheless, my overconfidence got the best of me, and I failed the exam. I tried again, and this time, I passed. I finally became an agent/financial advisor. My first policy was on me and my wife. I also wrote a policy on my mother-in-law and my sister-in-law. I regretted it later.

I got my driver's license. A few months later, I bought my first car—a red Toyota Corolla. My in-laws were kind enough to put a down payment. The finance manager at the dealership convinced me to buy an extra warranty, costing me another 5,000 dollars. I was naïve. That purchase was quite expensive.

One day, I was reversing the car from the driveway, and I hit another parked on the corner of our driveway. It was a minor hit, but I panicked. I am not a neuroscientist, but I have learned that when we are under stress, our brain releases a hormone called Cortisol, which

86

increases the adrenal level and clouds our thinking, blocking the prefrontal cortex from functioning effectively. That is what happened to me. I was born with the 'worry genes.' I kept reversing the car. My car got severely damaged. I got my first taste of the accident and recognized how poor a driver I was. I was embarrassed by my stupidity. If I had taken a few seconds to think before I moved my car, I could have easily avoided that costly damage to my vehicle. This has been my thinking pattern for years since childhood—I react quickly.

I was not happy about continuing my insurance career path. My interest all along was to find a job on Wall Street. I heard a lot about the position of a Wall Street analyst. The job was well-paying, had a high profile, and did not require many sales skills.

In the meantime, I had to move out of my in-laws' house. To cover our living expenses, I was accruing credit card debt. While working, I enrolled for my Master's in Business and also incurred some student loans. I learned some basic accounting and took more finance courses to prepare for a job as an analyst on Wall Street.

I went to a boutique firm on Wall Street. The firm had both investment banking and research divisions. They would take companies public, and the analysts would write research reports on those stocks. Brokers used this research and pitched stocks to their clients. It was a brilliant business model, and the environment appealed to me, given my passion to be a research analyst.

I was offered a job working alongside an experienced broker for $1,000 monthly. Money wasn't my motivation. I knew I couldn't sell water in a desert. My primary motivation for this role was to learn more about the stock market and eventually transition into an analyst position. I was determined to make the most of the opportunity. My responsibilities involved cold calling potential clients from 8 in the morning until 7 in the evening, all while working towards securing my licenses. On my first day, the broker gave me a script to follow, which I memorized and practiced with him. Although initially challenging, I gradually became more comfortable with the process and started making some successful calls.

The licensing exam day had finally arrived, and I was nervous. It was a grueling six-hour exam determining my future success as a broker. I knew I had to pass the test to build my book of business instead of relying on cold calls for a broker. The pressure was immense, and I could feel my heart racing as I completed the test and hit the submit button. That few seconds of waiting for the results felt like an eternity, and then I saw the word 'pass' on my screen. I was relieved. I knew that all my hard work had paid off. I was finally on a path to achieving my dreams.

I was licensed to pitch stocks and was responsible for contacting the qualified leads I created and pitching them a stock the firm was promoting. The same firm underwrote the stocks, and they were called "house stocks." These stocks were bought and sold within the firm by another broker, which allowed both brokers to cross-sell each other. The stocks needed more liquidity, and this was based on the demand and supply within the same firm. I spent countless hours sitting at a table and making hundreds of calls to pitch these stocks. Some individuals listened to me, and I qualified the leads for the broker.

A few months later, I was finally given the green light to open my accounts and work independently. However, I soon realized that my previous salary of $1000 had been taken away, and my new role was known as the "eat what you kill program." I had to work hard to make sales and generate commissions. Despite the added pressure, I persevered and built a small client base over a few months.

While working as a stockbroker, I simultaneously pursued a junior analyst position within the same firm. Regrettably, my lack of focus on the sales role led to my termination from the company, extinguishing any hopes of securing the analyst position I had been striving for.

Over two tumultuous years, I faced the harsh reality of unemployment and underemployment, which had a severe impact on my mental and emotional well-being, as well as my finances. During this trying time, I took on odd jobs to make ends meet and dedicated myself to improving my skills for a research analyst role. Moreover, I enrolled in the CFA program to enhance my qualifications and passed the level 1 exam successfully. I applied to numerous junior analyst programs, eager to put my newfound knowledge to work, but was met with silence.

My journey continued, with each step leading me closer to my dream job. The road ahead was long and winding, but I was determined to keep moving forward.

I was going through a tough time trying to make both ends meet. One day, my landlord, who also happened to be a relative, came to me asking for his rent. I had no other option but to go to a bank and borrow $3,000 on my credit card, the maximum available cash credit, with an interest rate of 21%. The teller at the bank gave me a look and said,

"This is quite an expensive living."

As I ponder upon my past, it dawns on me that I had a tough time dealing with stress, which negatively impacted the overall home environment. I regret having moments where I would hurl objects, bang my head against the wall (knowing all too well that the wall always wins), and yell and scream. It was like there was a devil inside me that I couldn't control.

MARRIED LIFE

Married life was an incredible journey for me—mixed emotions. Becoming a father at a young age brought me so much joy, but it also meant that I had to face the challenges of supporting my family. Financially, I wasn't quite prepared for building a family. Nevertheless, I made the audacious decision and allowed my wife to stay home during her pregnancy and beyond. Despite the immense financial strain, having her at home was immeasurably comforting. It was a decision made out of unconditional love for my wife and unborn child, as I couldn't bear to see her go through the stress of work and travel.

The decision required many sacrifices, as I had to borrow more money to cover her health insurance and other household expenses. This was a significant change from the traditional 50/50 marriage model—the merger of equals (*matchers become match-makers*). In my family, there was no such thing as 50-50—I cooked, cleaned, and paid the bill happily and proudly.

To make life even more miserable, one of my credit card companies put a hold on my bank account for defaulting on the payment. I had $800 in my bank account. I paid $500 to the credit card company, and the bank charged $100 to remove the hold on my account. I ended up with $200 in my account.

I even used my wife's credit cards to pay some bills. I learned painful but valuable lessons about borrowing from family members and apologized for putting her through all the mental agony. From that moment on, I made a conscious decision never to borrow money in her name again, even when it came to significant investments like purchasing our first home.

I consolidated all my debts with a debt consolidation company, paying a fixed monthly payment. My credit score was below 500. My struggles to make ends meet only seemed to grow bigger. Our landlord wasn't too pleased with my financial situation, and we had to find a new place to live. We moved out to a new place, paying a few hundred dollars more when I had over $100,000 in credit card debt and student loans.

I FOUND JESUS—I HIT THE ROCK BOTTOM

The burdens I carried seemed never-ending. I found myself entangled in a web of substantial financial and emotional hardships. The weight of my responsibilities grew heavier as I struggled with the daunting task of supporting my family while simultaneously contending with missed credit card and student loan payments. These struggles unfolded against a backdrop of unstable and tumultuous financial markets.

The situation became even more distressing when my family chose to distance themselves from my precarious circumstances. It was tough when the family I thought I could count on turned their back on me in difficult times.

"A transactional approach blurs the meaning of love in a relationship. Our character defines the values and principles we live by daily, and these same values form the essence of nurturing valuable relationships, especially in a marriage."

Approaching a relationship with a transactional mindset distorts the true essence of love and turns *matchers into mere matchmakers.* In doing so, we risk losing sight of the deeper relationship at the core of any healthy relationship: recognizing and appreciating each other's unique value and worth.

I love my family for "who they are, not what they can bring." This principle is what truly defines the nature of genuine love and respect.

It's unfortunate that in our world, money and material possessions often take priority over genuine love, especially in a marriage. I had compassion for my family; they were too conditioned to view relationships through a transactional lens, where money was the primary factor in a marriage.

"Count the money, not the blessing."

In the book, I delve into the damaging effects of religious institutions on our families, particularly how they instill a conditional relationship and create hardships (see Chapter 16, pages 325-328). It provides powerful evidence to support the destructive consequences of deceptive religious claims.

My financial hardship was a highly challenging and stressful situation to deal with. It left me feeling overwhelmed, helpless, and in the throes of deep despair. I was suicidally depressive.

"I hit the rock bottom."

But I was a hustler. It's still a mystery to me how I managed to summon remarkable resilience.

It was during this trying period that I stumbled upon a piece of advice that resonated with me:

"The true measure of success is how often you can bounce back from failures."

When you focus on something you truly love and work hard to improve your skills, the money will eventually follow.

I had been out of affiliation with a broker-dealer for nearly two years. As a result, my licenses were on the verge of expiring. I walked into a boutique broker-dealer to see if they were hiring cold callers. A broker took my resume and asked me to come back the next day so he could speak with his boss, Paul. The following day, he called me and offered me a cold-calling job for $500 monthly. When I arrived for work, Paul wanted to meet me. I went to Paul's office, and he took out my resume, remarking how impressed he was with my qualifications. I was honest with him. I told him, "I am broke and broken—I am fiscally broke and emotionally broken: deep in credit card and student loan debt." He said, "Your education will pay huge dividends."

He told me about his whole career and life. He was a humble man who owned a brokerage firm employing around 50 people. We talked for hours about my recent piece on telecom companies, and he seemed interested in my take on the industry. It was no surprise, given the intense interest in telecom companies in 2000 when the dot.com bubble was in full swing and stocks were skyrocketing. What was surprising was that he offered me a job as an equity research analyst on the spot without me having to do any cold calling for the broker. He suggested that I work with other professionals in the company to cover telecom companies. I was so excited and emotional, saying, "You are like God to me." He replied, "We are all created in the image of God."

I dressed in my best suit and tie the next day and headed to work. I still couldn't believe that Paul offered me a job as a research analyst. He handed me a $10 bill and told me to get my fingerprints taken at the nearby police station as part of renewing my license. Walking down the street towards the station, I couldn't stop thinking about what had just happened. It didn't matter whether I was working for a top-rated Wall Street firm or a boutique firm where I could fail and learn from my mistakes. All that mattered was that I had achieved my goal. Wow!

I felt so relieved that I could comfortably make a living. I put a lot of effort into my work, going in early and staying late, sometimes even working weekends. It felt like I was burning the candle at both ends. My willingness to go above and beyond the call of duty was a testament to my commitment to improving my skills. I ended up building a great relationship with my boss, Paul. We bonded over our shared interests in books and knowledge. One Saturday morning, while printing out my research reports, Paul complimented me on my dedication, saying that it's a part of who I am, regardless of who I work for.

He was so helpful in proofreading my reports and offered some constructive feedback. I didn't have much experience with research reports, so his input was incredibly valuable to me. He was kind in pointing out areas where I could improve my writing skills.

STRUGGLE AND SURVIVAL

Wait. I am not done with my beautiful life. The early 2000s saw Wall Street facing significant challenges, with dot-com stocks crashing. Our firm was in a tough spot due to our exposure to dot.com stocks. A few people had to be laid off as a result. One morning, Paul called me into his office. I felt I was next on the chopping block. But instead of letting me go, he explained the situation to me. He said he fired his accountant and asked if I could take over some of the accounting work in addition to my current role as an analyst. I realized I would likely be out of a job if I didn't agree to do the accounting work, and perhaps I would've been unable to share this story today. Although I had a finance background, I didn't have any experience in the financial controller's job, which included making journal entries, reconciling payroll and bank statements, and preparing financial statements.

"When backed up against the wall, the only way is forward. We can do amazing things with this positive mindset."

95

As usual, I took the plunge and decided to do the accounting work too. Paul assigned a CPA to help me with the accounting tasks. After a month of training, I created all the necessary financial statements and functioned as an accountant.

I did two jobs for the same salary. While I put great effort into both, I became more engaged with my research work over the weekends and evenings. I learned how to present my research reports to brokers in the morning, who then pitched those ideas to their clients during the day—a typical Wall Street way of doing things.

One day, Paul introduced me to his new hire, a young Jewish American. He was born and raised in Brooklyn, New York. His father worked as an insurance broker, and he started his career in the stock market when he was 18 years old. I was fascinated by his impressive sales skills. He could sell ice cream to Eskimos. He was an exceptional salesperson, able to sell anything to anyone with his smooth talking and quick thinking. Despite our differences in backgrounds and personalities, we became good friends. I was amazed to witness the friendship between a reserved Indian with a thick Indian accent and a Jewish American with exceptional sales skills.

It was a good fit: we complemented each other's weaknesses. I was good analytically, while he was natural at salesmanship. Together, we made a great team.

Things couldn't be emotionally worse. One morning, when I went to the office, I saw everybody with a sad face. It was like a dark cloud had descended upon the place, and it was hard to shake off the feeling of gloom that seemed to permeate everything. Something terrible had occurred, and everyone was feeling the impact. They told me Paul had passed away. He had a massive heart attack the previous night. I could not control my emotions. I went to his office and spent a few moments looking around. Plenty of books and company reports are all on the floor exactly how he left them. Paul is no more!

As I pondered the state of our existence on this earth, the words from Genesis 6:3 echoed in my mind.

"My spirit won't remain with human beings forever because they're truly mortal."

The realization that our time here is limited and our mortality is inevitable struck me deeply. I remembered what Paul said on the first day of our meeting, *"We are created in the image of God."*

I had a new boss. I continued to do both my accounting and analyst jobs. One day, my boss called me into his office and expressed gratitude for all the accounting work I'd been doing. He then asked me to pay myself a $1,000 bonus in the next payroll. I was grateful for his generosity, especially considering my financial struggles with student loans and credit card debt. A month later, he gave me a two-year forgivable loan of $10,000 to help pay down some of my credit card debt. I also received the same financial support from my Jewish-American friend. It was a huge relief. I was so grateful for their kindness.

TALES OF OVERCOMING ADVERSITY

I transitioned from analyst to investment banking while keeping up with my accounting work. This shift opened up a whole new world of opportunities for me. In investment banking, I helped companies secure funding and provided valuable advisory services. Not only was it rewarding in terms of experience, but it was also financially lucrative.

I enjoyed that opportunity since I was able to use my analytical skills. I felt confident communicating effectively with management, conducting due diligence, and analyzing and valuing companies. It was a great experience to take on all aspects of a deal. I did everything from 'soup to nuts' and manufactured ready-to-sell deals.

I worked with my "friend and colleague." He and his team were in charge of closing all the deals. The work was challenging as the products we sold were under intense regulatory scrutiny from the self-regulatory agency—FINRA. This meant that we had to follow all the procedures and policies carefully. This often led to heated arguments and screaming matches with my "friend and colleague." Sometimes, I was worried that my licenses were on the line. But at the end of the day, we managed to resolve our issues. Despite our differences, we were able to work together effectively.

I used to be the one who would often start arguments with him. But he understood me and my intense emotional outbursts. I was rough and tumbled on the surface, but I cared about him, and so did he. It was more of a task-oriented conflict, not a relationship issue.

I've had my fair share of challenging experiences with others at work, too, and I know how frustrating it can be when dealing with people who think they know everything. I've always found that there's so much to be gained from learning from others, and it's hard to do that when you're constantly being bossed around by someone incompetent and selfish. It drove me crazy. Trying to get along with people at work was tough when my emotions got in the way.

I did all the heavy-duty analytical work and manufactured deals. We did our first deal, raising 10 million dollars for a small publicly traded company. We received reasonably decent cash fees and warrants[5]. So, we also participated in the stock's upside, besides the cash compensation. We got $1 million in cash fees from the company. For the first time, I saw the real investment banking business. I paid myself $150,000, more than enough to pay off all my debts. We continued to do deals and brought in fees. As a banker, I made over a million dollars in the first two years. It is like the expression, *"setbacks are nothing but a setup for a comeback."*

As my journey unfolded, I witnessed a gradual transformation in my life. The weight of debt that had once burdened me was lifted, allowing me to breathe freely and envision a brighter financial future. My credit score markedly improved, a tangible testimony to my disciplined efforts to manage my finances more effectively.

With this newfound financial stability, I felt a refreshing surge of motivation to push myself even further. Pursuing my career goal to become a Wall Street professional took center stage. Along the way, I diligently amassed a wealth of experience and knowledge in key areas, arming myself with the tools necessary to navigate the competitive landscape of the financial world. Each step forward became a building block, solidifying my path toward achieving my aspirations. This journey, marked by its ups and downs, ultimately reinforced the invaluable lesson that one can overcome financial

---

[5] Warrants are financial instruments that allow the holder to buy an underlying security at a predetermined price before a specified date.

challenges and lay the foundation for a prosperous future with determination and persistence.

PERILS OF YOUTH

One day, my 5-year-old daughter asked me, *"When are we buying a house?"* She had this dream of living in a spacious home. We finally purchased our first house in the summer of 2005, comfortable enough for our small family.

I wanted to fulfill my child's wish of living in a big house and my insatiable desire to impress people. I had such a low sense of self-esteem. I purchased less than half an acre of land near a small city in India and built a beautiful house overlooking a lake. I was the conspicuous consumer in the history of conspicuous consumption in the village where I grew up—and grew up poor.

My love for conspicuous consumption didn't end there. I went to a Mercedes Benz dealership and purchased my first luxury car—an S550 in 2007. It symbolized my hard-earned success. It was something I envisioned when I was working for the insurance company. One of my colleagues had a snapshot of a Mercedes Benz in his workspace. A decade later, I had the privilege of owning a more expensive model.

"Overnight success is a lifetime making."

Achieving anything significant in life takes years of hard work, dedication, and persistence.

As I write this book, I'm compelled to reflect on our powerful emotional drive to impress others with our wealth. It's a destructive force that ultimately brings no meaningful value to our lives. It's caused me to question my sanity—the constant urge to find freedom externally with our hard-earned money and take little time to seek the freedom within. The dopamine in my brain was pushing me for more *short-term pleasure.*

Consider for a moment the allure of material wealth—the shiny new car, the lavish house, the designer clothes—all gleaming symbols of affluence that beckon us. We strive tirelessly, pouring our blood, sweat, and tears into the pursuit of financial success. Yet, as the dust settles and we find ourselves amidst the trappings of wealth, we must ask:

Does this accumulation of wealth truly enrich our lives? Does it bring us lasting happiness or a sense of profound fulfillment?

I have contended with these questions, often wondering about the state of my own sanity. The constant desire for external validation through our finances is like a hedonic treadmill or a hamster running on a wheel. We never get anywhere with our insatiable desire to please others. We chase the illusion of internal freedom, believing that wealth will be the key to unlocking the doors to our dreams and desires. Yet, in our relentless pursuit, we may inadvertently neglect the pursuit of inner freedom—the kind that doesn't depend on the size of our bank accounts or the value of our possessions.

It's a paradox that resonates with many of us. We tirelessly work to amass wealth, often at the expense of our well-being, relationships, and personal growth. We invest so much of our time and energy in impressing others with our material success that we sometimes overlook true happiness—like spending quality time with loved ones, nurturing our passions, or simply finding solace in the stillness of our thoughts.

Chapter 6

My Crusade to Educate My Child

"If the decisions you make about where you invest your blood, sweat, and tears are not consistent with the person you aspire to be, you'll never become that person."

—*Clayton M. Christensen*

I had the insatiable desire to succeed in life. I believed education was the only way to get ahead and stay ahead. Academic success was everything for me and my child. Do I ever recommend any parent to follow what I did to educate my child? The answer is a resounding NO. I am lucky that my child persevered through and accomplished precisely what I had envisioned for her.

My decision to educate her was the classic idiomatic expression, "I took a plunge"—from selling our house at a considerable loss to switching three places and a near-death experience to a colossal failure—as always, success wasn't linear.

Many people might identify with my tale, particularly those "helicopter parents." I had a reputation for being a controlling and invasive parent.

When we knew we would be blessed with a beautiful baby girl, I brainstormed a "name" for her. I had three criteria:

—Reflect my Indian heritage

—Reflect the unconditional love of her father

—A name that can easily be pronounced in America.

So, I came up with the name "Preeya" (meaning 'love'). It's pronounced exactly the way it is spelled. It is a unique spelling. The typical Indian name is spelled "Priya." Then, I decided to add my full name as her middle and last name: "Preeya Shajan Ninan." She is mine, and she is unique!

On June 30, at around 4:20 AM, my child was born. I was not at the hospital at the time she was born. I wasn't that mentally strong. The following day, I went to see her. I saw this beautiful baby sleeping soundly in a crib. She was gorgeous. I took her in my arms. I immediately realized she took after her father in every way except her mother's wide-broad, beautiful eyes.

The nurse asked me to send the baby's name two days later. It was like "set, ready, go." So, I quickly faxed it over to her. But then, I received a call from her, and she couldn't help but laugh. She said, "You have a 6-pound child, and you got a six-inch name for her." That's when I knew I needed to make some changes. I decided to go with 'Preeya S. Ninan.' When I spoke to the nurse again, I told her that 'S' stood for Shajan.

I had a broad vision for my child before she was born, a path broad enough for her to build a solid career and create a fulfilling life. When she turned four, we enrolled her in Pre-K at a Catholic school, Notre Dame, to guide her onto a disciplined Christian path at an early age. Around this time, we also enrolled her in Indian classical dance—Bharath Natyam—and passed on her mother's dream for our child to fulfill.

I remember watching my child's growth with fondness and wonder. It's funny looking back, as I realize now that children form opinions at a very young age. As my daughter grew up, I couldn't help but notice how the world around her shaped her thoughts and opinions. I remember she came home from pre-kindergarten and told me about a classmate who had been "mean" to her. Hearing her say, "She was so mean," with conviction and innocence, was adorable.

I have always been amazed by my daughter's thoughtfulness. Even at a young age, she possessed an inspiring level of maturity—a precocious child. I have always admired her ability to consider others' thoughts and feelings. Furthermore, unlike many other children her age, she never acted out or threw temper tantrums when frustrated. I was constantly impressed by her poise and composure.

A CURIOUS, AWKWARD FATHER

Sister Mary Ellen was her teacher, and during our parent-teacher meeting, I couldn't help but ask how Preeya was doing compared to her classmates. Sister Mary Ellen kindly reminded me that they don't compare children in their classrooms, but she said, "She was sometimes a little talkative."

My awkwardness continued…. It was a heartbreaking moment for me.

One morning, I was dropping off my child. Her teacher, watching the children coming to the class, told me that Preeya had asked her friend to bring 20 dollars. That child's parent had notified the school, and I was distraught with my child in front of other children in the schoolyard. I regretted my reaction and wish I had handled the situation differently.

Later that day, we took our child to the principal's office at school. Witnessing Mommy's emotional state was difficult. No parents want to face such a situation. But we knew we had to confront the issue. We sat down with our child and explained the consequences of her actions, ensuring that she grasped the seriousness of what she had done. I may have been strict with my child as a parent, but I intended to instill discipline and responsibility. It's crucial to remember that early childhood is a significant social and emotional development period. I now realize I should have been patient and empathetic while disciplining my child. It is still a lingering thought. I meditate on it.

It's natural to want the best for our kids and teach them important lessons. But I've realized that I might have missed a beat or two in the hustle and bustle of parenting. Those tiny humans are like sponges, soaking up everything around them. And it's during those early years that they're learning how to navigate their emotions, relate to others, and what it means to have someone they can trust and confide in.

So, when I look back at some of those disciplinary moments, I'm bound to wonder if there was a better way. Maybe if I had taken a deep breath and tried to see things from their perspective, it could have been a more valuable teaching moment. In the journey of life, we often encounter moments of reflection. It's not about dwelling on regrets but recognizing that we all make mistakes and grow from them. These experiences shape us, molding our character and leading us toward personal growth and wisdom. Embracing our imperfections allows us to approach life with resilience and an open heart, ready to face new challenges and opportunities with grace and understanding.

INVISIBLE FATHER: A VISION FOR MY BABY GIRL

My vision for my child was to get her a degree of freedom—*the promised land*—that opens up any door for her to do whatever she is passionate about without subjugating her to the servitude of the male-dominated environment.

Since my child was born, I have been building a dream to get her the best education possible. I was 100% focused on that goal.

When my daughter was young, she had a natural talent for poetry. I wanted to nurture her abilities, so I created a website where she could showcase her work. It was a joy to see her share her imagination with others. As she grew older, her interests expanded to music, art, and dance. Watching her explore these passions has been a delight. I've kept all her artwork and the things she made for me. *Those are the precious gifts from my precocious child.*

I couldn't stop thinking about how to make my dream of her attending Harvard a reality. It seemed like such an impossible task, and I knew it would require much sacrifice. But I was fixated on this goal and willing to do anything to make it happen. She would need a strong high-school education to get accepted at Harvard. So, I decided to get her into one of the top specialized public high schools in New York City, the Bronx High School of Science. We spent countless hours preparing her for the SHSAT test, thinking this would be key to the promised land. We sold our house in Long Island and moved to Queens so she could attend school there. Our hard work paid off when she took the test and was accepted into the prestigious Bronx High School of Science.

Now begins the hard work!

For a father, it was heartbreaking to see my child going through some emotional hardships: I pulled my child out of her comfort zone and put her in a new and rigorous environment.

The first day of school was quite challenging for her. When I picked her up from the bus station on the first day of school, I noticed she was tired and unhappy.

I told her, "When you get home, hug Mommy. Mommy is the source of Oxytocin, the chemical of unconditional love, and Daddy is the source of Cortisol, the stress chemical."

She had a ton of homework assignments for the next day. She stayed up till midnight and had a few hours of sleep.

I was a supportive yet demanding parent. I remember, rather painfully, criticizing her for wearing a tiny outfit to school. I regretted later doing that to my child.

There are a few things I had envisioned for my child besides getting her a solid academic background. Like many children growing up in this country, she, too, had the comfort of mommy or daddy dropping her off at the school a few minutes from our house. I wanted to get her out of that comfort zone, build friendships, experience some tough times, and learn to deal with real life, which is not a linear process.

One day, I talked to the mother of my child's friend about the challenges I faced while raising my child, including moving her to

The Bronx High School of Science. During the conversation, she asked me,

"You are the one behind the scene?"

The Shepherd's Way—I was hands-off when it came to all school activities or graduations, so it was easy for others to assume that I wasn't involved in my child's life.

I continued to remain invisible.

NEAR DEATH EXPERIENCE

One day, I called my mother and said, "I am returning to school." She said, "You are not a kid anymore; educate your child." I replied, "That is precisely why I am returning to school: I can feel like a kid again and educate my child." I attended Harvard to get a legacy status for my child.

One night, I was driving back to New York from Cambridge. The long drive had exhausted me, and I ended up dozing off in the car. I hit the concrete divider on I-95, and when I woke up, my car was facing north, and the engine had stopped. Despite the shock of the accident, I could exit the car and assess the damage. I felt okay, but I noticed that the front tire had blown up, and I knew I had to move the car to the side of the highway and replace the tire. I stepped back into the car and tried to start the car. Luckily, I could start the car and move it to safety. I then saw the exit right in front of me. I took the exit, and it led me to a gas station.

It was around 1 in the morning. A gentleman came over to me

and asked if I needed any help. I said, "I just had an accident and needed to replace the tire."

He replaced the tire for me and said,

"Drive slowly; you will be fine."

I felt like angels were speaking to me in the middle of the night. I got this amazing perspective: that accident could have killed me and a few others on a busy highway at night. I said to myself, "I feel so lucky to be alive. God pushed me to the cliff's edge but pulled me back." I survived that crash miraculously and unscathed.

The convocation ceremony holds a special place in my heart as it was a truly memorable event for me and my family. I put my cap on my child as a symbol of my unwavering ambition to send her to Harvard. I couldn't resist capturing the moment she wore my cap; she looked adorable! It was a touching moment that I will always cherish.

WARNING SIGN AND STOP SIGN

My child had been struggling with a vigorous routine: she had to wake up early every day, take a long bus ride to school, spend all day in classes, and then stay up late into the night to finish homework. On top of that, she was under a lot of pressure to do well in her studies.

Yet, I remained undeterred. It was time to apply for college. I wanted her to apply to Harvard's Restrictive Early Action program. She prepared all the common app's application materials but did not want to complete the application. I was devastated.

Seeing my child's resentment towards me for pushing her hard to get into Harvard was one of the most challenging things I've ever endured. It hurt me deeply to know that my actions had caused such a rift between us, but at the same time, I believed that getting her a great education would be the best thing for her future.

I told her, "We sold a house at a huge loss, moved to Queens and live in a small apartment, took you to local schools in India, secured every recommendation I could obtain for your community work, and encountered a near-death car accident." I said, "Complete the application and send it." She did.

I told my child, *"The outcome doesn't matter; you applied. I am happy and proud of you."* It was a heartbreaking experience for me to put my child through the suffering she endured. I believed in my child more than she ever believed in her abilities. I saw in her the potential for a successful career very early on.

A month later, she got an email from Harvard with the subject line "update on your application." The application was deferred to a Regular Decision. I was disappointed. My child was literally on the floor crying over the decision from Harvard.

"It was a flashing red light for me; stop pushing her anymore."

Early applicants are highly competitive. I said, "you are deferred, not defeated." I still hoped she might get accepted into its Regular Decision program. I kept her on track to the 'promised land.' She applied to all eight Ivy League, Stanford, and other colleges.

March 31, 2016: I anxiously awaited the decisions from all Ivy League schools. None of the Ivy colleges accepted her, including

Stanford. She was accepted at a few other colleges. She decided to attend the Macaulay Honors program with a full scholarship.

I felt all my efforts were in vain—a colossal failure.

WHAT DID I LEARN FROM MY JOURNEY TO EDUCATE MY CHILD?

My child was doing excellent in Levittown school in Long Island. She was consistently on the 95-99th percentile throughout middle school. For her to perform better at an Ivy League, I thought she needed a more rigorous program than the one offered at Levittown School. So, I chose a highly competitive school to prepare her for the demanding curriculum of an Ivy League college. A few of our family friends suggested that moving my child to The Bronx High School was a bad idea. They were right if my only focus was to get her to an Ivy League college. It wasn't. I wanted her to build a holistic view of life beyond grades—a growth mindset.

GROWTH MINDSET

I call myself a below-average individual. I am not trying to be ostentatiously humble, but I stay with the problem longer. We must create a "can-do attitude" or a growth mindset to succeed. It empowers us to come up with new ways of thinking and rethinking.

According to Stanford psychologist Carol Dweck, a "growth mindset" is a belief about our intelligence or talents. A growth mindset means that we firmly believe in our ability to improve through hard work, perseverance, and a willingness to learn from our mistakes. People with a growth mindset tend to be more resilient and open to new experiences, which can lead to greater success and happiness in life.

Having a fixed mindset can harm our growth and development as individuals. This mindset involves believing that our intelligence and abilities are fixed and cannot be improved. This way of thinking can be self-limiting and prevent us from taking on new challenges. It can also lead to a fear of failure and a lack of motivation to push ourselves out of our comfort zones. A fixed mindset can be a major obstacle to personal growth and success. We limit ourselves and fail to reach our full potential. This mindset is highly resistant to change and can hold us back in all areas of our lives, from our careers to personal relationships.

Dweck has a different approach that might help break through a certain barrier.

Her secret? Harnessing the power of "yet."

Even young children can understand this lesson. Dweck narrated the story of a Chicago school where students must pass several courses to graduate. If they didn't pass the test, they received a "not yet" grade instead of a failing one. Dweck argued that "not yet" showed a learning curve and path into the future, whereas a failing grade would leave them nowhere. "Not yet" also gave her critical insight and a turning point in her career as a psychologist. In her study on how children cope with challenges, Dweck found that giving them problems slightly too hard for them resulted in some reacting positively, with comments like "I love the challenge." These students understood that their abilities could be developed—*that's the growth mindset story.*

On the other hand, students who reacted negatively ("tragic," "catastrophic," etc.) felt that their intelligence was being judged, and they developed a *fixed mindset*. One study even found that they were more likely to cheat instead of trying to improve. So, instead of asking, *"Why me?"* it's better to focus on asking, *"What* can I do to improve my grades?"

"Did Shajan get paid for doing nothing?" Well, technically, yes.

A few months back, while checking my bank account, I noticed some deposits from a university where I used to work. The first question that came to my mind was, *"why me?* Why all these tests, dear Lord." I took a few minutes and meditated on it. I heard a voice in my head that said, *"Instead of dwelling on 'why me,'* ask yourself *'what'* you can do to alleviate your suffering, Shajan." Feeling empowered, I emailed the payroll, asking, "What are these deposits for? I don't work at the university anymore." The payroll team apologized for the deposit error and asked if they could reverse the transactions. I replied, "sure." A few days later, I checked my account and found they had left a few thousand in it. I shared this story with my students to teach them the importance of honesty, integrity, and the power of *"what."*

It's important to remember that emotions like fear or shame hold us back from achieving our goals. This is the brain's default mode and the negative side of neuroplasticity. Instead of succumbing to a survival or scarcity mindset, it's essential to cultivate an abundant attitude that allows us to take action toward manifesting a desirable outcome[6].

I don't usually say that I've mastered anything because having that mindset limits me from learning and growing. It's like saying I know everything when there's so much to discover. Instead, I have an open mind keen on learning new things daily. I focus on what I can control and what interests me, and I build my career and life around it. This helps me gain more insights and broaden my horizons.

By remaining curious and humble, we can expand our knowledge and become better versions of ourselves.

Did my affirmation to my child that "she is the best" hurt her confidence? Did I create a fixed mindset in her?

The "*The best is yet to come*" approach could have opened her to experience failures. My child's self-confidence, self-esteem, and self-worth were eroding at The Bronx High School. She faced students who were far more competitive than her.

Referring to Malcolm Gladwell, it can often backfire when promising students are placed in an elite environment surrounded by exceptionally brilliant and competitive students. In the context of that environment, my child lost her confidence. She was intellectually capable, but the environment caused erroneous confusion about her capabilities. Sociologist Samuel Stouffer called this phenomenon *"relative deprivation,"* which is the belief that a person will feel

---

[6] Tara Swart, "The Source"

deprived or entitled to something based on the comparison to someone else. It's like moving from a 'poor neighborhood' where you're the richest to a 'rich neighborhood' where you're the poorest. In my child's case, her classmates were her "frame of reference," and her intelligence was a function of the intelligence of those around her. It's the classic *"big fish in a small pond vs. small fish in a big pond"* syndrome. My child was only in the 90th percentile at The Bronx High School.

She knew well that she would not get accepted into an Ivy League school with her performance at The Bronx High School. Hence, her anger towards her father for pushing her to the extreme.

ALL-STAR EFFECT

The same theory applies to the teams with the most all-stars. They tend to perform the worst. If you have a team of all-stars, no one wants to compromise because everybody wants to win. There has to be a loser for others to win. Malcolm Gladwell called it an "elite institute cognitive disorder."

Pushing my child to my best choice (Bronx High School) was not in my child's best interest. She would have been readily accepted to an Ivy League college, if not Harvard, had she stayed at Levittown School. The best predictor of success in a competitive environment is your relative level of intelligence (class rank), not absolute intelligence (SAT or ACT score). It was the classic example of an inverted U-curve.

The Inverted-U Theory was created by psychologists Robert Yerkes and John Dodson in 1908. I quote it directly:

"The Inverted-U Theory gets its name from the curve created when the correlation between pressure and performance—peak performance is achieved when the level of pressure we experience is appropriate for our work. When we're under too much or too little pressure, performance declines, sometimes severely. There is a threshold point above or below which performance varies."

My child's high school experience was way too intense for her. She told me she would try for her graduate program at an Ivy League while doing her undergraduate program. During her senior year in college, she took her GMAT and applied to a few universities, including Yale University.

She was admitted to the Silver Scholar MBA program at Yale School of Management. I felt a sense of accomplishment. I put my child through enormous hardships and challenges. I literally saw the writing on her wall. She could have easily slipped into anxiety and depression.

It was a massive amount of cognitive dissonance on my part to put my child through all the pain and suffering to get an Ivy League degree when I was doing fine with my humble upbringing. My parents never bothered about where I went to school or whether I got a degree or not. In retrospect, my relentless pursuit to get her to the *"promised land"* is quite shocking. I was lucky my child persevered through all.

Although I did not have Western parenting skills, everything I guided her through with my distressed brain turned out to be "right on the money." I ventured her into The Bronx High School of Science to help her build social and emotional skills and face the real world out of Levittown High School. Her agonizingly painful four years of high school were a blessing in disguise.

She was fully prepared for college after going through all the challenges at her high school. She learned to manage time very well and engaged actively in college clubs: she was the editor of the college magazine and president of the Indian dance club. She uncovered her leadership potential, became a great dancer, built solid social connections, developed grit and resilience, and succeeded academically.

It is not that my self-esteem was wrapped around the Ivy League. However, I was worried about our patriarchal society—gender inequality. As a father, I did not want my child to call herself a "victim" of gender inequality. She has a "degree of freedom" now.

Our beautiful God-given gift accomplished her mommy's dream of becoming an accomplished Indian dancer and her father's dream of earning an Ivy League degree. I watch from a distance that a beautiful version of us is building her beautiful life. That is the proudest moment in my life.

Howard Gardner, a psychologist at the Harvard School of Education, explained that education's single most significant contribution to a child's development is to broaden the spectrum of talents and help that child towards a field where her talents best suit her. It's not just about textbooks and grades; it's about nurturing every child's unique strength and gift, helping them become a better version[7] of themselves. This, I believe, is the essence of true

---

[7] The best version creates a fixed mindset.

accomplishment in education.

As a parent, it's natural to want the absolute best for our children to envision grand futures filled with prestige and accomplishment. But sometimes, life takes us on unexpected detours, leading to destinations we never imagined. We live in an uncertain world full of opportunities. In those moments, we learn that the name of a diploma doesn't define our children's worth but the passion, determination, and potential they carry within them.

MY CHILD'S BIRTHDAY PARTY: PERILS OF EMOTIONAL DEPENDENCE

My intense emotional attachment to my family was the source of my unhappiness. As my child grew older, I could feel her detachment from me.

Here is a special day for me and my family. June 30 marks the birthday of my beloved child, and I always look forward to this day. As with every birthday, I collected some pictures of my child growing up, made a photo collage, and posted it on Facebook with some beautiful words.

But the birthday shattered my expectations.

I returned from work in the evening, and we all went to my daughter's favorite restaurant, Applebee's. More than anything else, my child loved the chocolate meltdown they served there. But I was surprised that neither my child nor my wife seemed hungry. I had thought they were starving all day and waiting for me to come home from work. A few days later, I found out that they had arranged a birthday party with her grandmother and cousins that afternoon. It tipped me over the edge. As a neurotic person, I was furious and worried about my child's decision to have a birthday party without my knowledge. I spoke with my best friend and colleague—my only Jewish American—for advice. He immediately said, "That is an atrocity." He understood how I felt. His daughter and my daughter are of the same age. He knew I was going through some serious emotional turmoil. Whenever I was emotionally distressed, he connected me with his life coach, Katrina. He had his life coach contact me that night. She told me it was unusual for a child to behave this way and asked me to talk to her about what led her to make that awful decision.

I was distressed by the insensitivity of my child's behavior, and my emotions got the best of me. As a father, my child means everything to me, and it was hard to understand how a 15-year-old could treat her father this disrespectfully. It made me wonder if she even realized how much this day meant to me and if she truly understood the importance of family.

I asked my child why she decided to have a birthday party without me.

As I gazed upon my child's sorrowful expression and the overwhelming emotions that consumed her, she told me that she was not entirely aware of the gravity of her actions. It was clear that her surroundings had influenced her thought process. Despite feeling disheartened, I found myself compelled to empathize with her situation. At around 10 PM that night, I went to Walmart and bought an 'I am sorry' greeting card. And I wrote, "Happy birthday, Umma, love you, Daddy," and gave it to her. I apologized for my rage over her behavior—my inability to regulate my destructive emotions. I believed my behavior was unacceptable. My jealousy caused my anger—how could a third party take away that moment of happiness on my child's birthday?

My fear of losing my child's love triggered outrage, released the stress hormone in my body, and made me emotionally weak and distressed. My family, who I thought was a secure attachment system, was amping up my fear of losing that emotional support, the perils of emotional dependency.

I've realized that my overwhelming emotional attachment to my child was the root cause of the outrage, not the situation itself. It was my own thoughts and feelings that got in the way. Ultimately, it doesn't matter whether my daughter had a party with her father before or not. I wanted to do something special for her because that's what I love to do as a parent. It was unfair to expect her to reciprocate in any way, and I regretted putting that pressure on her.

We need to understand what motivates others to show that semblance of love. It is often conditional: material wealth or other short-term pleasure by being with that person. Nothing lasts forever. It is learning to develop a mindset that allows us to be aware of the universe's impermanent nature and let things go when things unfold unexpectedly.

My moral outrage over my child's birthday party left me thinking about what I have accomplished—created a tumultuous and unhealthy environment, and I ended up apologizing to the ones who did the atrocity.

The lesson I learned was that we are constantly moving objects—the impermanence or temporary nature of life. We turn into different forms, shapes, and looks as we grow, and one day we decay. Do we ever realize our fragility and the beauty of being alive and happy?

Yet, within this impermanence lies the exquisite beauty of being alive. It's a reminder to cherish each moment, embrace our vulnerability, and find solace in the present. It starts with loving and accepting ourselves and our flaws so that we can extend that same love and forgiveness to others.

We often seek fulfillment in external sources, expecting love and happiness from outside ourselves. But true contentment springs from within. It's a journey of self-discovery, a process of understanding that our well-being is a cornerstone to fostering meaningful connections and experiencing genuine joy. We must embrace our impermanence and find joy in the present moment.

Chapter 7

Lessons from My Failed Startup

Quoting Adam Grant, "We live in a culture of worship at the altar of the hustle and pray to the highest priest of grit. Find a different mountain to climb." In other words, broaden our horizons. Our paths should be broad enough to accomplish our goals. This is particularly important regarding our career path or when building a business as an entrepreneur. The lesson I learned from my failed business:

We often hear the cliché "Don't give up." That is the classic boiling frog syndrome. It may be too late to rescue ourselves from the slow boiling pot. Our quest to prove ourselves becomes dangerous. I only had a few years in my quest to prove to myself and others that I made a suitable investment. I doubled down on a wrong decision. "Don't give up" means rethink a failing decision—broaden your path towards accomplishing your dream.

I made the bold choice to aid in my child's preparation for the "promised land," the Ivy League, which resulted in a happy accident. In 2012, while she was preparing for her Special High School Admission Test, I noticed a pattern—I could do the same or offer a better-quality service using an online platform using teachers from India. In November 2011, I started a private limited company to provide online tutoring to students in the US. The idea was to use tutors from India to offer quality services to American students. It took a lot of effort to make this plan a reality, from building the website to registering the company and leasing office space in India. However, things didn't go as planned, so I switched gears and focused on in-class training instead: I started offering IELTS coaching in a nearby center, even though many other similar programs were already available. I trusted my employees to build the business and spent most of my time hiring teachers rather than finding students. I wasn't very selective with my hiring process and relied more on people's backgrounds and experiences—I hired pretty much anyone willing to work for us and paid a decent salary.

Despite months of effort, our business was yet to attract any students. We attempted to offer English-speaking coaching to school children, hiring a salesperson to secure contracts with various schools. However, we quickly encountered numerous issues with this approach. Most schools were in remote areas, requiring us to cover travel expenses. Furthermore, our fees were insufficient to cover the cost of our trainers, who consistently failed to deliver quality training. Their unreliability was further compounded by a salesperson who embezzled the money we collected from schools. Adding insult to injury, our landlord unjustly kept our deposit despite us fulfilling all our contract terms. Despite these setbacks, I remain steadfast in my commitment to providing quality education to those who need it.

After relocating the company, I searched for someone to lead the business. I was fortunate to come across a promising candidate, a young lady with a degree in psychology and previous experience running a similar center. I hired and placed her in charge, hoping her expertise would turn things around. However, to my disappointment, she followed the same old model of taking school contracts. Although she was more assertive and responsible than her predecessor, the business struggled to stay afloat. Every month, we lost money, our employees lacked commitment, and schools hesitated to pay our fees. With slim margins and a highly competitive market, expenses continued to rise. Clearly, many flaws existed within our business model, and I realized that I could have approached people and situations with better tactics.

When I first had the idea to use the English-speaking, well-educated pool of tutors to offer coaching to the students in the US at a much cheaper cost than what was available in the US, I was so excited. The prospect of providing a high-quality education to students who might not otherwise have access to it was gratifying. I knew that this was something that I had to pursue.

I thought setting up an online platform, enrolling students in that platform, and matching trainers based on the student's needs was the perfect solution. Unfortunately, I failed to test the viability of the service to a small group of students and collect feedback from that test. I didn't understand the operational capabilities required to offer quality service, which was a critical mistake. I realized the business needed a committed team with diverse experience and backgrounds. However, we hired employees without proper hiring procedures, especially not evaluating the expertise in their respective subjects and skills to deliver the content. Monitoring them took work, too. I didn't realize how little I knew about the human condition. I tend to trust people too much. My relationships with employees were very open, and they felt I was a friendly, naïve, selfless individual who could easily be manipulated. In other words, I was coerced into things that may not be right for the company.

In terms of quality, system usability, etc., the technological capabilities and trainers were woefully inadequate to provide several 'need-to-have features.' I needed to have more faith in my ability to provide services of a high caliber.

I grossly underestimated the competitive environment. A few competitors offered the same services at a lower price and better quality than ours.

Having a growth mindset is similar to how successful entrepreneurs operate. They always keep their initial success from getting to their head. Even if you believe your business idea is excellent, it's important to remember that successfully executing it is challenging. If you aren't focused and don't build on that momentum, the early results could evaporate soon.

They are curious to know what they don't know—a sign of intellectual integrity. They have that humility and discipline to learn from others and shape their thinking—see the gap in their knowledge. They take startup strategy as theory, customers' response as hypothesis, and MVPs (minimum viability products) as prototypes to experiments to test the hypothesis. Our curiosity opens up an opportunity for new ideas and helps us experience the joy of learning. This approach, in turn, allows us to build confidence and remain humble about what we didn't know or still don't know.

We validated the demand by simply getting the visitors to register for a program on our site without any purchase commitment. It was a flawed assumption to ask visitors on our site what they need since they need to know what they need or how to express their needs.

The idea of acquiring a large number of customers before

validating the business model is expensive, and it can damage the startup brand if the functionality and operational capability are flawed or show no minimum viability. Entrepreneurs get far more reliable feedback when they put an actual product in the hands of existing customers in a real-world setting.

The "Just do it" slogan was a great success for Nike, but as an approach, using some random opinions turned out to be costly and time-consuming detours for us. I needed to focus on the core vision of the business.

George Bernard Shaw said,

"The reasonable man adapts himself to the world; the unreasonable one persists in trying to adapt the world to himself. Therefore, all progress depends on the unreasonable man."

The trait of disagreeableness is a powerful force in innovation and progress. It's the courage and conviction to stick with a plan, even if other people may think it's crazy or outlandish. Those with this trait often challenge the status quo, paving the way for groundbreaking discoveries and advancements. They understand that it's not about seeking approval but about believing in the potential of their vision, even in the face of skepticism. This unwavering determination can lead to transformative changes that reshape industries and societies. Steve Jobs is a classic example of this trait.

I lacked the essential personality traits of a successful entrepreneur—the discipline and the focus to bring an idea to fruition and the courage of conviction in the face of contempt. I didn't feel the need to adhere to beliefs and behaviors considered normal.

Lack of assertiveness was a flaw in my business and my life. I couldn't face the problems in the business, was not hands-on with daily issues, hired the wrong people and paid whatever they demanded, and needed a clear conviction into the idea. The test-and-invest approach would have helped us determine whether to persevere, pivot to a revised model, or abandon altogether before expending too many resources. Managing human beings was the biggest challenge in my business—we are constantly searching for happiness. In January 2022, I closed down my business.

PIVOT AND RETHINK

Many of us are taught to persist and persevere to achieve our goals. However, as Adam Grant suggests, we must keep the path broad enough to fulfill our dreams and know when to grit and quit. This principle applies to many areas of life, including our decision to stay in a miserable job, a bad relationship, or a lousy investment. We've already seen the consequences of not making a suitable investment in innovation (see pages 183-189, "DISRUPTIVE INNOVATION") in the downfall of companies like Blockbuster, Kodak, Blackberry, Sears, Toys R Us, and Digital Equipment Corporation. By recognizing when to pivot and when to persevere, we can make better decisions and achieve tremendous success.

Maintaining a "never give up" attitude is an excellent approach to life. It is like a compass guiding us through life's twists and turns, especially for those who might lean on others more than we assert ourselves. It's about recognizing the incredible potential within us while acknowledging that we can also learn and grow, even when we're not the most assertive voices in the room.

It is crucial to incorporate both fixed and growth mindsets, emphasizing our strengths while continuously seeking ways to enhance ourselves. The fixed mindset celebrates our strengths, reminding us that we already possess unique qualities and abilities that can take us far. It's like acknowledging the bright spots on our journey. But the magic happens here: the growth mindset encourages us to seek ways to improve and stretch beyond our comfort zones. Sometimes, it might feel contradictory. We're essentially saying, "I'm good at this, but I can be better." It's a dance between self-assurance and humility, and it's all about discovering more effective paths to our goals.

Here's the natural beauty: when we find ourselves on a path that isn't quite working or doesn't align with our strengths, we have the power to pivot. It's like realizing that you're not a great swimmer but an excellent climber. So, instead of endlessly treading water, you find a more promising route up the mountain.

The key is to stay motivated and determined, even when facing the unknown. Change can be daunting, especially for those of us who might rely on others for support or guidance. But we often find new strengths and opportunities we never knew existed within change.

We must comprehend our capabilities while recognizing our boundaries and having a receptive outlook. It may seem contradictory, but it's all about finding better and different ways to achieve our goals, not giving up. Sometimes, that means letting go of a path that isn't working (in that sense, "never give up" is a flawed approach), or we are not great at it and finding a new, more promising one. It's all about staying motivated, determined, and open to change.

FIXED MINDSET VS. GROWTH MINDSET

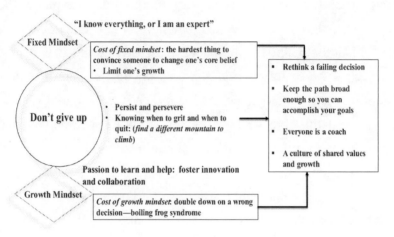

"I know everything, or I am an expert"

Fixed Mindset

Cost of fixed mindset: the hardest thing to convince someone to change one's core belief
- Limit one's growth

Don't give up
- Persist and persevere
- Knowing when to grit and when to quit: (*find a different mountain to climb*)

- Rethink a failing decision

- Keep the path broad enough so you can accomplish your goals

- Everyone is a coach

- A culture of shared values and growth

Passion to learn and help: foster innovation and collaboration

Growth Mindset

Cost of growth mindset: double down on a wrong decision—boiling frog syndrome

Source: Adam Grant and author

Part Two

My Academic Career

Chapter 8

Love What I Do or Do What I Love?

"The only way to be truly satisfied is to do what you believe is great work. And the only way to do great work is to love what you do. If you haven't found it yet, keep looking. Don't settle. As with all matters of the heart, you'll know when you find it."
—*Steve Jobs*

Achieving success is not solely dependent on passion. It demands consistent efforts toward progress and persistent commitment to hard work. Building resilience and determination is crucial in attaining our aspirations. Sometimes, that means pushing ourselves out of our comfort zones and developing grit and resilience. We can achieve anything we set our minds to, fueled by our unwavering focus and determination.

Becoming an educator was a challenging journey for me. Still, my years of practical experience, guest lecturing in India and the US, and experience in academia have provided me with a unique perspective I share with my students. My commitment to bringing intellectual thoroughness into the classroom and finding meaning in my work gives me a fulfilling and rewarding experience.

My commitment to self-improvement has been unwavering in all my years as a teacher. While there's often a pursuit of being the absolute best, I've understood that genuine growth springs from steady dedication to becoming a better version[8] of oneself. It's about embracing every opportunity to learn from missteps, actively seeking feedback, and experimenting with fresh ideas in the classroom.

Every day in the classroom is like a blank canvas—a chance to paint a better, more vibrant picture than the one I created yesterday. This pursuit of becoming a better teacher fuels my passion and keeps me on the path of continuous growth and self-improvement. It's not about chasing perfection; it's about the journey of evolving and positively impacting my students' lives.

I realized that passion alone is not enough. However, passion got me going regardless of the challenges, hardships, and setbacks. I call it grit and resilience. Angela Lee Duckworth, at the University of Pennsylvania, did excellent work on grit. She highlighted that perseverance, hard work, and tenacity make a person succeed in life and career. According to her, grit is "working hard and long enough." She has beautifully explained this in her book, "Grit: The Power of Passion and Perseverance." Learning is not how quickly and easily you learn things. Instead, it is a continuous process of change for the better. The Japanese term for this is "kaizen."

I do have a slightly different perspective on grit. Although grit is undoubtedly significant, emotional intelligence is equally vital for success. I have encountered numerous challenges, and I acknowledge that my absence of emotional intelligence has contributed to several

---

[8] Striving for perfection (the best version) leads to complacency and a fixed mindset. Instead, focus on continuous growth and improvement. We can cultivate resilience, adaptability, and a sense of purpose by embracing a growth mindset (a better version).

of them. It can be arduous to navigate through difficulties when one lacks the knowledge to manage one's emotions and react appropriately. Developing self-awareness is an imperative aspect that can aid us in conquering obstacles and accomplishing our objectives.

My passion for teaching emerged while I was in college. I stood before a small group of students during lunchtime while they had their lunch. I took a few minutes and explained some concepts I had learned in the class. My underlying motivation was to gain some confidence in public speaking.

MY FIRST PUBLIC SPEAKING OPPORTUNITY

On Nov 15, 2015, I was invited to speak at a leadership summit organized by a business school in India. I often envisage myself giving speeches in front of a large group, and it has been yet another dream of mine since childhood. It is my nature that I rarely say 'no' to anything. Therefore, I was delighted to accept that invitation. I took the plunge.

I prepared for my speech, mainly related to my life experience and career on Wall Street. I practiced my speech a few times, speaking to myself. The night before the speech, I was terrified of speaking to a large audience and media. I couldn't sleep. I was nervous. I didn't feel like I was experiencing imposter syndrome or self-doubt. I am passionate about what I do and take pride in my skills. However, speaking to a large audience for the first time was nerve-wracking.

Nonetheless, I decided to go and give my speech. I sat in the front row and listened to the speakers before me. I felt I had a far better speech than them and was fully prepared. That gave me enough confidence. It's like students who do poorly on an exam and then find comfort in knowing that their friends did worse. It's human nature to find joy in others' misfortune. I thought about the positive impact my words might have on the audience. That drive strengthened my resolve to do better and pushed me forward.

My turn came. I gave a 30-minute presentation and answered a few questions from the students. As far as I could tell, 'I nailed it.' This opportunity was a seminal moment in my life regarding public speaking. Since then, I have been actively engaging in public speaking. I have given guest lectures at many IIMs (Indian Institute of Management) as part of my interest in bringing my practical world experience into the B-schools in India. My practical experience and confidence in public speaking provided me with a solid academic career path.

I truly believed I could help shape students, teach them how to apply the theories and concepts, and prepare them for a life beyond the classroom. Referring to the wisdom of Carol Dweck:

"There are no diamonds in the rough in my class. All students are diamonds."

In January 2018, Fordham University offered an opportunity to teach as an adjunct faculty. I taught two sections of the financial management course to undergraduate students. Teaching students from different socio-economic, ethnic, and cultural backgrounds was an exciting experience for me.

I went to my first session nervously and delivered my lecture with a slight 'Indian accent.' I wasn't very much satisfied with my performance. However, I gained some clues regarding the pace with which I delivered my lecture. I was better prepared for my following lecture immediately after the first session.

My teaching style was mainly lecture-oriented, with the use of PowerPoint. I have this habit of giving a small talk about my life experience and providing some advice at the beginning of my lecture. In that, I said:

"You are all teenagers, just out of high school, and college campuses offer opportunities to build valuable connections. Reach out to people. Most of us have an uncertain career path. So much of our career success emanates from serendipitous meetings—you know somebody, they know somebody, they hear about a job, and then they think of you. Ask for help. When you approach somebody with the right attitude, they will respond kindly. Spend time on an actual conversation over the phone or in person rather than sending emails or texts. The email could be intimidating or lost in translation. I had no such guidance from my teachers when I was your age. Even worse, I had little interaction with society. The value of connections is far more important than your 4.00 GPA."

The materials were intimidating with numbers and formulas. And the concepts were complicated and often confusing as well. At the end of the day, I reflected on my lectures and improved my delivery. Still, I wasn't entirely comfortable with my teaching style.

I assumed that students knew everything I was teaching. I was wrong. My communication wasn't very effective, and I spoke faster than students could catch up.

It's a common pitfall we educators can fall into. We get so passionate about our subjects that we forget what it's like to be on the receiving end of all that information. We assume that our students are right there with us, grasping every concept effortlessly. But the truth is, sometimes, we need to slow down, break things down, and create a learning environment where everyone can thrive.

I realized it's not about how fast we cover the materials but how well students understand and retain them. So, I made a conscious effort to improve my communication, be patient, and actively check in with my students to ensure they followed along.

"WE ARE NOT TEENAGERS"

The end of the semester brought about a range of emotions for me. After a few weeks, I decided to read the student evaluation. I was disappointed to find that my rating was below average. While some students complimented my teaching style and the insights I shared, others took offense to my use of the term "teenagers." They expressed that they didn't identify as teenagers and even suggested that I should be removed from the campus. It was disheartening to see that some students placed so much sensitivity on certain words like "teenagers." My intention with my small talk was to encourage students to connect and build social capital.

As part of my profession, I receive evaluations from my students and peers every semester. Students download their thoughts, emotions, and feelings onto their phones (which I call emotional regulation or journaling) and then upload them to the online faculty evaluation system, with some even sharing them on the web.

I was, to put it mildly, disappointed. I was surprised by the emotional insecurity expressed by some of the students. It was sophomoric.

A few weeks later, the priest announced a presentation on motivating adolescents and teenagers at my church. As a teacher of sophomore students, I found the topic quite interesting, so I decided to stay after the church service. The presenter claimed to have a Ph.D. in adolescent and teenage mindset. At the end of the session, he asked if any *teenagers* were present and to raise their hands. I couldn't help but chuckle at his request because I knew from experience that none of the teenagers would raise their hands. It made me wonder what he had learned from his Ph.D. I asked myself how he could have missed the crucial part of teenage development and how children's brains respond to certain triggers. Unfortunately, many psychologists and psychiatrists lack emotional intelligence, making it challenging to impact others positively.

Daniel Goleman and Michele Nerveaz wrote an article on how to boost your EQ with three questions:

First question: *What is the difference between how you see yourself and others?*

In Chapter 1, I emphasized the significance of self-awareness in developing emotional intelligence. It's an essential component of EQ that cannot be overlooked.

In this exercise, I aimed to see how I see myself (self-perception) and how others see me (my reputation). We all have blind spots, dark sides, or weaknesses and are often cognitively biased (confirmation or implicit bias). I felt I was listening to the cues and answering students' questions. Still, the feedback showed that I wasn't— flipping slides quickly and not connecting with the students. Students are, in fact, my coaches, and it is better to get perspectives as to how my actions impact the students in my class. That requires introspection. I am still learning.

Second question: *What matters to you?*

As a teacher, I find student evaluations to be an invaluable resource. However, I often focus too much on negative feedback, even if it's just a few comments. I dwell on it too much since I want to improve my teaching.

Amos Tversky and Daniel Kahneman coined the '*Small Loss vs. Big Gain*' concept in their Prospect Theory: we asymmetrically feel losses greater than an equivalent gain. It stems from our 'loss aversion.' They *suggested* that we value losses about 2.3 times more than gains of the same value. Simply put, it's a psychological phenomenon in which the pain of losing something is more than twice as powerful as the pleasure of gaining something of equal value. This means we are more likely to take risks to avoid losses rather than pursue gains, even if the potential rewards are the same. For instance, losing $50 can be more painful than finding the same amount on the street. It's like saying that I started with nothing and built a successful life, but I still worry about a small loss in my investment account. *Loss avoidance or loss aversion* is also known as *negativity bias*. We humans tend to be more concerned about the pain and disappointment of failure rather than the joy and satisfaction of success. It's an instinct that sometimes keeps us from taking risks and pursuing our dreams.

"Our brain's default position or primary survival mechanism is to avoid risk or loss. Changing that default mode is too scary for the brain. This is the negative side of neuroplasticity."

The memory (hippocampus) and emotion (amygdala) centers of our brain work together to bring all the evidence of past mistakes to the forefront of our minds to prevent us from repeating them. This constant focus on survival, rather than creating and thriving, can lead to a negative bias and a tendency to worry more about what went wrong than what went right.

When I was discussing the current two-party system in the US and how it has been hijacked by the elite with their influence on the politicians, one student said, "We cannot change the system." I explained that this is a classic negativity bias or loss aversion phenomenon. However, I also pointed out that neuroplasticity works both ways, so it is possible to retrain the brain to see things differently and create positive change.

Despite many positive comments, dealing with negative feedback from students took a lot of work. It often bruised my sense of self and made it difficult to maintain a positive outlook.

But the *loss aversion* did not make me *risk-averse*[9]. Instead, it catalyzed me to explore alternative paths to improve. I firmly believe that failure or loss is not something to be feared but rather an opportunity to learn and grow. I have overcome countless obstacles by embracing this *abundant mindset*.

---

[9] Tara Swart, The Source.

Third question: *What changes will I make to achieve these goals?*

I improved my listening skills. I asked students if I needed to rephrase certain concepts so they could understand them better.

I kept pushing myself forward. My Department Chair was very supportive. I was progressively getting better with my teaching style. Students never questioned my knowledge, but they expressed dissatisfaction with my teaching style: feedback like "learn how to teach" on their evaluation form reflected their dissatisfaction.

I am struggling. But I am getting through. At the beginning of every semester, I read some of the feedback from my previous students. My intention with this approach was to create a culture where it is safe to admit that *'I am not perfect and students are my coaches': learning to teach is a continuous process.* It helped me build my resilience.

We learn from our mistakes, adapt, and grow together. Learning is a collaborative effort; we're all in it together.

UNLEARN

Empty the old tea cup before you put in the fresh hot tea.

"It is easier to carry an empty cup than a cup that is filled to the brim; the more wealth we possess, the harder it is to protect."
-Lao Tzu

As an educator, I try to instill a 'how to think' approach in my students.

There is an excellent story about a Zen master welcoming a

recruit. The following is taken directly from the "Empty Your Cup, Unlearn Before You Learn" article by Francois Lavallee:

"The new guy is shy and timidly sits before the old master. When offered some tea, it took some time for the new guy to realize that he had to serve it to the master and himself, starting with the master. A smarter apprentice would also have noticed the look of impatience from the old master, but he was new to this. He started pouring the master's tea, waiting to be told when to stop, and the master started talking. The cup was almost filled to the brim, and the apprentice slowly reduced the pouring rate, still waiting to be told to stop. The inevitable spill occurred, nonetheless."

The problem we observe in this case is cognitive laziness.

Much like the cup filled with its own opinions and ideas, we often carry our preconceived notions into new experiences. This story serves as a valuable reminder of the necessity to unlearn before we can truly learn and grow. Embracing fresh perspectives requires us to approach each opportunity with an open mind, ready to shed our preconceptions and make room for the wisdom that comes with humility and receptivity. In doing so, we open ourselves to transformative experiences and a deeper understanding of the world around us. We often hold on to our deep-seated beliefs and unwillingness to change our minds.

We believe questioning our way of thinking makes our lives unpredictable, following the masses is easy and less threatening, and changing our views and opinions can damage our identities. We tend to hold on to our beliefs, ideas, and ways of thinking, even when they no longer serve us. We cling to what we know, fearing the unknown and the uncomfortable. But to truly learn and grow, we must be willing to empty our cups and unlearn what we think we know before learning something new.

However, we hardly take the time to reflect on our behavior—we often lack self-reflection. To be self-aware, we need to unlearn what we have learned. Then, we get the freedom to rethink. These days, the fragile nature of college campuses reflects students' resistance to rethinking—pampering our younger generation like a toddler.

I mentioned the classic boiling frog syndrome in my failed business venture: It will be too late to fix it if we are unaware of the danger of our resistance to rethink our thinking. As Adam Grant eloquently said in his YouTube video,

"The warm bath becomes a death trap."

Just as we have our minds, we have the organizational mindset: The sum of all the individuals and their mindsets shapes an organizational culture. Often, we don't recognize that, but organizations and universities are like people. It is where we create future leaders with heightened receptiveness to all kinds of information and navigate any situation they encounter. Every situation is an opportunity, not a threat or hindrance, to learn and develop in a world of constant change and disruption.

The belief that we don't change what is working is a dangerous premise. We often forget the hidden danger of this approach. We rarely question a story but accept it as accurate. In his book "Think

Again," Adam Grant described the cognitive tools we use every day: habits, assumptions, and instincts or opinions. That is our identity. We rarely keep that open mind central to transcending our sense of self or identity or amending our cognitive tools.

Learning is a continuous process—the best is yet to come. The more we try to be perfect, the more fragile we become. There is a Japanese philosophy called 'Wabi-Sabi,' which is centered on appreciating the imperfect, transient, and incomplete beauty—an appreciation of forces of nature, the ephemeral nature of our very existence on this planet. Perfection is our perception of an event, a thing, or a person devoid of the realities of our nature.

One of the most crucial steps is to stop judging yourself and others so harshly. Understand that there's no such thing as a 'perfect' life. Life is a journey filled with ups and downs, imperfections, and unexpected twists. In these imperfections, we often find the most beautiful moments and opportunities for growth.

The pursuit of perfection is a disease in today's world: perfect family, perfect body, perfect house, perfect job, and perfect children. Chasing a perfect life is like the hamster on a wheel. We never get anywhere with it, and it is a constant struggle. We often forget that there is nothing permanent in nature.

I have always believed that the truth is not what others consider perfect. Instead, I view perfection as a subjective concept that varies from person to person. It is vital to remember that others' opinions about us are shaped by their experiences and perceptions of the world around them. So, it does not matter much as to what others think of us. Our thoughts and beliefs about ourselves drive our decisions and actions, not the situation we find ourselves in: *question your thought processes and build a growth mindset.* By doing so, we can overcome our destructive emotions and embrace challenges as opportunities for growth and learning.

> **What did I learn from my classrooms?**
>
> *"Learning to teach is a continuous process."* As an educator, I employ different teaching approaches to cater to the varying needs of my students. While some are focused on simply passing the course, others wish to understand how the concepts they learn can be applied in the real world—something I bring to the classroom based on my industry experience. Additionally, I have students who wish to delve deeper into the subject matter and explore the existing ideas and beliefs. I encourage them to question and *'rethink'* their knowledge or beliefs in such scenarios. This book is designed for unlocking that new level of consciousness—self-discovery and personal growth.

PURSUIT TO GET BETTER

I am not devoted to a single method of instruction. I reflect on it and consider different ways to teach and interact with students. I continue to bring up some of the worst comments students made on their evaluations and read them in class. This may seem unreasonable, but I intend to make my students feel more comfortable expressing their opinions and suggesting ways for me to improve my teaching style. By doing this, I want to show my students I am comfortable with my limitations.

The best way to prove myself is to improve myself. It takes courage and vulnerability to admit I have room for improvement. I hope to model this confident humility to my students. I am someone who is intrinsically motivated to improve my performance.

COMPASSION FOR MY STUDENTS

In the spring of 2022, after the midterm exam, one looked quite worrisome among the many emails I received from my students about the exam. A young lady in that email said, "I did not do well on the exam. Can we talk privately on Zoom?" I arranged a Zoom session. She was very emotional and said she was struggling with mental health issues, primarily due to the loss of her grandparents.

Millions of children at schools, colleges, universities, and elsewhere suffer from depression, anxiety, panic attacks, and other challenges. They often flee to safety without looking left or right, creating symbolic tunnel vision—losing a sense of 'who they are,' closing their minds to alternatives, and destroying their creative insights.

Just as we need the right soil conditions for plants to grow sustainably, we need the right environment for children to grow and build positive mindsets.

The interesting thing in that Zoom meeting was that a week before my Zoom session with this student, I was upset with students in my class for smiling at their laptops and paying no attention to the lecture.

She brought that up in our Zoom session and said, "I use my laptop to take notes, but I will turn it off." I immediately thought of a situation my child experienced years ago when she was in middle school.

My child told her mother when she used the money to buy soda in her school: "Mommy, I will not buy soda again. I will drink water." I wasn't as tough as her mother. I was heartbroken to hear that from my child. I look at my students through that lens.

Let me digress. I take responsibility for instilling the soda-drinking habit in my child:

As a toddler, she used to get her body temperature up occasionally. Doctors recommended we give her some Motrin every four hours until the temperature subsides. The issue was that she hated medicine, and getting her to take Motrin was a struggle. So, I decided to try something different. When we were at the regular visit with her doctor, I asked the doctor if we could give her some soda. The doctor said, "Maybe a tiny bit." I thought I could mix Motrin with soda so she would drink Motrin. We showed her the soda and had her taste it first, then mixed some soda with Motrin. But she refused to take the mix and ended up drinking soda.

There is a parallel story of students using computers in the class. I had no problem with students who use their computers to take notes. So, I let them use it. They become addicted to the device, especially when listening to finance lectures. When I wrote this book, I had decided for students not to use their computers during lectures or exams. I had to strike a balance between compassion and effectiveness in the classroom. While my initial inclination was to be understanding and accommodating, I began to realize that this well-intentioned compassion was inadvertently doing a disservice to the students.

In many ways, it's a lesson in compassion going slightly off course. Sometimes, what appears compassionate on the surface can lead to unintended consequences. We want the best for others, but we also need to consider the bigger picture and the impact of our actions.

GROWTH MINDSET IN THE CLASSROOM

How do I create a growth mindset in the classroom?

Often, I use the concept of *desirable difficulty* in my lecture. Cognitive psychologist Robert Bjork at UCLA coined the term "desirable difficulties."

He describes counterintuitive concepts as ways of learning that may feel less effective and lead to more errors during the learning process but produce better performance in the long term.

The concept of desirable difficulties describes the idea that students need tasks that challenge them to the right degree to learn better.

My approach to teaching consists of active engagement by students discussing a few concepts that provide them with a strong base, which in turn supports their subsequent course. Also, they can carry that knowledge base to their real-world activities. I test those concepts mainly through quizzes.

The idea is to cover a concept and show how it relates to different fields. It bothered many students. They were upset with my approach. Since the focus is primarily on grades or rapid progress, such an approach may be unappreciative. I told them this approach was desirable since it enhances their long-term knowledge and memory retention, although challenging when acquiring knowledge or skills. It is a slow process. If students think otherwise, it becomes an undesirable difficulty. I firmly believe that education isn't just about conveying knowledge; it's also about preparing students for the realities they'll encounter beyond graduation. It's about equipping them with the tools to navigate the complexities of the world, even when it gets uncomfortable.

OUR CHALLENGES ARE DESIRABLE DIFFICULTIES

Amazingly, I have experienced how students with learning disabilities do better in my courses. Students find my courses quite intimidating, so I humanize complex concepts and theories with some stories. Also, I cold-call students to get them engaged.

One day, this young lady in the back told me, "I cannot cold call." I considered her behavior rude. A few weeks later, we had the midterm exam. She came to me and said that the disability center closes at 5 p.m., and she cannot get the extra time (students with learning disabilities are granted extra time to complete their exams.) I told her to sit in the classroom and take the exam with other students. Then she said, "I may need more time." I said, "I will stay as long as you need." I canceled my intercampus ride and proctored the exam. She sat right in front of me. While she was taking the test, I was thinking why she said I should not cold call. She finished the test a few minutes earlier than the other students and left. I had to wait another hour before getting a reservation on my ride back to the other campus. I laughed at my ordeal and said, "no good deed goes unpunished." She did well in the exam and got a straight 'A' for the course. Her learning disability was desirable. She succeeded because of it, not in spite of it—her adversity forced her to succeed.

Children with no apparent advantages refuse to take the notion of underdogs and be passive. It is like a worthy rivalry situation where one feels insecure and creates a heightened competitiveness. Was she an in-secured over-achiever? Her insecurity got her into a better performance. She did not internalize that insecurity. Instead, she internalized a desire to succeed, producing great success and happiness.

The story teaches us that struggles and challenges are desirable difficulties that help us succeed. By facing them head-on, we can grow and develop into more robust, resilient individuals.

I go with the philosophy that educational institutions are places for students to learn about themselves—an apprenticeship model— learn the mechanics of life in general and acquire the tools needed to do a job—a place to create a growth mindset.

My parenting style largely led to my child's lack of internal sense of self-esteem, self-worth, and self-confidence. On many occasions, I noticed my child's insecurity. One day, I was introducing my child to a group of young ladies at my church. I said to them, "This is my baby girl." She was so upset with me and said, "Daddy, you said I am 20. Why are you still calling me a baby?" I said, "oh, I said you are 20. I changed my mind. You are my baby." Immediately, she said, "drop me home right now." That ruined my day. I created a video and posted it on my Facebook on her 20th birthday, saying, "Happy birthday to my young lady."

I don't hold my child responsible for her apparent lack of self-esteem and self-awareness at an early age. I protected her from everything that could go wrong, creating a moral dependency and spiritual void (*my version of spirituality is finding peace within, discussed in Part Four*). In the process, I eroded her ability to think independently, solve problems independently, and deal with all the dark forces around her, such as bullying, teasing, insults, conflicts, etc.

One day, while I was driving her to school after my angry outburst at my child or the classic parental melt-down over her interest in pursuing her Ph.D. in theology. She told me, "I must face some failures in my life." But I wasn't ready for her venturing into things the way she wanted. Indeed, a Ph.D. in theology would only further create a fixed mindset and suffering (discussed in Part Four). Hence, her characterization that I am a "control freak."

As a parent, I've come to understand the consequences of being overprotective. Scientifically speaking, our brains don't fully mature until our mid-20s. While shielding our children from negative influences and dangers may seem right, it can have the opposite effect. When they become young adults, they've internalized the fear and insecurity we've instilled in them, causing them to become more fragile and less capable of handling life's challenges. They may suffer from anxiety, depression, and other mental health issues. They strongly seek protection from anything violating their belief, identity, or sense of self we created for them.

I always tell my students, "We live in a world full of opportunities, but be aware of the dark forces of destruction."

The perceptions we create for our children must change—less dependence on scholars who often twist the interpretation of religious or political philosophies that suit their narratives and more focus on questioning our way of thinking. It is a delicate balance. Instill more independent thinking: *question everything (unlearn) and rethink.* This practice requires concentrated efforts by parents and educational institutions, the environments that mainly influence their thinking.

I advocate building self-awareness and improving our mental health: activating the brain's cognitive side and being critical of our thinking. In other words, a rational approach: question our beliefs and views and look for evidence instead of creating a victimhood mentality.

SOFT SKILL IS THE HARD SKILL TO MASTER

Aaron Temkin Beck, a pioneer in Cognitive Behavioral Therapy (CBT), noticed that people who are depressed experience negative feelings about themselves and the world around them. I, myself, had experienced the same anger and resentment towards the world. Breaking up from that distorted thinking is questioning our beliefs and looking for evidence to support our core beliefs.

In my case, I journal all my negative thoughts and figure out how to improve the quality of my thoughts.

Our beliefs are the manifestation of everything we experience in our environment. It's so easy to fall into the trap of *confirmation bias*. We tend to seek information confirming what we already believe while ignoring anything contradicting our beliefs. It's a dangerous habit to get into because it can lead us down a path that isn't based on reality.

We must be open to new ideas and willing to challenge our assumptions, even if uncomfortable. I kept emphasizing this approach of rethinking throughout this book: it is *acceptance and compassion*. Accept that we have control over only our thoughts and emotions and come to peace with the nature of reality. It's easy to forget that our perception of reality is subjective and biased, and we must be mindful of this as we navigate our lives.

The current environment at educational institutions is not often favorable for students to question their and others' views more compassionately. Many forces inside and outside schools, colleges, and universities perpetuate the status quo and discourage meaningful change. Even teachers who try to encourage independent thinking in their classrooms are often punished or silenced. Understandably, the course correction approach seems an existential threat to these educational institutes.

Chapter 9

Wokeism and Fragility

Teaching the younger generation has always been my unwavering passion. I felt it was crucial to foster self-awareness and inner peace in them. In today's world, there's an unrelenting clash between wokeness[10] and victimhood culture and anti-wokeness and insensitivity to human conditions. I focus on finding the intersection between wokeness and anti-wokeness, where we can all learn from one another and build resilience.

"Get woke, grow broke" anti-woke sentiment is picking up steam on the Right—the Red America. "Get woke, play victim," pro-woke and progressive idea is gaining ground on the Left—the Liberal and Progressive America in which victimhood is reinforced and stimulated. I believe the solution to our collective well-being is humanity: The God-fearing, Church-going, Gun-owning, Family people on the "Right" need to understand that tribalism is antithetical to the truth in the Bible—we are all children of God. Instead of empowering people to think and act encouragingly towards peaceful coexistence, they are planting the seed of hatred—caught up in a 24-

---

[10] Wokeness refers to being sensitive to genetically inherited injustices like race, gender, or sexual orientation.

hour news cycle of fear and paranoia perpetuated by news media and social media. For the Liberal and Progressive cohorts, being sensitive to genetically inherited injustices—sex, gender, and race—in society is not enough. It is far from solving our social and environmental problems. The solution starts with empowering our younger generation to deal with adversities. It is all about building self-confidence and self-worth in them. They are not *"supposed to be victims."* They should be provided a platform to openly debate their thoughts and be less sensitive to certain 'trigger words' they dislike.

It's sad to see how anger, prejudice, conflict, hatred, and resentment can arise when two opposing forces collide. This *"us vs. them"* mentality is rooted in our natural tendency to create distinctions and form groups, often leading to discriminatory behavior towards those different from us. It's vital to remember that such practices are unhealthy for our collective well-being. Anger and hatred only lead to stress, which is not helpful to a healthy lifestyle. Instead, we should all strive to find freedom within ourselves, regardless of what others say or think about us.

Humanity is not a zero-sum game, where one group's gain is another group's loss. Instead, it's a collaborative effort where we can all thrive. The idea that the exaltation of one group over other groups is necessary to protect individual freedom is false. It goes against the spirit of freedom and liberty, especially on college campuses.

I use tribalism and identity politics interchangeably. The way I define identity politics is the fight for individual freedom, liberty, and the pursuit of happiness. I favor identity politics in college campuses as long as it is practiced under an over-arching framework with a defined mission. A mission to expand and positively transform human conditions, a mission for the collective well-being of humanity, not "us vs. them," and a culture of shared value, regardless of the color of our skin, religious affiliation, ethnicity, gender, race, or sexual orientation. That framework drives open debate and discussion on college campuses—embracing the culture of oneness: we need to work together to solve our intractable problems for the common good.

However, a significant worry puts doubt on the validity of this framework: the looming possibility of an intentional effort to manipulate and control the opinions of bright and promising people—Children. This tactic may be an attempt to portray these people as the victims of innate genetic traits, or "wokeness," which is a phenomenon. Such a project can undermine legitimate intellectual discourse and impose polarizing beliefs that might prevent serious debate and critical thinking. It emphasizes how crucial it is to maintain fair and impartial debates that enable the study of many viewpoints without undue bias or manipulation. Such debates foster intellectual growth and the refinement of ideas, ultimately contributing to a more enlightened and balanced society.

Although freedom of speech is a fundamental right, it should not be employed as a shield for discriminatory remarks against individuals who hold different religious views.

It's essential to recognize that our words carry weight, and that weight comes with responsibility.

College campuses have been grappling with the issue of reconciling free speech and hate speech for quite some time. It begs the question of who holds the power to determine what is appropriate and inappropriate to say when we are all biased. It is undeniably concerning to learn that wealthy donors are wielding their financial power to influence affluent universities and even going as far as to ensure students holding dissenting opinions are deprived of job opportunities in firms run by these elites. Such actions are a blatant violation of the principles of academic freedom and integrity.

Instead of just creating a facade of social responsibility with their donations to wealthy universities and indoctrinating the younger generation, donors can make a real difference by investing their resources in developing emotional intelligence in the younger generation, particularly in underprivileged inner-city schools and colleges. This is where their donations will have the most significant positive impact—*empower the next generation to be self-aware and become assertive and compassionate individuals who can contribute towards creating a just and equitable society.*

Determining what is acceptable to say and what crosses the line is virtually impossible. Our environment shapes our beliefs. We believe we have the freedom to express our opinions, but how often do we acknowledge that our perceptions and biases heavily influence our opinions?

Our thoughts and emotions are molded by our experiences and beliefs, shaping our opinions. That's why it's important to question our way of thinking and address the root cause of our biases: *our environment.*

We must understand that we live in an uncertain world, and the truth is not always evident. Therefore, we can acknowledge our biases by cultivating a compassionate view of humanity.

Ultimately, free speech becomes truly meaningful when coupled with compassion and recognition of the harm that hate can cause.

Wokeness, in the present form, only builds a victimhood culture—" I am a victim of my race, gender, or ethnicity." Our younger generations are front and center of this movement. The moral underpinning of this movement is laudable. The question our younger generation should be asking is what we are doing with this woke culture. Unless each one of us takes responsibility for affecting positive social change, wokeness becomes a cancer in our society.

WHY ARE WE SO SENSITIVE?

"Don't let others discriminate against you; take control of your thoughts and emotions."

I strongly believe in the importance of studying history. To truly comprehend how our historical experiences have shaped our perspectives, we must question what we can do to transform ourselves and our beliefs. Our past actions and decisions provide valuable insights to help us learn and grow. No one has the authority to degrade us without our permission. We empower ourselves and serve as an example for others facing their own struggles by freely discussing and sharing our experiences with both physical and mental adversity.

In the context of racism in the U.S., the Civil Rights Act of 1866 and 1964 bring some perspective. Civil Rights Act of 1866 was the first federal law to affirm that all U.S. citizens are equally protected under the law. The passage of the Civil Rights Act of 1964 marked a milestone in the long struggle to extend civil, political, and legal rights and protections to African Americans, including formerly enslaved people and their descendants, and to end segregation in public and private facilities.

Still, we see racial tensions in our society. The Whites argue against learning black history and critical race theory in schools and colleges. They fear that by acknowledging the past and its implications, they will be perceived as guilty. Guilt and shame are part of our life and an opportunity to learn and grow—*learn the history in black and white.* After all, we cannot move forward and live in harmony unless we accept and learn from our past. If we don't know where we are coming from, it's impossible to know where we are going.

"The power to achieve greatness is within us."

The progress made by the Black community in the United States is nothing short of remarkable. We have had a black president for two terms, a black woman serving as our Vice President, and countless black individuals achieving success in media and business. These role models are not only inspirational but also provide us with valuable insight into what it takes to succeed. In my own classrooms, I have seen black students excel, driven by their strong family backgrounds and an unwavering belief in their abilities. Despite facing discrimination, they have thrived and proven that nothing can hold them back. It's time to acknowledge our incredible progress and continue to work towards a more equitable society where everyone has the opportunity to succeed.

How often do we misjudge others? Humans are prone to cognitive biases, a systematic error in our thinking that can cause us to deviate from rationality in our judgments. These biases can impact our perception of information and others, leading to inaccurate judgments and illogical conclusions.

Americans have this unhealthy obsession with color-coding people:

One evening, I was walking out to my car parked on the street. A white lady approached me and asked, "Do you live around here?" I said, "Yes." I knew where she was going with it. She then asked, "Where do you live." I said, "Right around that corner."

I thought that asking her the same questions would escalate the situation. Instead, I gave her enough time to rethink her way of questioning. I was soft-pedaling the seriousness of the situation. She looked at me and said, "Sorry."

We all have a beautiful side buried beneath our conscious awareness. Here is why I did not react to her questioning:

When someone hurts you, it's easy to think it was intentional. It may appear to be a deliberate act. However, it's crucial to keep in mind that they may struggle internally with stress, negativity, and other issues. When you change your perspective and understand human conditions, you can start to feel compassion for that individual, ultimately leading to love, forgiveness, and kindness toward them.

I smiled at her and left.

Malcolm Gladwell, in his book 'Outliers,' talked about Sandra Bland:

Sandra was an educated, church-going child who had her own podcast. Listening to her voice on her podcast, I truly believed she was a blessed child.

I want to address this situation in two ways:

A white police officer in Texas pulled over Sandra, a young African-American woman from Chicago, for failing to use a turning signal. She was there for a job interview. The conversation between them escalated into an altercation. She was pulled out of the car, arrested, and imprisoned. Three days later, she committed suicide in her cell.

Our perception can significantly influence our reaction to a situation. It's essential to recognize and overcome biases and preconceived notions to accurately and impartially perceive the situation at hand. Failure to do so can result in an inaccurate and unfair assessment of the situation.

Both of their behaviors were wrong in this context. But the Police officer had all the power.

Mr. Gladwell, in his podcast, stated that she sat in her car and lit a cigarette to calm herself down and potentially de-escalate the situation.

She refused to put out the cigarette and comply with the officer's order, making the officer furious. The fact that she was driving a Honda signifies her class in society. What if she was driving a Benz? Would that change the perception the police officer had about her? What if a white lady is driving a Honda? Is it a black lady traveling to another state and driving a Honda in a white neighborhood that triggered the police officer's fear, or is it a stereotypical view among white people about blacks in general that Black people are an unintelligent inferior species and have a genetic tendency toward violence?

Sandra was the product of everything she consumed while growing up regarding how she viewed the world: *she felt insecure.* When a police officer confronted her, she felt the officer was there to get her. She reacted with that mindset. The officer had the same fear. That is the way racism is embedded in America. The issue of racism has plagued America for thousands of years, and despite significant progress, racial disparities persist.

We must make an intensive effort to develop self-awareness and strive towards a fairer future for all members of our community. I wished she had been taught in her church or community that she should not feel bad about her upbringing, race, or ethnicity. She should have been proud of her color and upbringing—we are all children of God. The black and white read the same bible: "We are all created in the images of God." We are all valuable.

She should have followed the officer's order and shown compassion for the officer for his suffering—his fear and insecurity. They both needed to be self-aware.

The perception is that you will suffer if you are a Black or Brown American (communities of color). That is the victimhood culture. Black and Brown are led to believe that they are supposed to be 'victims' of racial injustice. In other words, it is a miracle if they succeed in life. There is no truth to this cultural ideology. I, an Indian American, never felt I was a victim.

Twenty-seven years ago, I immigrated to the US from a humble upbringing with a few hundred dollars and big dreams—dreams of getting a quality education and supporting my family. I'm proud to say that I've accomplished both. Nowhere on earth can I find the opportunities this country offers to those who work hard, long enough, and persevere through all the ups and downs. I owe a great debt of gratitude to this most remarkable nation on earth.

In my class, a student raised the question of whether we all have the same opportunities. To answer his question, I discussed the idea of loss aversion. We all have equal opportunities to survive and thrive, just like anyone else on this planet.

The key is to rewire our brains for abundance rather than wiring ourselves to be victims.

Unfortunately, our society, particularly political forces, constantly pushes a culture of victimhood. Regardless of our genetically inherited characteristics, America is a land of opportunity for anyone.

A STRONG CULTURE CAN TRANSFORM SOCIETY

I am referring to the book "What You Do Is Who You Are" by Ben Horowitz:

Over time, culture can overcome seemingly invincible structural barriers and transform the behavior of social systems. The persistent strength of culture can undermine even the most difficult structural barriers, changing societal norms and institutions. In the 1970s, many kids from the Bronx created a new art form called 'hip-hop.' In a single generation, they overcame poverty, racism, and massive opposition from the music industry to build the world's most popular musical genre. They changed the global culture by inventing a culture premised on openness, hard work, and a hustler mentality.

ALL STUDENTS ARE BLOOMERS

An environment where minorities (communities of color) struggle to get ahead builds self-doubt or self-criticism. They only overcome that by trusting in their confidence and ignoring others. People perceive our confidence level based on where we come from, live, or what we do.

We put so much value on people working in the Ivy League vs. elsewhere. To a large extent, that is true. I see this pattern of behavior among educators in non-Ivy league colleges. They don't often find a lot of motivation to do better since they think students are weak, and they don't try to raise the bar.

I remember one professor stating in my peer evaluation, "I need improvement. I teach like I am teaching at an Ivy League school. Our students are weak." Is that a virtuous cycle for Ivy League students, where teachers are motivated to do their best and provide the best for their students? The answer is a resounding "yes."

In contrast, students in a non-Ivy league were treated as 'weak.' In my class, every student is an Ivy League student. They have enormous potential. All they need is hard work, tenacity, perseverance, and the will to confront challenges head-on.

The study led by a Harvard Psychologist, Robert Rosenthal, showed what happened to students when teachers believed they had high potential in a random selection of 20% labeled as bloomers and 80% as a control group. Students labeled as bloomers achieved more than 50% intelligence gains in a year tested by examiners unaware that the experiment had occurred. The students labeled as bloomers continued to show gains after two years. They were being taught by entirely different teachers who did not know students had been labeled as bloomers.

The students labeled as bloomers scored more than others due to the self-fulfilling prophecies created by the teachers' beliefs. Our expectations and beliefs significantly impact how our lives turn out. Knowing this power enables us to deliberately create abundant mindsets, giving us the confidence and resiliency to face life's challenges.

If we believe something true, we'll act as if it were true. When teachers believe their students are bloomers, they set high expectations for their success. As a result, the teachers engaged in more supportive behaviors such as communicating warmly, giving more challenging assignments, calling on them more often, and providing them with more feedback, which boosted the student's confidence. That is the growth mindset I referred to earlier.

The study showed that teachers' expectations are crucial for improving the grades and intelligence test scores of low-achieving students and members of stigmatized communities. When teachers believed in their students' potential, they acted in ways that made students' potential a reality. The supportive behavior of teachers boosted students' confidence and catalyzed self-fulfilling prophecies.

As an educator, I believe all humans have the potential—to empower people to overcome genetically inherited biases and succeed.

When someone says, "I don't have a racist bone in my body," that person doesn't understand that racism lives deep within. We are judgmental. George Floyd's situation was crystal-clear evidence of racism in America.

Being aware of the influence of images and narratives on our perception of the world is incredibly important. Neuroplasticity works positively and negatively—meaning that our brains can change and adapt to our experiences, for better or worse. It's essential to be mindful of the media we consume and actively seek diverse perspectives to broaden our understanding of the world. Doing so can broaden our horizons and help us become more empathetic, compassionate, and informed. It requires courage to listen to others, rethink how we think about humanity, and approach our lives differently; we are all human. We don't believe that it is not our fault that we are born with a particular cultural, religious, or ethnic heritage. Embrace it.

BEWARE OF THE SMART MINORITY AND THEIR INFLUENCE ON PUBLIC POLICIES

Whenever there are racial tensions, companies issue solidarity statements aligning with social justice activism. Those statements are their reaction to racial injustice or police brutality without having to change their internal cultures. What is missing are the needed changes on organizational, leadership, and individual levels, making them committed to creating a more just and equitable workplace, not making *politically correct* statements that show a gesture of solidarity to the woke or victimhood culture. Companies often prioritize their public image while ignoring or dismissing the same voices (minority voices) they profess to care so much about.

Corporations (*I use corporation and company interchangeably*) are not soulless money-making entities but rather made of individuals with shared values—profits are the outcome of successful strategies rooted in a 'noble purpose.'[11] That noble purpose is to foster human connection and make everyone feel they belong. It matters significantly for the overall success of a corporation. Simply making a hollow show of solidarity aligning companies with social justice activism, employees, and consumers is not enough. However, changes that companies can make on the organizational, leadership, and individual levels to show that they are committed to creating a more just and equitable workplace are far more critical to building a diverse community.

Corporations understand the cost of silence is much higher than woke washing—a powerful marketing tool for corporations. Corporations often capitalize on this movement, distract, and prey on us. We see this corporate behavior of rushing to advertise their commitment to support the cause, usually when there is social unrest

---

[11] ("Woke washing" your company won't cut it, by Erin Dowel and Marlette Jackson, HBR, July 27, 2020)

over gender and racial issues. *Companies are savvy to capture those moments and capitalize on them.*

In Churchillian terms, CEOs of corporations rise to the occasion—appear focused, strong, and uncompromising. They pledge a few billion dollars to address social or environmental concerns, put some token minorities as heads of Diversity, Equity, and Inclusion divisions, plant a tree in Harlem, donate money to progressive movements like BLM, temporarily cut advertising dollars to media who criticize the movements, and fire people who use politically incorrect statements. Often, corporate statements of solidarity gloss over internal inequities. They create a semblance of corporate social responsibility (CSR) without dismantling the system that created these social, environmental, and governance problems. These managers (I hesitate to use the word 'leaders' since leadership is about making a positive difference in other peoples' lives) have fallen short when addressing racial, income, and gender inequality.

The rich and the powerful should be responsible for embracing this notion of humility and humanity, not just showing a semblance of social responsibility and riling up people's emotions using social media and news media—brain-wash, woke-wash, and green-wash the young generation. Greenwashing refers to companies portraying themselves as environmentally conscious but failing to fulfill their commitment to offering environmentally friendly products. It is like fashion companies promoting recycling initiatives while contributing to plastic pollution.

Why would they create a semblance of environmental consciousness?

It's fascinating how we tend to accept the motives of others without questioning them. This habit of creating a meticulously crafted public image is no different from politicians discussing patriotism, family values, or gun control. However, they cannot live up to anything they say in public. They do not genuinely believe in these values, only going along with them to fit in and further their agendas. As I often say, *"people who are happy within don't hurt others."* They are battling their inner demons—lacking self-awareness. But we have the power to choose not to be naive— *question our way of thinking.*

Chapter 10

A Holistic Approach to Teaching and Learning

I believe in a holistic approach to education that focuses on academic achievement, personal growth, social skills, and emotional well-being. It helps develop well-rounded individuals who are better equipped to handle challenges in life. By encouraging students to question themselves and each other, show humility, and remain curious, we can instill a culture of self-discovery and growth. One effective tool in this pursuit is introducing concepts that challenge students to think and rethink their understanding of the world.

Learning is such a crucial part of life, and it goes far beyond just acquiring knowledge about one specific thing. For example, achieving excellence in school isn't just about putting in the time and effort to learn a concept. It's also about understanding how that concept applies to other areas of study, internships, or jobs. It's a genuinely transformative mindset that can open up countless opportunities for growth and success.

When students are encouraged to think creatively and apply what they've learned in practical ways, they retain the information better and develop a sense of self-motivation. It's vital to foster an environment where students can explore ideas and concepts hands-on, as it helps them see the relevance of their learning and how those concepts can be applied in the real world.

My teaching career continues to evolve. I design my course with a few essential concepts I want my students to master and create an open debate in the classroom. Then, I explain the theoretical underpinning of those concepts and connect them with my practical world and life experience.

I am not an expert in the concepts I teach: I learn with my students—discover new and better ways to educate my students.

In my classroom, I borrowed the idea of promoting a mini-TED talk from Professor Adam Grant at the Wharton School of Business. Students pick a concept, work in small groups, and record a short presentation—usually a 5-minute-long talk. Students are encouraged to challenge the concepts I covered in the class and guided to provide a thoughtful presentation.

I believe that grades are not a strong predictor of job performance—focus less on the grades and more on the learning process. I would rather hire students with a C average, who have the emotional maturity and collaborative attitude, *'who can get along and get things done,'* than their straight-A counterparts who have a *'been there done that'* attitude or a fixed mindset. It is all about humility and curiosity to learn. *Humility and curiosity* are essential allies in the quest for success.

Being humble keeps us grounded and encourages our desire to learn from our errors and those of others. Curiosity, on the other hand, feeds our hunger for knowledge and innovation, encouraging us to venture into unexplored territory and gain new insights. When cultivated, these qualities open the door to long-lasting success and personal development.

I continue to encourage the socially and environmentally conscious generation to rethink their approach to learning:

Ask whether capitalism is alleviating or exacerbating human hardships.

DEMOCRATIZATION OF CAPITALISM

Democracy is built on providing equality and fairness to all, and it strives to ensure everyone has a say in the decision-making process, leaving no one behind.

Democratization of capitalism refers to making economic opportunities available to more people instead of just a select few (the elites). It creates a fairer, more sustainable economy that benefits everyone.

Capitalism could be defined as *either,*
A social system based on individual rights that unleashes the power of the human mind—Inclusive Capitalism.

If a system inspires its people to seek their true value and worth and instills ethics, integrity, honesty, morality, humanity, and humility, it can create a society where democracy and the free market thrive, and everyone can achieve their dreams.

Or

Capitalism in terms of **capital:**

A socio-economic system based on private ownership of resources or capital—Extractive Capitalism.

In this system, the power lies in those who own and manage the capital, which is often the institutional or owner class. This has led to the birth of elitism in capitalism, where a select few hold excessive power over the rest of society.

However, what we witness today is a Democracy, which is a product of manufactured consent[12], where people are conditioned, curated, and indoctrinated through news media, social media, politicians, and religious organizations.

The excessive concentration of power among institutions that own and manage hedge funds, private equity funds, pension funds, and mutual funds—*capital they own and what they manage for others*—has led to an alarming level of control over the media and democracy. The wealthy associated with these institutions use their vast resources to manipulate the press, distort the truth, and influence public perception in their favor. Their misery and suffering become the suffering of society. We are conditioned to consume what media produces, and the politicians have become mere puppets in the hands

---

[12] In the book Manufacturing Consent, Noam Chomsky and Edward S. Herman delve into how the American media portrays events and creates stories that cater to the interests of the country's political, economic, and social elite.

of these elites, resulting in a democracy under the control of the elites.

The elitism has even seeped into college campuses, threatening the freedom of speech and dictating who can say what—an environment that is supposed to *nurture the values and worth of every student and unleash the power of human minds.*

As a nation, the United States has made great strides in advancing from the *Iron Age to the Stone Age to the Gilded Age and now to the Information Age (the Digital Age).* Yet, our hardships and sufferings are increasing on an alarming level: *Income inequality, racial inequality, gender inequality, hopelessness, homelessness, depression, anxiety, alcoholism, drug addiction, and gun violence, to name a few.*

Capitalism in terms of *Capital*:
A historical Perspective

Stone age

Modern capitalism
- *Dollar: The world's reserve currency*
- *End of Gold standard*
- *Print money: Modern Monetary Policy*
- *Trickle down economics*
- *Bubbles: Too big to fail syndrome*
- *Stock buyback*
- *Corporate power and the rise of elites*

Information age
(Digital age)
- *Cloud computing*
- *Quantum computing*
- *Machine Learning*
- *Artificial Intelligence*
- *Wi-Fi and connectivity*

Gilded age
Industrial Revolution
- *Turn of the 20ᵗʰ century*
- *Immigration and urbanization*
- *The wealthy tycoons held the most political power*

Worsening human hardships
Racial inequality, gender inequality, income inequality, hopelessness, homelessness, gun violence, depression, anxiety, suicides, alcoholism, drug addiction, etc.

Source: Author

The gross federal debt of the United States has surpassed $33 trillion (as of November 2023). The United States of America enjoys a powerful position in the world of its reserve currency status[13]. This powerful status allows America to borrow cheaply and squander it—the easy money policy. In the process, we create a market economy where the rich get richer. They are the *"owner-class"* who benefit from the enormous spending by the *"worker-class"* stimulated by reckless fiscal and monetary policies. The ones suffering the most are people experiencing poverty who pay more for the goods and services from the real economy—higher inflation due to more money and less supply of goods and services. Supply and demand is an economic model of price determination in a free market and stock market—price determines what we produce and how much we produce. As corporate profits skyrocket, so do the stock prices.

It's hard to ignore the fact that the leader of the free world is leading by an example of economic disparity. This disparity was much pronounced during the COVID-19 times. The number of billionaires has increased, and the gap between the rich and poor has widened, leading to the rich becoming even richer while millions lost their jobs.

The Dow's best week since 1938. More than 16 million lost their jobs in 3 weeks (source: CNBC. April 9, 2020)

---

[13] The US dollar has long been the world's primary reserve currency, widely used by central banks and governments globally for international transactions and foreign exchange reserves. This affords the US a significant advantage in issuing debt, allowing it to borrow in its own currency at lower rates, keeping borrowing costs low for the government.

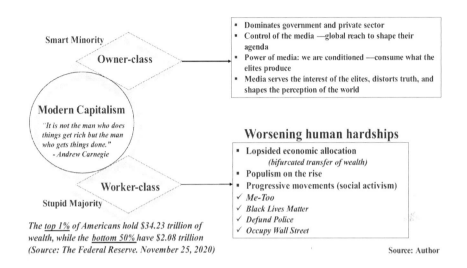

The *top 1%* of Americans hold $34.23 trillion of wealth, while the *bottom 50%* have $2.08 trillion (Source: The Federal Reserve. November 25, 2020)

Source: Author

Needless to say, the influence of the elites in the media and politics has a toxic effect on building an inclusive society. The media shapes people's beliefs and views. *Can we stop consuming what they produce?*

THE PURSUIT OF SHORT-TERM PLEASURE

As I stated at the beginning of this book, there are no best practices. Nothing is right from the outset. It evolves. American capitalism is evolving: a move away from Keynesian economics or expansionary fiscal policy—government spending boosts consumer demand—as the standard model in advanced economies after the Great Depression of the 1930s. Neoliberalism—a model of free-market capitalism favoring the shift of economic control from the government to the private sector, shaped in the 1960s and 1970s, is present in the United States and other economies today. This term was later used by Milton Friedman, a classical liberal economist, in his 1951 essay "Neo-Liberalism and its Prospects." This model itself was a shift: A defining moment for this shift was Milton Friedman's 1970 article for the New York Times, in which he argued that,

"The social responsibility of business is to increase its profits."

Can corporations pursue the dual goal of corporate *purpose* (profit) and the *mission* to affect positive environmental and social changes?

Given the younger generation's concerns about building a cleaner environment and a healthier society, I would like to discuss a few concepts relevant to these noble goals and my take on what is missing in their thought process—*the challenges of creating market capitalism where everyone enjoys prosperity, let alone sustaining it.*

The key question is how the policies within and forces outside a corporation can help us bring about positive social and environmental changes. Forces like corporate governance, disruptors who threaten market capitalism, and the role of the younger generation interested in sustainability goals such as ESG but are completely and utterly confused about how to think about positive changes.

I don't want to paint all CEOs with the same brush. Let me give you a brief idea of the concepts first. Then, I would like to provide my perspectives.

Since the 1970s, the overwhelming convention in the business world was *shareholder capitalism*—maximizing shareholder value. So, corporations are there to maximize shareholder value—a fancy way of saying 'make shareholders rich.' If companies fail to pursue that fundamental duty of shareholder capitalism, it becomes a negligence of their fiduciary duty to those who have invested in their companies.

Fiduciary duty is a legal obligation that requires one party to prioritize the best interest of another party. This duty arises when one party has more knowledge or expertise than the other. For instance, a financial advisor has a fiduciary duty to act in their client's best interest when offering investment advice.

The rationale behind shareholder capitalism is that when shareholder value is maximized, we all will be better positioned to pursue our personal, environmental, and social goals. According to this approach, shareholder capitalism is the path toward stakeholder capitalism—it addresses the interests of other *stakeholders, like employees, communities, government, suppliers, and customers related to corporations or firms.* This argument makes intuitive sense: higher profits attract more funding from investors, create more jobs, and potentially benefit the community.

Creating customer value and generating profits or earnings per share (EPS) are crucial for long-term shareholder value maximization. By delivering high-quality products or services that meet or exceed customers' expectations, companies can build a loyal customer base and differentiate themselves from their competitors. At the same time, generating profits and EPS is crucial for the business's long-term sustainability and maximizing shareholder value. It allows the company to reinvest in itself, expand its operations, and reward its shareholders.

Earnings per share (EPS) is a measure of a company's profitability that indicates how much money it earns for each outstanding share of its stock. Investors tend to view a higher EPS as a positive sign because it suggests that the company is generating higher profits relative to its share price, which may lead to higher demand for its shares and a higher stock price.

The measure of a company's success should not solely rely on quarterly EPS but instead on its ability to create long-term value for all stakeholders. By adopting a more inclusive approach, businesses can positively impact the environment and society and ensure their longevity and profitability. Sustainable business practices that benefit all stakeholders, not just shareholders or shareholder activists, should be measured more than quarterly EPS.

Corporations incentivize managers with hefty incentive packages like *stock options* to align the interests of managers (otherwise known as agents of shareholders) and shareholders (principals). These managers have more knowledge or expertise than the shareholders.

Stock options are a type of employee compensation that gives the holder the right, but not the obligation, to buy company stock at a specified price within a certain time frame. As an example, if the exercise price of the option is set at $5 per share and the current market price is $10 per share, the holder of the option has the right (no obligation) to purchase the stock for $5 per share and earn a profit of $5 per share. A stock option is a valuable tool for attracting and retaining top talent, as it offers the potential for significant *financial gain if the company's stock price rises.*

But the question is,
"Can a company be more conscious of the implications of their strategy with a stakeholder framework, not just shareholder focus or quarterly EPS?"

Empowered stakeholders can empower communities, employees, customers, and shareholders, delivering sustainable fiduciary results and inclusive growth.

In other words, the basic idea is that businesses must be stewards of the environment, uphold human rights throughout their global supply chains, and pursue sustainable shareholder returns that don't sacrifice the future *(long-term value creation)* for the present (*share price*). In doing so, the power shareholder activists wield (shareholder activism) to undermine stakeholder-centered strategies will diminish. In simpler terms, the price we pay in the present is based on the cash flow we expect in the future. So, there is no point in being financially concerned about small EPS (Earnings Per Share) hits when the goal is to create larger profits in the future. For building and maintaining shareholder value (rather than a get-rich-quick scheme), companies must invest in long-term projects that can create value (generate cash flows)—return exceeds the cost of capital or the return investors expect from a project given its risk profile.

Referring to an article by McKinsey[14], value creation is not limited to maximizing share price. Often, share price reflects a company's short-term success—mostly quarterly performance measured in earnings per share. Measuring value maximization (shareholder value or share price) rather than value creation[15] is the benchmark.

This fixation on short-term gain goes entirely against the principles of creating value, as it blurs the lines between short-term EPS and true value creation. It's nothing more than a shortcut for managers seeking to become wealthy quickly.

In many cases, managers are too *scared to take risks* and invest in long-term innovative projects simply because they fear they won't meet the EPS guidelines set by investors, which drives share price.

Investing in innovative projects (in an environment where companies get disrupted by innovative technologies) that create sustainable competitive advantage for companies requires short-term sacrifices, like getting rid of (writing off) obsolete investments. These write-offs appear on the income statement and can lower EPS, potentially driving down the share price in the short term. Staying ahead of disruptive technologies and ensuring long-term success is necessary.

---

[14] "Long-Term Value Creation Can—And Should—Take Into Account The Interests Of All Stakeholders"

[15] Creating value for a company involves increasing revenue, reducing costs, improving efficiency, enhancing customer experience, and fostering innovation.

DISRUPTIVE INNOVATION

The story of David and Goliath is extraordinary, emphasizing that with faith and courage, even the smallest and weakest among us can conquer the biggest and strongest challenges. The battle between the Israelites and the Philistines is a perfect example of the fierce competition between *new entrants and incumbents* (existing competitors) in today's business world. Like David, new entrants must face well-established industry giants with a significant market share.

Nevertheless, new entrants can vanquish the incumbents and emerge victorious with the right strategy, innovative ideas, and unwavering perseverance. The story of David and Goliath is a timeless reminder that determination and self-belief can make anything possible.

The battle between the Israelites and the Philistines was intense and nerve-wracking. Both armies were standing on their respective mountains, separated by a valley. Goliath, the champion of the Philistines, was a towering figure over nine feet tall, wearing body armor and wielding a massive spear. He challenged the Israelites daily to send one warrior to fight him in single combat. The victor would decide the winner of the battle. The Israelites were terrified of this mighty warrior, but a young shepherd accepted the challenge. Armed with a sling and five smooth stones, he marched forward to face Goliath. The giant was insulted by the sight of a small boy with a stick in his hand. The shepherd boy said, "I come to you in the name of almighty God." With the spirit of the Lord, he hurled a stone from his sling, hitting Goliath in the forehead. The giant fell to the ground. The shepherd boy ran to him, took his sword, and cut off his head. The Israelites emerged victorious. The Philistines fled the battle. That was the story of David and Goliath—the one-in-a-million long shot—the underdog and the overwhelming favorite.

Was David the underdog? What doomed the favorite?

Let me bring a parallel story from the business world. Clayton Christensen, in his book "The Innovator's Dilemma," explained with his *disruptive innovation* model, *"Why success cannot be sustained"*:

The mainframe computer was the first manifestation in the computer industry 60 years ago. It was complex and expensive, costing around a few million dollars to have one in our offices. Only a few big businesses could afford one. IBM was the leader in that space. Then came something called mini-computers. A few companies were operating in that space, with Digital Equipment Corporation (DEC) leading the way. They made good computers better for the same customers for a high-profit margin. The margin was around 40%. Christenson called this *"sustaining innovation."* But then came the game-changing *"disruptive innovation"*—making a historically complicated and expensive product or solution accessible and affordable to large segments of society, not just those with lots of money and skills.

The concept of disruptive innovation is fascinating to consider. It involves more than just enhancing existing products or services. Instead, it's about creating solutions that are more affordable and accessible to a broader audience. The aim is to entice those who do not use established companies' goods (referred to as "the low end of humanity" by Christenson) by presenting them with something that satisfies their needs at a lower cost. These disruptors can slowly gain momentum over time, eventually overtaking the incumbents. The ascent of Netflix over Blockbuster, smartphones replacing standalone cameras, and the bankruptcy of DEC are perfect illustrations of this phenomenon. It is critical to remember that this process is gradual, not an event, and often goes undetected by established players (incumbents) until it is too late. Universities today are experiencing a similar disruption that demands transformation. Universities need to foster an environment that motivates their leaders, faculty, and students to challenge their long-standing beliefs, enables them to express their opinions freely, and dissuades them from conforming to societal pressures.

Disruptors from the bottom of the market crept up to the top, destroyed the incumbents, and made computers more affordable and accessible to large segments of society. Today, we have moved from mainframes to mini-computers to PCs to laptops to smartphones, transforming how we communicate. It was not the management's ineptitude that led to DEC's demise. The company's leadership was so fixated on serving its affluent customers that they failed to recognize the disruption taking place at the bottom of the market. It's understandable, though—the allure of high-profit margins can be too tempting to resist, even if it leads to short-term gains at the expense of long-term success. This is the *short-term pleasure* I was referring to earlier.

What does this story have in common with the story of David and Goliath?

David was fighting the unconventional war with a modern technology called the 'sling.' He did not have the sword, shield, or body armor of the mighty warrior, Goliath. There was no head-to-head combat either. And yet David won the war.

It's important to acknowledge that our traditional methods may not work in today's uncertain world. Goliath-like entities that rely solely on conventional cognitive tools are at risk of being disrupted by those who adopt more unconventional approaches. It's essential to have an open mind and remain adaptable to new tools and strategies that may prove effective in certain situations. Disruptive innovation suggests that while individuals may not evolve, populations will. Similarly, business units may be unable to evolve due to specific customer bases and strategies. However, corporations can establish new business units with different strategies to compete with disruptors. IBM is a great example of this adaptable approach and has thrived over time.

The story is also a reminder that investment in innovation—not quarterly EPS—is essential to build a sustainable competitive advantage.

It is paramount to recognize the seduction of quick wealth and the need for social acceptance. These goals unintentionally promote negative neural patterns in our brains that encourage impulsive behavior and jeopardize long-term well-being. Rewiring our neural pathways towards healthier, more long-lasting objectives and contentment can be accomplished by emphasizing patience, developing a balanced viewpoint, and valuing significant successes over instant gratification. While indulging in short-term pleasures may bring us temporary satisfaction, it has been proven that it often leads to more misery and suffering in the long run.

As discussed in Chapter 14, true happiness cannot be achieved through these quick fixes. It is important to be mindful of the harmful effects of dopamine and cortisol that can come with 'get-rich-quick' schemes, as they can lead to addiction and further harm to our mental and emotional well-being.

Does the shareholder value maximization argument incentivize managers to respond to important societal, environmental, and economic challenges?

The truth is that the incentive system (stock options) often leads to conflicts of interest called *agency problems or principle-agent problems*—managers are hired as agents of the shareholders (principle).

The principal-agent problem is common when two parties have different priorities—the principal and their agent. When the principal owns assets but hires an agent to make decisions on their behalf, there can be a conflict of interest if the agent's interests do not align with the principal's. This divergence of interests can lead to unfavorable results for the principal.

This principle lays out the heart of the heartless economic principle: *self-interest and greed.* I call it 'human conditions'—*the pursuit of short-term pleasure.*

Let me say this: Corporations are people (the word "corporation" comes from the Latin word "corp," which means "body"). Managers use accounting or financial gimmicks to boost short-term EPS and beat analysts' EPS estimates. For example, inflating revenues or deflating expenses, shifting ordinary business expenses from the income statement to the balance sheet, not recognizing asset impairment, etc. EPS drives share price. So, managers can benefit by exercising their incentive options or shares. *This is the quarterly capitalism that drives American capitalism.*

The chart below thoroughly explains the concept:

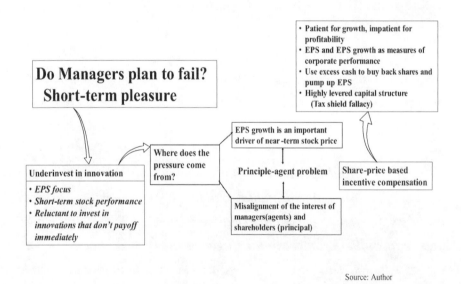

Source: Author

Incentivizing and motivating managers to enhance shareholder value is a practice in the corporate world—the agency cost.

The truth is that this incentive system rewards temporary success and encourages optimism. This practice often leads to skewing estimates toward unrealistically rosy outcomes, manipulating financials to meet that rosy target, and even firing and downsizing to protect their pay.

Despite the mechanisms to align incentives of managers and shareholders, the past two decades were filled with a seemingly unending series of scandals, from Enron to WorldCom to Tyco to Lehman Brothers, to name a few, signaling the crisis in corporate governance, ethics, and integrity.

Corporate governance is the system of rules, practices, and processes by which a company is directed and controlled. It involves balancing the interests of a company's many stakeholders, such as shareholders, management, customers, suppliers, government, and the community. Corporate governance ensures that a company operates ethically, transparently, and accountable while creating shareholder value.

The 2008 financial crisis is a prime example of the flaws in incentivizing managers to prioritize shareholder capitalism and hoping it will trickle down to the rest of the stakeholders. Large corporations follow an incentive plan to compensate their CEOs (agents) through equity-based pay, minimal salary, and short-term stock options. Short-term stock options are one of the ways managers game their companies' stock prices to the disadvantage of long-term shareholders, often engaging in deceptive accounting practices or not investing in projects that generate future cash flows.

189

*The real question is who benefits from this type of shareholder
capitalism or short-termism.*

Sadly, it's usually the large shareholders—hedge funds, pension
funds, or other institution investors—and executives who can reap the
rewards of this *get-rich-quick* scheme. They rarely hold onto their
shares for more than a year, leaving other shareholders to bear the
effect of any negative consequences. It's a far cry from the more
responsible approach of stakeholder capitalism.

ARE PROFIT AND PURPOSE MUTUALLY EXCLUSIVE DECISIONS?

In business, there has been a long-standing debate about whether
profit and purpose can coexist or are mutually exclusive[16]. Some
argue that corporations should prioritize their social responsibilities
and pursue a purpose beyond just maximizing shareholder value.
Others believe that a company's primary responsibility is to its
shareholders and that maximizing profits is the best way to achieve
this. However, growing evidence suggests that profit and purpose are
not mutually exclusive decisions. Companies that prioritize purpose
and social responsibility often see improved financial performance
over the long term. Studies have shown that purpose-driven

---

[16] "Mutually exclusive" refers to two or more events or conditions that cannot happen at
the same time. In other words, if one event occurs, the other event(s) cannot occur
simultaneously.

companies have better customer loyalty, higher employee engagement, and stronger brand recognition, which can translate into improved financial results.

Back in 1970, Economist and Nobel laureate Milton Friedman argued that the social responsibility of businesses is to increase their profits—a corporation's sole or primary responsibility is to its shareholders. Maximizing long-run value in highly competitive product and labor markets is impossible without taking care of all stakeholders—treating employees, suppliers, and local communities fairly in a competitive market.

As long as we understand that Friedman was referring to the maximization of long-run profits (value maximization) and not the next quarter's EPS, as many of Friedman's critics seem to assume, I think Friedman is still pretty much right.

NO GOOD DEED GOES UNPUNISHED

As the saying goes, "no good deed goes unpunished," this is especially true for companies prioritizing social responsibility and purpose alongside profits.

Despite the fact that many business leaders have recognized the importance of being socially responsible and have incorporated sustainable practices, ethical standards, and community involvement into their business models, they still face severe backlash from shareholders and activists.

CEOs committed to leading their corporations with purpose and humanity can be penalized by shareholders looking to 'get rich quick.'

To put it bluntly, if the stakeholder-centered strategies fail to translate into higher stock price movements, then CEOs can lose the support of shareholders, which in turn creates a breeding ground for shareholder activism. These activists seize on that opportunity in the form of a proxy fight, an attempt to persuade shareholders to use their proxy votes—shareholders of a public corporation may appoint an agent to attend shareholder meetings and vote on their behalf. That agent is the shareholder's proxy.

At a minimum, these investor activists can make it difficult for CEOs to devise and implement stakeholder-centered strategies. These investor activists can swing neutral shareholders. For example, passive investors are those who invest in index funds. These indexers outsource their votes to proxy advisors.

We might ask ourselves:

Why is it so challenging to implement stakeholder-centered
strategies, even when we have so many great ideas?

It's a question akin to asking why the United States struggles to pass common-sense gun laws. The truth is that CEOs are incentivized by metrics such as revenue, EPS, and stock prices. Fund managers who invest in these companies are rewarded based on their performance relative to the market, whether active or passive. And boards of directors are tasked with protecting the interests of shareholders. There are instances where we find directors are in cahoots with the managers—*Get rich, too.* It is the short-term pleasure that drives their decision.

So, how can a CEO shift their attention from revenues, EPS, and stock prices to ESG goals, for example? In other words, focus on maximizing shareholder value while keeping the ESG goals in mind.

'ESG' stands for environmental, social, and governance responsibility—the commitment of the CEOs to lead their corporations for the benefit of all stakeholders. This popular management theory has been picking up steam given the alarming climate crisis and increasing social challenges like income inequality, racial inequality, and gender inequality.

Promising ideas by entrepreneurs get funded by public investors and banks at different stages of their business plans. All of these investors expect to be rewarded with financial returns. Government-mandated accounting standards and all valuation matrices are created with shareholders in mind. For example, companies have the choice as to how they recognize expenses. Companies can defer expenses like devaluation or repayment in the income statements and increase EPS.

Companies can forgo long-term value-creating projects or put aside investment in innovation, not worried about disruption and ESG mandates, for fear of underperforming in the short term. Accounting standard setters have yet to come up with a framework for valuing investment in innovation like intellectual capital (systems, procedures, or policies), human capital (competencies, diversity, ideas, experience, motivations), or social capital (shared values, norms, gender, race, etc.) that addresses ESG concerns.

But investors have tools to punish companies considered unethical, immoral, or harmful, like companies in the alcohol, tobacco, gambling, weapon, or narcotics sectors. The *concept of return and risk* apples right here by placing constraints on those companies. Lower their price by using a higher discount rate or cost of capital (your higher expected return requirement given the risk profile of the investment), making less capital available to the company and less demand for their stock. Investors might demand higher expected returns to deal with more risk and will have to sell their shares for lower prices, getting lower returns on them. Put differently, there is a trade-off in which companies have to accept a lower rate of return or forgo the company's near-term stock returns in their goal to adhere to stakeholder-centered strategies. Furthermore, consumers can make their choices clear to corporations that engage in practices that only benefit the rich (focus on EPS) by stopping consumption of their products.

Consumers, corporations, and the government must join forces and collaborate toward a common objective to make a meaningful impact on environmental and societal issues. It cannot be dealt with by individuals or corporations alone. Can the US regulate its meat consumption? Let's shut down all fast-food chains. It is not good for the environment, individuals, and animals.

DIVERSITY, EQUITY, AND INCLUSION

It's essential to recognize that having more individuals from diverse communities in managerial or leadership roles within a corporation won't necessarily solve racial or gender inequality.

To create a cohesive environment with a skilled and diverse group of individuals, corporations must cultivate a corporate culture that attracts, mentors, and develops talented employees from all backgrounds. Achieving this goal requires a structural revolution within corporations, where a leadership-from-behind approach is practiced—*the shepherd's way.*

Professor Linda Hill, the chair of the Harvard Business School's High Potential Leadership program, has a marvelous article in the Harvard Business Review on 'leading from behind' and 'leadership as a collective genius.' Leadership in the future, she says, will require 'leading from behind' to create environments where people working in teams can contribute their skills for collaborative problem-solving and innovation through the joint creativity of diverse teams.

She compares this procedure to being a shepherd. Shepherds usually led their flocks from behind, providing protection and creating a space where the more agile could go first, allowing others to follow. To ensure that everyone succeeds in their various tasks, a leader must nurture the people on their team, set boundaries, and resolve problems.

Nelson Mandela, a leader admired worldwide for his strength of character, explains the true meaning of 'leading from behind.'

"It is better to lead from behind and to put others in front, especially when you celebrate victory when nice things occur. You take the front line when there is danger. Then people will appreciate your leadership."

— *Mandela, Long Walk to Freedom, 1995, 22*

Empowering others to lead alongside you is a powerful strategy that demonstrates strength and confidence. This approach involves taking proactive steps to lead the way while creating opportunities for others to share the success. By 'leading from behind,' you can inspire others to become leaders in their own right, creating a culture of collaboration and growth that benefits everyone involved. So don't be afraid to step back and let others shine—a strategy that can lead to great things!

MODEST RETURN, HIGHEST IMPACT

The underlying motivation for stakeholder capitalism is to make sure capitalism is working for humanity in general, not just one class of society, the shareholders. I have purposely used the term 'class'— the worker and the owner classes—to bring your attention to the lopsided economic allocations.

How do we scale our self-compassion and address our human hardships in the context of a business model?

We can become more understanding and empathetic toward others by addressing human hardships and being gentle with ourselves.

Connect the societal problems to business models.

We all know that only business can create wealth. However, communities around the world question the legitimacy of businesses for the right reason: the disparity between the rich and the poor is widening, resulting in a massive divergence between a business's success and a community's success. This well-known concept called Corporate Shared Value (CSV)[17] challenges the traditional belief about the role of business in creating societal good.

CSV aims to create a synergy between social and business values. By considering the impact of their business decisions on society, companies can create economic value and contribute to the greater good. However, a deep tension is inherent in creating shared value, especially in light of the business's focus on shareholder capitalism—a company's first and foremost responsibility is to provide a positive return to its shareholders. Milton Friedman supported this view and famously said,

"The social responsibility of business is to increase profits."

CSV approach allows us to rethink these tensions, examine traditional beliefs and biases, and identify strategies to maximize social activities' positive effect on business value. Why not rethink our decision to build a sustainable solution to social and environmental problems instead of merely paying lip service to them?

---

[17] Institute for strategy and competitiveness, Harvard Business School. Corporate Shared Value is a business approach that prioritizes policies and practices aimed at improving a company's competitive edge and profitability while also contributing to the betterment of the social and economic conditions in the communities in which it operates. This concept goes beyond traditional notions of corporate social responsibility, philanthropy, or sustainability and presents a new, innovative way for companies to achieve economic success.

We need a paradigm shift in defining a business school's mission—to bring students with the passion and capacity to learn fundamental business concepts and transform them into the new generation of leaders and entrepreneurs for building great businesses and strengthening our society. We measure our success by improving our competitiveness to ease the world's pressing problems.

From the outset, a successful business model must address a "customer's pain"—the implications of not solving that problem and the size of the addressable market. These are not 'nice-to-solve' problems but rather 'must-solve' problems.

There is no shortage of 'pain' in a world with over 8 billion people. We have massive social problems—poverty, climate change, pollution, lack of clean water and healthcare, run-down schools, discrimination, systems that torture, imprison, and kill innocent men, women, and children, and so forth. That opens up massive opportunities. We have yet to make any large-scale impact in addressing them.

One way to tackle complex social issues and create more jobs while building a stable local community is by establishing a model for change. This model requires a strong focus on business dedication to societal issues, which can attract a diverse range of participants. The key is to start by understanding the community and its needs. Instead of arriving at preconceived notions, we should have a long-term vision of how we hope to see the community change in the years ahead. To make this happen, we must leverage the resources and ecosystem of the community. This involves tapping into the imagination, energy, and passion of the people living there and identifying a solution that can make a real difference in the lives of a significant portion of the population. By connecting social problems to business models, we can create a sustainable model for change that benefits everyone involved.

Alleviate human hardship: Profit with Purpose

One effective way to alleviate human suffering is by promoting innovative business models prioritizing social impact and environmental sustainability. To achieve this, politicians can collaborate with their wealthy donors and establish a multi-trillion-dollar fund to support businesses that benefit society. For example, companies that provide affordable healthcare, education, and housing can significantly improve the quality of life for individuals and families. Additionally, businesses that prioritize sustainable practices, such as reducing waste and emissions, can help mitigate the adverse effects of climate change. By combining profit with purpose, we can create a better world for all.

I invite you to join me in embracing a vision of modern business education that values gentleness, kindness, and love for humanity. Without these qualities, billions of people will continue to suffer.

WHY IS SUCCESS HARD TO SUSTAIN?

Corporations are people with their unique personalities and values. However, it can be challenging to innovate and stay ahead of the curve in the business world, given our intense desire to find *short-term pleasure.* Pursuing short-term pleasures may temporarily boost dopamine, but they often come at the cost of creating more societal problems.

It's disheartening to witness once-thriving corporations suddenly crumble after years of success, and the same can be said for personal relationships.

Professor Clayton Christensen's insights on merging personal life and corporate strategies are thought-provoking. He emphasized that even though none of us enter into a marriage with the plan of getting a divorce, we often implement a strategy entirely different from what we plan to pursue. This statement underscores the significance of execution - the constant endeavor to maintain success in our personal and professional lives, which is as important as planning. Pursuing short-term pleasure or dopamine-driven happiness can adversely affect our personal and corporate lives, leading to disastrous outcomes.

As an educator, I relate my life experience to my teaching. I am driven mainly by the logical framework: attempting to tap into rules of cause and effect. This framework teaches me that every action has an equal and opposite reaction, and it's essential to understand that each action I take will have a good or bad consequence. The positive side of this framework is that I can always ask myself how my behavior affects those around me, take responsibility for my actions, and learn from my mistakes. This logical thinking is necessary to maintain a healthy state of mind. However, it's important to note that our logical thinking can also make us risk-averse[18] (the enemy of risk-taking), which can be detrimental in a business setting. To apply this theory in a practical business setting, we must understand that every decision we make will have positive and negative consequences.

Most financial concepts I teach in class are metaphysical— beyond my comprehension and highly abstract, from quantifying risk to measuring the return to forecasting cash flows to valuing companies whose cash flows are stretched forever. It is a naïve realism: turning something abstract into a concrete mathematical model as truth when humans struggle to predict the future and our perception is biased.

In my earlier discussion on profit maximization (see page 184, "The Innovator's Dilemma"), I referred to the practice of short-termism on earnings per share as the primary driver of the share price. This practice diverts resources from investments where the payoff lies far beyond the short-term horizon and creates a systematic bias against innovation and bias towards quarterly EPS. If a company is solely focused on immediate gains, it may overlook potential investment opportunities in innovation that could be highly profitable in the long run.

As mentioned, managers are often reluctant to invest in

---

[18] The source by Tara Swart, P 172-173

innovation, given their focus on short-termism. Building new capabilities entails writing off the old assets. However, this can often come at a cost to their quarterly earnings, leading to managers' hesitation. Disruptive entrants to the industry do not face this challenge and, as a result, can quickly adopt new technology and gain a competitive edge. This is the classic conflict of interest I discussed earlier—senior executives' compensation packages are heavily weighted toward share price improvement. As a result, EPS and EPS growth remain the key metrics for corporate performance.

Why do successful people stumble?

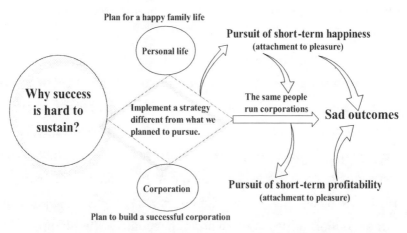

Source: Clayton Christensen and author

The takeaway from this analysis is that we intend to create a happy and fulfilling family life. But we follow a different path: short-term pleasure—*attachment to material well-being*. The same people run corporations and pursue short-term happiness—*short-term profitability*. The result is often disastrous in both cases.

202

AGENTS OF CHANGE

If you're looking for ways to truly make a difference in society, consider becoming an *"agent of change."*

Agents of change refer to individuals or groups who challenge the status quo and implement innovative ideas to tackle social, economic, and environmental issues. Becoming an agent of change requires a combination of education, awareness, and action. It's not enough to be aware of our problems; we must take action to create real change. By becoming an agent of change, you can inspire others to do the same, creating a ripple effect of positive impact that can spread throughout society.

"Instead of aligning ourselves with political ideologies like progressivism, liberalism, or conservatism, focus on humanism."

By putting humanity first and working towards a common goal of improving the lives of all people, we can make a real difference in our political system.

The US democracy in its present form only serves the interests of corporations, the rich, and the two major political parties, a sham of democracy. Thoughtful public policies are paths to a habitable climate and peaceful society—the bedrock of an economic system that delivers prosperity in the long term. Implementing robust and effective public policy frameworks requires collaborative efforts of business persons, politicians, consumers, and independent voters— voters who are not glued to TV channels or listening to politicians who indoctrinate us.

Independent voting blocs elect representatives who can wield all the power to shape the voters' social, environmental, and governance agendas, especially the socially conscious younger generation. I have always believed a few independents in the Senate and House could make a massive difference in making the needed regulations possible. We need a third powerful, independent voice in our political system to succeed. Otherwise, we will continue to see the two parties bashing at each other without much benefit to humanity.

Before we get too worked up on our environmental and social concerns, *'rethink'* and understand what causes what and why. That is theory. If we are looking for personally and globally sustainable solutions, then what is good for us is good for our society.

Suppose our younger generations are hungry for change. In that case, simple lifestyle changes can have a profound positive impact on society, individuals, and the environment:

By limiting our fast food and processed consumption, we can positively change the behavior of corporations. We save money, eat healthily, save our animals, and it is environmentally friendly. By killing helpless animals and eating that meat for our healthy diet, we are killing ourselves and destroying the environment. The power is within us. That is how morality works. We don't need activists or pontificators—*keep environmental consciousness on the side and go for that Big Mac and Happy Meals.* That only creates a moral void.

I encourage my students to make healthy and environmentally conscious choices. I often remind them to moderate their meat consumption to help save the planet, save animals, and live a healthy life. That being said, getting through to some students can be challenging. I remember when a student retorted, "*You are not our parent.*" It was pretty humorous, but I still replied, *"You look like my child."*

Our younger generations have often been led to believe that living separately from our parents shows their independence. They are validating their experience. They can live with their parents, cook, and eat together instead of paying someone's mortgage. This behavior is environmentally friendly, too: we build fewer buildings. If our younger generation is so into charity, they can save plenty of money to help those who need our help. They can also volunteer for a non-profit or foundation instead of working for them and draining their resources.

One of my students asked me a question that has been on my mind for a while: Can we create an equitable society where everyone can access the resources they need to live a healthy life? Despite the economic principle of scarce resources, my response was a resounding "yes!" There are enough resources to give everyone a fair shot at a healthy life. But we need to shift our mindset from one of *scarcity to one of abundance.* To make this happen, I suggested setting up a multi-trillion-dollar impact fund, funded by philanthropists and taxing the wealthy, and the money would be used to finance promising business ideas from business schools nationwide. However, some of my students were skeptical, arguing that it would be difficult to convince politicians to adopt such policies, given their close ties to the elite in our society. I recommended that the younger generation support a third party and use their position to shape our public policies toward addressing our lopsided economic system and making it fair and equitable for all.

Chapter 11

Optimism: The Perils of Ignorance

"The omnipotent God is not benevolent enough for human beings to attain omniscience."

I always find that optimism drives me into more misery and suffering unless I am humble enough to understand that humans cannot predict things. So, while keeping a positive spirit, why not accept the perils of our optimism and be skeptical? Embracing ignorance is not typically considered a politically correct stance, but it helps me stay informed.

If I think I am "all-knowing," I am hopelessly naive. I recognize that the universe is uncertain, and uncertainty can be an opportunity for growth. With this perspective in mind, I strive to approach the future with an open mind and confidence in my ability to adapt to whatever may come my way.

In a constantly changing environment, it's easy to believe we know everything and make decisions based on incomplete information. But this often leads to mistakes which require us to revise our decisions with new information. Even then, we can still be wrong. Therefore, confident humility is crucial for effective decision-making. By being willing to admit when we're wrong and open to learning, we can improve our decision-making process and make better decisions in a fast-paced world.

A significant revelation is realizing that the success of one's choices depends on the delicate balancing act of *self-assurance and humility*. The connection of self-assurance with an open, receptive mindset is represented by confident humility. It recognizes that while bravery to act comes from self-assurance, humility keeps one anchored in the awareness that knowledge is never absolute. This dynamic equilibrium enables decisive decision-making while maintaining an open mind to new information, criticism, and the potential for error. Individuals who embrace confident humility are better equipped to handle complexity with grace, which promotes lifelong learning and development.

Adam Grant[19] summed it up brilliantly: Confident humility is being secure enough in your expertise and courageous enough to admit your ignorance and weaknesses.

I proudly call myself an 'ignorant' since it pushes me to continuously learn, grow, and improve. Sure, it is politically incorrect to use it in my classrooms. During the break, one student came to me and said, "Professor, I love you; it is politically incorrect to use such words." I do use it regardless. The very reason we go to schools is that we are ignorant. That perspective will help alleviate the tension in my classrooms. If I don't believe in confident humility, I can never be convinced enough to say, "I am right." That makes me pivot and rethink.

---

[19] An author and professor of organizational psychology at the Wharton School of the University of Pennsylvania.

Daniel Kahneman said,

"The idea that the future is unpredictable is undermined every day by the [misleading] ease with which the past is explained."

There is a consensus. That consensus is often wrong. Of course, hindsight is 20/20: Why things did or didn't work out is always apparent after the fact. Then, we sense that we learned something and won't repeat the same mistake.

We build a causal relationship that experience increases confidence in predicting events. But the question is how accurately we can predict things. Considering human nature, we are making a grave mistake by trying to predict human behavior. While we develop expertise through experience, experience alone isn't enough.

THE FALLACY OF DATA-DRIVEN EVIDENCE-BASED APPROACH

"People often think the best way to predict the future is by collecting as much data as possible before deciding. But this is like driving a car looking only at the rearview mirror—as data is only available about the past."
— *Clayton M. Christensen, How Will You Measure Your Life?*

In probability theory, we learn that random events result in some predictable manner. In other words, we use historical information to predict the future.

The 2008 financial crisis violated the independent assumption in probability theory—which focused on the central tendency—and ignored the oddity, small events, or outliers. Those small events became a significant force and manifested into a bubble and major crisis: from sustained increases in housing prices to toxic securitized subprime mortgages (loans to the least credit-worthy borrowers, primarily underserved communities) to bail out banks and insurance companies. Thousands who had taken out a mortgage were failing to make payments. The shadow banking system—a collection of investment banks, hedge funds, insurers, and other non-bank financial institutions and banks collapsed. The crisis rattled the world economy unprecedentedly. The world became frighteningly clear about how far we are from reality.

The common denominator of the 2008 crisis was not public debt but rather the dangerous fragility of an overleveraged financial system primarily funded by short-term financial instruments and high yield (high interest rate). The mismatch in maturity—borrowing short and lending long—proved extremely dangerous. This crisis revealed our greed and desire to *"get rich quickly,"* which provided only short-term pleasure (immediate gratification) while causing long-term damage.

It is humbling to realize that despite having access to years of data, economists always seem to miss the signs of an impending crisis. Take the example of AIG, a major insurance company that needed to be bailed out by the US government during the 2008 financial crisis. Ironically, an insurance company that relies on accurate risk assessment failed so spectacularly.

It makes you wonder about the supposed infallibility of human intellect.

FAST FORWARD: THE FED SAID, "INFLATION IS TRANSITORY"

On June 16, 2021, Federal Reserve chair Jerome Powel said, "There is a possibility that inflation could be quite low. The high inflation that we know will start to decrease."

On November 13, 2021, Mr. Powel made an announcement that surprised many. After five short months, he declared it was time to retire the word 'transitory' from his vocabulary. This decision was based on the fact that the risk of persistent inflation had risen significantly. Despite Mr. Powel's impressive credentials and years of experience in economics, his expertise and the experience of other economists suddenly became worthless to the Federal Reserve.

It's interesting to hear that U.S. Treasury Secretary Janet Yellen believes[20] that the economists who predicted high unemployment to tame inflation are wrong ("eating their words"). According to her, the labor market and consumer demand show little weakness while prices moderate, proving that high unemployment was not necessary to bring down inflation.

People are very loss-averse and optimistic. We don't like taking risks; we keep an optimistic view of the world. They don't work very well together. Khanamen's theory is that:

"Given that people are optimistic, they don't realize how bad the odds are."

---

[20] Yellen says economists 'eating their words' after predicting high US unemployment | Reuters. December 5, 2023.

PAST SUCCESS IS NOT A PREDICTOR OF FUTURE SUCCESS

Shareholders elect corporate boards, thinking that they possess the proper business judgment.

Why do they fail to exercise their fiduciary duty to shareholders?

Here is a classic example of past success that was highly over-rated and had no predictive value:

A case written by Harvard Business School titled "Ron Johnson: A Career in Retail" clearly articulates the danger of architecting a change effort in the images of one's past success. The overconfidence of JCPenney's Board shows the perils of relying on past success to predict future success. Ron Johnson's past success charmed the Board. Their decision to hire Ron Johnson was grounded on his prior successes at Apple and Target.

JCPenney was one of the oldest department chains whose core customer group comprised price-sensitive, middle-class suburban mothers. Continued price wars from big box retailers like Sears, Kohl, and Macy's and pressure from small new mass merchandisers like H&M and online rivals like Amazon have caused JCPenney's customer base to dwindle.

It's hard to watch the epic failure of someone like Ron Johnson, who was admired for revolutionizing technology and department store retail at Apple and Target. His 'take it for granted' assumptions about engineering change at JCPenney were flawed. Instead of having a 'how little I know' attitude, he followed the 'I alone can fix it' attitude. He later explained how he experienced a form of 'situational arrogance'—a flawed expectation that one's prior success in one context will apply to another novel situation—in his effort to turn around and transform JCPenney.

Johnson faced the classic chicken and egg dilemma: The shareholders wanted to address the performance gap—what we should do to impress shareholders; a quick turnaround. But Johnson wanted to solve the opportunity gap—what we could do using the capabilities of JCPenney. He did not measure up to what the Board wanted. In other words, the typical short-term pleasure effect—shareholder capitalism. The Corporate Board has a fiduciary duty to its shareholders: turn around quickly.

Corporate culture is crucial in building value for all stakeholders, including shareholders.

IS THERE A RIGHT CULTURE FOR EVERY COMPANY?

In his book "What You Do Is Who You Are," Ben Horowitz described what culture is.

A culture reflects what the company is, what it does, and its aspirations. Employees have a key role in defining the culture. A corporate culture is something we build together: Know the things they agree on and those areas in which they differ. The fusion and interaction of all these factors create your culture. It is hard to identify a culture you want: figure out where the company is trying to go and the path it should take to reach that goal.

The culture that worked for Apple would never work for

JCPenney. At Apple, generating the most brilliant design is crucial to its success. It is not a culture of frugality where the CEO sleeps well at Red Roof Inn before he meets with the heads of State. At JCPenney, frugality is vital to its success. Johnson should figure out what works for JCPenney to reinforce that message. Business conditions shift, and your strategy evolves. So does the culture. Johnson needed time to execute his vision for JCPenney. He was in a race against time—the Board needed a quick turnaround.

Johnson adopted a radical change in all aspects of the business: its structure and culture, etc. He rebuilt the retailer's brand by remaking everything from the pricing to the merchandise to the overall store layout and design—a boutique-like shopping experience to replace their standard rows of overcrowded clothing racks. In the process, he created a conflict between brand and culture. That opportunity gap—failure to align the internal company culture, store look, merchandising mix, external advertising, and internal promotions with employee morale and training—was critical in delivering the brand experience to customers.

Johnson was trying to transform a conservative JCPenney corporate culture. Did he communicate his vision clearly to the Board that it would take longer to change the situation? His previous experience led him to adopt a bold and radical change without transforming the mindset of internal (employees) and external stakeholders (customers, for example). It was radical because he ended discount sales in a department store known for its markdowns. Suppose we ask the children how their mothers would wait for the Sunday newspaper to arrive so they can clip out those coupons for their shopping at JCPenney each week. Johnson alienated the core customers by removing weekly coupons. His failure could be attributed to cognitive bias and organizational pressure—limited time to show his performance.

Bearers of bad news tend to become pariahs (outcasted) in the context of quarterly capitalism or quarterly Earnings Per Share. Pessimistic views are suppressed, and optimistic views are rewarded, undermining long-term organizational performance. The optimistic biases of individuals become mutually reinforcing, and the group validates unrealistic views of the future—we fail to rethink. Johnson was eventually fired from JCPenney.

My takeaway on optimism is that we have limited capabilities. Adopting realistic optimism might serve as our compass in a world rife with uncertainty—recognizing the limits of our ability while maintaining a positive mindset. Utilize our skills and expertise to navigate the parts of our journey that are already known and concentrate on what we can manage and comprehend.

The book published by Harvard Business Review, "Realistic Optimism, The Awareness of Actual Circumstances" by Justin Menkes, explains the need to be acutely aware of the realities of challenges we face and keep a sense of realistic optimism and a sense of humility and humanity: letting yourself see the world for what it is and letting the world see you for who you are—create an awareness that we are human beings and be honest about our shortcomings.

Chapter 12

Memories of My Classroom

My classrooms are filled with valuable teaching moments. My semester starts with my wisdom talk: the lessons I learned from my life experience, a few power points about my four pillars of happiness, and a few minutes of mindfulness meditation with my students. This guided meditation is to help them practice meditation every day for a few minutes and write one page about how it transformed them.

COMPASSION FATIGUE: DID MY WORK AS A TEACHER MATTER?

An exciting and rewarding lesson from my teaching career is the sense of lasting impact I create in my students. This produces a buffer against all my stress and burnout.

Before transitioning into a full-time faculty, I worked at three universities for the last four years, teaching six courses on average. It was very stressful to deal with the classroom dynamics, given the intimidating nature of the courses, let alone managing students who go through intense depression and anxiety and the difficulty of disciplining students who are late to class or do not show up at all.

Here are a few stories:

In the 2021 fall semester, I implemented a revised attendance policy in my class to motivate students to arrive on time. To ensure accountability, I allowed a 5-minute grace period for latecomers. If any student came after this time, they were allowed to sit in the class but marked as absent, resulting in a loss of attendance for that day.

One morning after class, a young lady approached me and apologized for being a few minutes late. I assured her that it was not a problem and that she could take up to three absences without affecting her attendance. She seemed upset and told me she wouldn't attend my class anymore. I said, "You don't have to." Later that day, I received a long and angry email from her, criticizing my attendance policy as outrageous and accusing me of being rude. I was taken aback, as I had never received such a disrespectful email from a student. I read her email while going to another college and reflected on her words for a while. Despite her anger towards me and my teaching methods, I did not feel the need to respond. Instead, I reminded myself that my own child sometimes behaves worse than this student. I also considered that she may be going through personal struggles that she may not want to share openly. At the end of the semester, I was pleasantly surprised to read her mindfulness meditation paper, in which she expressed gratitude for the opportunity to meditate and write about her experience. She even referred to me as a "great teacher." I needed that dopamine boost.

In the same semester, while doing my final grading, I noticed that a few students could have done better in the course. I emailed them and said, "I know you could do far better than this." One of those students was suffering from a recent mugshot. Someone attacked her and stole her computer. She emailed me the situation, stating that her

218

homework would be late. My immediate response was to ask, "Are you okay?" Then, I thought about my child and how easily this could have happened to her. I noticed her academic performance was deteriorating, and she missed classes. When she wrote back to me, saying that a good computer costs a lot of money, I felt even more compassionate towards her. I said to myself, "I should buy her a computer." Instead, I wrote her that these life lessons only make you stronger and even better. I offered her a make-up exam and gave her a few days to study. She did amazingly well on the final exam and earned a good grade.

From my experience, I've realized that sometimes, my compassionate yet demanding approach to teaching takes time to truly resonate with my students. There have been instances where students who were upset over my teaching style contacted me years later and showed appreciation for my big-picture approach to teaching. It's incredible to feel that energetic shift and know that my impact on their lives was positive and long-lasting.

My welcome email to students

On August 18, I sent a welcome email to all my students:

Dear All,

Hello! Welcome to the Ivy League Club. You must be feeling quite confused after receiving an email from your professor with such ambiguity.

But let me explain what I meant by "Ivy": "I value you." You are here because you have proved your potential and have the talent and capacity to overcome challenges and be successful. However, there is still much to learn about yourself and your capabilities. Knowledge is what we don't know. We will learn together. As you advance your career, you will uncover endless opportunities to learn, rethink, and reshape yourself. "The best is yet to come."

In life and career, we are constantly faced with uncertainty, which makes life so beautiful and full of opportunities. We should embrace each step and appreciate the journey, not just the destination.

Success is leading a meaningful life, having self-awareness and curiosity to learn, and having the courage to face challenges. We must constantly seek ways to fulfill our desire for a happy life. This can be achieved through building positive relationships with our minds, which radiates out positively.

Thomas Edison said, "I have not failed. I've just found 10,000 ways that won't work." There are no failures in life. Often, we feel nothing seems to work despite our hard work and perseverance, but enduring adversity is our success.

College tests your character, passion to improve, and determination to succeed. I asked myself this question,

What does "getting along" mean?

Getting along with my life and others, especially in a college and work environment—brainstorm together, share credits, stop judging, and listen more. Create a growth mindset—an 'I can do' attitude.

Remember, learning is a social, emotional, and collaborative process. It's essential to build a life around the mindset of learning, not just focusing on grades or validation from others. You are already great and beautiful, the foundation upon which we build happiness.

FINAL EMAIL TO THE CLASS

At the end of each semester, after posting all grades, I take a few minutes and write a last email to all my students:

Dear Students,

I want to express my sincere gratitude for the privilege of teaching such gifted individuals like you. You each have a unique purpose and journey; being a part of it has been an honor. As we navigate the challenges and opportunities of today's world, it can be easy to feel overwhelmed. Our social and emotional struggles stem from a lack of control over our thoughts and emotions. However, if we can learn to trust and value each other, we can create a positive environment that helps us grow. Forgiveness and observation without judgment are powerful tools to cultivate a positive environment. It takes courage, humility, and curiosity to rethink our beliefs and learn from our mistakes. There are no best practices; it is a constantly evolving process. My own journey has been filled with struggles and sacrifices, but I channeled that energy positively and kept moving forward. I broadened my dreams and pursued them even when my plans failed. It was the small but consistent efforts that made all the difference. Your life must be transformational, not transactional. Success is not defined by external factors like name, fame, wealth, or societal status. Rather, success is defined by our effort to find peace within ourselves and achieve inner happiness.

MY TUNA SANDWICH STORY

Let me end this part with yet another story of success:

I want to share a story of success highlighting the importance of determination and perseverance in achieving one's goals. As an Equity Research Analyst, Investment Banker, and Educator, I have always set clear goals for myself and worked tirelessly to achieve them. I have learned that success is not always guaranteed, and setbacks and failures are inevitable.

I never thought walking into a boutique firm to do some cold-calling job to keep my licenses active for a broker would lead to my dream job. I was offered an analyst position with the firm. The 2000 dot.com crisis in Wall Street allowed me to find an accounting job, which I later transitioned into a lucrative investment banking opportunity. My intense desire to teach in business schools led me to do guest lectures in many IIMs and IITs in India. That experience helped me land a job as an adjunct faculty teaching one course, which I expanded into teaching six courses at three universities while working on Wall Street. I was relentless in my pursuit of securing a full-time faculty position. As an educator, I have created a network of faculty, department chairs, and students for over four years.

One experience that stands out is when I applied for a full-time job as a finance lecturer.

In 2022, I applied for a full-time job as a lecturer in finance at a university where I had previously worked as an adjunct lecturer. I compiled a resume highlighting my years of experience in various roles on Wall Street, my educational background, licenses, a few years of experience in academia, and three recommendations from department chairs at different universities. I was thrilled to learn that I had been shortlisted for the first 30-minute preliminary interview and even more excited when I learned that I had made it to the list of finalists. I put so much effort into preparing a 45-minute lecture, practicing it to ensure I stayed within the allotted time frame. I even cut my presentation to ensure I stayed on time. The interview was virtual, but I still dressed formally and felt confident. After the lecture and a series of interviews, I took a moment to reflect on my performance. While I felt good about my presentation, I knew I could have done better if the interviews and lectures had been in person. Now, I'm eagerly waiting to hear back from the Search Committee. They told me that I should expect to hear from them within 15 days.

I went out and got a tuna salad and celebrated that event. It was a small victory, but it felt good to treat myself. I then planned for another tuna sandwich and a can of beer in 15 days, assuming I would get the job. Unfortunately, I never heard from them, so much for my tuna sandwich and beer celebration. I was disappointed but contacted my referees to see if they had any insight into what had happened. They were reassuring, telling me it was a very competitive position and that I would get another chance.

Almost a year later, I underwent the same rigorous process at another college for the same position. The day-long process included lectures, interviews, and an in-person presentation. I was confident that I exceeded the search committee's expectations and left optimistic about my performance. A few months later, I received a job offer.

Finally, I had my tuna sandwich and beer. As I enjoyed my tuna sandwich and beer, memories from a year ago came flooding back. It was a mix of emotions, but I couldn't help but smile as I remembered the past. Each bite was a reminder of the happy moments and the wisdom gained from the past year. I savored every flavor, grateful for the present moment and all that has brought me to where I am today.

I am grateful for the unwavering support from my colleagues, department chairs, and deans throughout (I am thinking of titling my next book, "Vital Group: The Power of Relationships"). As an introvert, I surround myself with only a few vital groups of people. When I needed a few references for the application, I contacted them. They were quick to respond to my request. Sometimes, they wrote, "happy to help," or "I will do anything for you." They were pleased to respond when I was offered the position as a full-time faculty: "very well deserved."

Two things remained constant in all three of my career successes, from an analyst to a banker to an educator. Firstly, I was determined to achieve my goals no matter what obstacles came my way. Secondly, the paths that led me to accomplish everything were the least expected ones. It's incredible how life can take us on twists and turns.

My unwavering desire to succeed and willingness to face challenges have been the keys to my success. Using the language of neuroscientists, utilizing both a 'vision board' and 'action board,' and an abundant mindset was incredibly beneficial in achieving my goals. It was not my ideal fantasy, and I passively hoped for my goals to come to fruition magically. I remained centered and driven by creating an overarching vision of my future and outlining concrete steps to achieve it. The path was broad enough to reach my goals. Additionally, there's a spiritual aspect to everything in my life, as if it's all part of a greater plan orchestrated by a Higher Power. It helps me stay grounded and grateful for every opportunity that comes my way.

As I reflect on my experience as an educator, I am reminded of many memories of my classroom. The sight of eager students ready to learn, the feeling of satisfaction when a student finally grasps a complex concept, moments of frustration and challenge to keep the attention of a classroom full of students or to find the right way to explain a complex topic—all significantly influenced my way of thinking. I am grateful for the opportunity to have shaped the minds and futures of many young people. The memories, lessons, and relationships formed in my classroom will always hold a special place in my heart.

"Know my students"

As an educator, seeing my students suffer hasn't been easy. It affects me profoundly when I see them arriving late, appearing uninterested, or missing classes altogether. It's challenging to comprehend their struggles from their melancholic expressions. That's why I've decided to take the initiative to get to know my students better and create a conducive learning environment. Judging a student's performance is easier than understanding their challenges. To that end, at the beginning of the semester, I ask all my students to submit a one-page summary of their background, including any mental, emotional, or physical struggles they may be dealing with, as well as their career goals, vision for the future, strengths and weaknesses, and their expectations for the class. I missed this part while educating my own child.

225

Part Three

Peace Within

Chapter 13

Life Beyond the Classroom

I begin my lecture by asking my students,

"How are you feeling?"
"Bored, Tired, Depressed...?
or
Joyful, Energetic, Compassionate, Loving...?"

The power of positive thinking and visualization can significantly impact our physical and mental well-being. When we focus on positive outcomes and visualize success, we set ourselves up for success and are more likely to take the necessary actions to achieve our goals. It's important to remember that our thoughts directly impact our emotions and behaviors, so it's essential to cultivate a positive mindset to lead a happy life.

While on a train, I struck up a conversation with a lovely young lady who happened to be a student at my university. I couldn't resist telling her that she reminded me of my daughter. She was kind enough to say that I looked very young. I told her I look at myself in the mirror every morning and say, *"Good morning, good-looking young man."* She found it hilarious and couldn't stop laughing.

Keeping a positive spirit is how I get closer to God and glorify myself.

"The kingdom of God is within you."

The hidden wisdom from this verse is that eternal happiness is *not* something we search for outside of ourselves but resides within us. The path to everlasting happiness can only be achieved through self-discovery.

I call myself a colossal failure and a success. At the outset, I am grateful for every hardship, setback, and failure. Those were my blessings, not sufferings. I am privileged to have gone through those experiences. That was the lens through which I saw my success. By getting in touch with my inner self, I not only make decisions that are truly meaningful but also develop a feeling of purpose that rises above outward appearances, which eventually results in a more fulfilling and peaceful life.

It's easy to get caught up in the idea that we need to become something or someone else to be the best version of ourselves. We are fixated on the idea of external freedom and search for ways to achieve it. We are being conditioned. Our upbringing, culture, society, news media, education, social media, and religion influence how we interpret things. These forces manipulate our perception of everything in this world—our brain shapes itself by repeated experiences from our surroundings. That is the power of neuroplasticity. Our perception transforms into thoughts and emotions, and once we label them, they become feelings that manifest into actions or behaviors.

Recognizing that our emotions do not stem from a conscious decision is crucial. They result from our unique perception, which is influenced by the environment we have encountered. These external factors can trigger various feelings, including anger, envy, sadness, and worry. Nonetheless, it is essential to remember that these emotions do not define *"who we are"* as individuals. Rather, they are a reflection of how we have been conditioned or *"what we are"* and how we habitually think. Our destructive emotions often lead to a negative relationship with our minds, causing us to feel inadequate or inferior.

Our society tends to equate pleasure with happiness, but this is a dangerous conflation.

The feeling of pleasure is ephemeral. It arises from the limbic system of our brain and often triggers intense emotions, cravings, and desires. Although it can provide a brief sense of joy, it can also become addictive and create an imbalance in the brain's reward system, leading to compulsive behaviors such as overindulging in food, shopping, gambling, substance abuse, and other destructive behaviors. But we can activate our brain's prefrontal cortex, enhance our cognitive abilities, and make pleasure more enduring. Mindfulness meditation is an effective method to cultivate awareness of the negative impact of addictive behavior on our health, social connections, and relationships (see pages 235-256 and conclusion). Genuine happiness is a gradual and ongoing process requiring consistent commitment and effort.

Our actions are primarily driven by external factors, like a desire for validation or material gain. Conflating short-term pleasure with true happiness and contentment is easy. Humans are wired to seek out short-term pleasures fueled by dopamine. The more we indulge in these pleasures, the more we crave them, leading to a vicious cycle driven further by the stress hormone cortisol. We live in the "now." If our rational brain or the prefrontal cortex is dysfunctional, cortisol takes over, and we become addicted to pleasure. We want more pleasure (dopamine) now (cortisol), and it's no wonder that many of us struggle with addiction and chronic depression[21]. The world around us is designed to make us miserable or grasp pleasure, and we become hopeless.

Can I say hopes sustain our lives?

It is true in my case.

On the other hand, it's important to note that happiness is long-term and strongly influenced by serotonin. This neurotransmitter[22] helps us to resist the urge to seek pleasure constantly. It instead directs our focus on building connections with others, cultivating a sense of belonging, practicing gratitude, valuing ourselves, and pursuing our passions. When we have these virtues, we feel hopeful for the future and excited about all the possibilities.

We often feel inadequate, perpetuating a sense of deficiency within ourselves—we are not good, rich, beautiful, tall, or smart

---

[21] Serotonin vs. Dopamine - 7 Key Differences Between Pleasure and Happiness - YouTube

[22] Neurotransmitters are chemical messengers that transmit signals between neurons and other cells. They are essential for transmitting nerve impulses across synapses and properly functioning the nervous system. Examples of neurotransmitters include dopamine and serotonin.

enough. And we want happiness. In other words, we say to ourselves, "We don't have it." The toxicity of our modern world only intensifies that deficiency within. Then we think our happiness is extrinsic, coming from somewhere else. Therefore, we have an attachment to pleasure—name, fame, wealth, or status and an aversion towards pain and suffering. We engage in all sorts of destructive behavior to alleviate our pain and get that dopamine-driven happiness (pleasure). Drug addiction and alcoholism are common and often lead to severe consequences, including fatal overdoses. These substances provide instant gratification or feel-good moments, grasping after pleasure and pushing away displeasure. This is the cause-and-effect moment— we become addicted to things that create the dopamine rush. The trial becomes a habit, and the habit becomes dependence. In the process, we enslave ourselves by the shackles of dependence on some external trigger to make our lives pleasurable.

So, who benefits in both cases: attachment and aversion?

Businesses, social media, and, to a large extent, religious institutions.

These forces not only create deficiencies within us—create a feeling of discontent that we don't have what others have—but also tap into our deficiencies and thrive on them. We outsource our happiness and create an illusion of happiness.

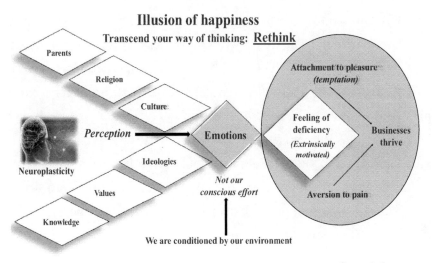

Source: Author

On my first day of lecture, I always start with an important message for all my students to hear. I look out at the faces in front of me and say, "I love you for who you are as a person." It's a simple statement but sets the tone for the entire semester. I want my students to know they are valued and respected in my classroom, regardless of their background or experiences.

I genuinely hope that this message can catalyze us to embark on a journey of self-discovery, where we take the time to understand our inherent value and worth as individuals.

Chapter 14

Four Pillars of Happiness

"I embarked on a spiritual path, where I channeled my emotions toward self-discovery. It was a grueling yet necessary journey to discover my true self and pursue happiness."

Society can be exceedingly cruel towards those who are mentally and emotionally fragile. I had struggled with my emotions, feeling anger towards everything I had experienced. Deep down, I was crying out for help. So, I developed a framework that ensures my well-being is not compromised at the expense of my environment. I refer to this as my *four pillars of happiness*—the way I define happiness. The purpose of this framework is to encourage a shift in my mindset and inspire personal growth. One of the core pillars is emotional well-being, which academic and religious institutions often overlook despite its significant positive impact on both individual and societal health.

PILLAR #1: EMOTIONAL WELL-BEING—EMOTIONAL INTELLIGENCE AND MINDFULNESS MEDITATION

"The idea that transcendence and science are mutually exclusive

is a false dichotomy[23]. Neuroscience has shown us that by focusing on our breath, we can deactivate the emotion center or limbic system and activate the prefrontal cortex. This ability allows us to achieve a state of meta-awareness or flow. This inward flow of conscious awareness is like the breath of God flowing through us, reminding us that the power above us is within us—the kingdom of God is within us."

I've been delving into the intersection of cognitive neuroscience and quantum science, providing fascinating insights into the nature of consciousness. It's particularly intriguing to see how these modern scientific disciplines align with ancient Buddhist philosophy, which has always embraced the importance of compassion. *Compassion is about finding inner peace and positively transforming our surroundings.* It is a powerful force that can unite people and help us overcome mental and emotional challenges. It's remarkable to witness how these seemingly dissimilar fields of study converge to unlock the mysteries of the human consciousness.

Having 'Emotional Intelligence' is a crucial skill that everyone should possess. *It entails understanding our own emotions as well as the emotions of others without being too hasty to pass judgment.* It's natural for our emotions to get stirred up when someone says or does something we don't like. This can create negative impulses in our brains, interfering with our ability to think clearly. Those triggers are like brain tumors pushing on our amygdala and interfering with impulse control. This negative impulse hinders our cognitive control

---

[23] It is a misconception that science and transcendence cannot go hand in hand.

and creates negative emotional reactions like angry or revenge thoughts. Those are not our conscious, compassionate emotions but rather biased perceptions about events or individuals we gathered from our external environment. Psychologist Daniel Goldman calls this phenomenon *amygdala hijack*—a set of neurons in our brain that creates the stress hormone called cortisol, which assesses every situation we face for a sudden reaction and gets us into a fight-flight or freeze mode. This is a primitive function that helped our ancestors (hunter-gatherers) survive in the wild. Our beliefs and feelings frequently change because emotions frequently outweigh reason. This is the madness within and around us—we *still live in the stone age.*

We live in a highly indoctrinated society where the truths are ignored, and lies are embraced. There is this famous quote:

"There are two ways to be fooled. One is to believe what is not true, and the other is to refuse to believe what is true."

All our social, emotional, financial, and familial problems stem from one source: we are not in control over our thoughts and emotions. The scripture clearly warns us and says,

"Do not conform to the behavior of this world but be transformed by the renewal of your mind."

Translation: transform our way of thinking and avoid falling prey to the negative influences of society.

Following the crowd or the majority only leads us into more chaos, misery, and suffering.

I HIT ROCK BOTTOM ONCE AGAIN

Let me tell you a personal story:

A few years ago, my daughter sent me a response to my series of messages indicating that I had been overly controlling and domineering in her life and career. A fancy way of saying, "I was a control freak." I focused solely on her education, ignoring her mental and emotional well-being. Looking back, I recognize how I raised my child had contributed to this characterization of me.

I emphasized the importance of emotional literacy in parents at the beginning of this book. As a parent myself, I was concerned about the gender inequality prevalent in society and how it could impact my child. Yes, it was true that I wasn't present with my child: *I was emotionally illiterate.* I did not know what caused my destructive emotions, and I ended up saying things I regretted later. Nor was I aware of the techniques to regulate my emotions. Therefore, I rarely asked my child *'how she felt'* or observed her emotions non-judgmentally. In hindsight, it was one of my most significant shortcomings or colossal failures as a father.

I had not experienced this type of response from my child before. I was totally unprepared. It had a disastrous impact on my emotional well-being. In his theory of positive psychology, psychologist Martin Seligman stated that we fall into three traps when something terrible happens to us. Those are the three Ps: *personalization, pervasiveness, and permanence. I immediately recognized that I fell into all of them.*

I personalized it; I internalized my failure. I felt it would spread to all areas of my life and last forever. I was pondering on it. I woke up in the middle of the night with heaviness on my chest. My anxiety and depression were so intense that I felt like a knife was twisting my heart. It was excruciatingly painful.

I sat on the couch and asked myself:

"Where did I go wrong with my life? Why didn't I think through it before I sent all those messages to my child? Is it right to apologize to my child as a parent?"

I was drowning with nothing to hold onto. It was an existential crisis for me.

"I hit rock bottom once again."

I felt I needed to master some resilience for my own mental and emotional well-being. From my perspective, apologizing was the best way to model appropriate behavior for my child. After a brief moment, something incredible happened. I had this epiphany:

I said to myself,

"Glad I experienced this trauma. I can empathize with people who go through mental and emotional hardships. Now I know how wrong I was in making assumptions about human conditions."

I journaled the same on my phone and went to sleep. That was the turning point in my life.

This experience truly changed my perspective and shined a new light in my darkness. My Jewish American friend and colleague once told me something that really stuck with me, even though I didn't fully comprehend its meaning then. When I was upset with the people around me, he said, "You are doing it to yourself."

This experience fueled my curiosity and desire to explore and comprehend the complexities of my way of life. I began to examine my own thought patterns and gained a deeper understanding of my way of thinking:

Forces drive my thoughts and emotions; my sense of insecurity and the urge to validate my experience; my decisions based on false perceptions of the realities and the consequential effect of those decisions on me and others around me; and ways to unify my emotions and to find meaning and purpose in my life.

As some suggested, I felt I should consult a psychiatrist and get some anti-depressants or even turn to psychedelic substances. Somehow, I could not bring myself to either option and continued my search for alternate ways to reevaluate my thoughts and behaviors without any form of medication.

One day, I came across a YouTube video on meditation that completely changed my perspective. It introduced me to mindfulness meditation, which helped me realize why I was suffering. How did this help? Instead of using medication to suppress my emotions, meditation led me toward my suffering. Meditation gently comforted me with the catalysts behind my suffering and allowed me to sit with them, acknowledge and accept them. I have learned that my emotional dependence and lack of awareness of my own biases were major contributors to my pain. As a result, I failed to cultivate self-love and compassion for others, further worsening my suffering. My perspective about my life and spirituality has changed since then.

My anti-depressant is mindfulness meditation. The best part? It is free, and it has no adverse side effects. Also, I began taking walks, cold showers, and prioritizing healthy eating, all while meditating regularly. I even donated my TV to charity and limited my news media exposure.

And the best thing of all? I wrote a book about my experiences, turning my sufferings into something positive for myself and humanity.

I firmly believe that I must return to the basics and focus on my physical, emotional, and spiritual well-being. Personally, the Holy Trinity of well-being consists of caring for my mind and body and finding inner peace.

I started to reflect on my destructive emotions. I wrote many long emails to my child, apologizing for my emotional distress. In some cases, I wrote many pages and attached them to the email about what went wrong with the emotional side of my life and how I used my depressive rumination to bring my mind to the present moment.

This entire part was one of the emails to my child. That shows how much I was concerned about my own and my child's mental and emotional well-being. And I look at my students through the same lens and practice mindfulness meditation in my classrooms. I create a safe and supportive learning environment that fosters growth and success by being compassionate toward them and supporting their mental health. When my students feel seen, heard, and valued, they are much more likely to engage with the material and retain what they've learned.

I have to admit that I have no expertise in mindfulness

meditation. I have never been to any meditation retreats or Buddhist monasteries. As I said in my introduction, my retreat is facing and experiencing life head-on. However, I have listened to a few monks and experts in neuroscience about the science of spirituality and the true nature of reality. Meditation practices have been around for centuries, tested, and refined over time. They remain just as relevant today, particularly in a world bombarded by social and news media and various religious institutions trying to influence our thinking.

Our limbic system is a powerful recorder of our past experiences, cataloging our thoughts. These thoughts then transform into emotions, which in turn become the feelings that we experience. When you think about it metaphorically, thoughts and feelings are like the languages our minds and bodies use to communicate.

Our body responds to our mind based on the triggers we encounter. We worsen our negative feelings by continuously calling ourselves victims (subjects). To put it more clearly, we give away the power of our minds to someone or some objects.

When I was sick, lonely, depressed, or angry, did I ever ask myself what caused it? Or what could I do to control my negative thoughts? Instead, I resorted to temporary solutions to fix my lack of inner sense of peace—the problem was within. I didn't see my inner world.

Not demonizing but humanizing my flaws, weaknesses, and mistakes leads me to heal my mind and body. By being consciously aware of my subconscious mind, I can break the habit of living in the past—the unlearning process. Stated differently, break away from the habit of victimization: the "subject" and "object" thoughts—someone or something is causing me to behave in certain ways. Nobody is

causing anything. I am doing it to myself. *It is acceptance*: I have no control over my environment but can control my thoughts and emotions. This is not to say, "I have failed in my life." Rather, it is a success: the courage to say to myself, "I made some bad decisions and behaved in rather erratic or violent ways on many occasions."
I started to ask myself,

"How can I cultivate a positive mindset?"

Then, the healing process begins: change how I respond or react to my thoughts instead of being controlled by my environment (triggers). This is my relearning process, and it is a breakthrough moment—watch what I say and how I react to certain triggers. At the end of the day, I self-reflect and ask myself, "How did I do today? What did I learn? How did I turn my loneliness into something emotionally rewarding?"

It is a fantastic subjective experience: I started self-regulating my emotions. I have learned to improve my thoughts and emotions positively. My relationship with others changed positively as well—turning a vicious cycle into a virtuous one. It is changing me chemically (eat right), physically (exercise), and emotionally (meditate) as well.

Mindfulness meditation became an eye-opener for me. It helped me break free from my dark emotions. *Mindfulness refers to conscious awareness of our body and mind in the present moment in a non-judgmental way: not ruminating on the past or worrying about the future but rather being in the present moment.* It is a secular— non-denominational practice—to regulate and transform our disruptive emotions. *It is the science of consciousness—compassion towards our mind (self-compassion) and compassion for others.*

Mindfulness practice is a constructive way to develop self-awareness and emotional regulation, helping one achieve meta-cognition. By creating a space between our impulses and reactions, we can learn to control negative thoughts and emotions effectively.

Our reactions are suppressed emotions.

"Treat the cause, not the trigger"

One technique I use is to focus on my breathing. In other words, stop the painful rumination (negative self-talk, shame, guilt, anger, etc.), bring my mind to the present moment, turn my attention to the sensation of my breathing, and constrain the amygdala. Maintaining awareness of the object of attention—breathing—is crucial in mindfulness. This practice can be highly effective in keeping us anchored in the present moment and controlling our emotions.

Whenever I have episodic memories or depressive ruminations, I focus on my breath for a few minutes. This simple technique helps me to stay centered and calm, and it allows me to bypass my limbic system and activate the cognitive side of my brain. By deactivating my stress hormones (emotion center) and activating the cognitive side of the brain (prefrontal cortex), I get into a flow state[24] (fully present). I maintain a meta-awareness or meta-cognition, neither expressing nor suppressing my thoughts and emotions but simply observing them without judgment.

---

[24] Flow state is a mental zone where a person is fully immersed, energized, and focused on a task, feeling a sense of complete absorption.

It's fascinating to contemplate the correlation between waves in the ocean and our thoughts and emotions. Our thoughts and emotions are much like the waves in the ocean, metaphorically. However, we cannot eliminate those waves, but we can traverse them and connect with the stillness beneath. Similarly, we cannot ignore or push away our problems or distress, but we can pass through them and connect with the tranquility in our hearts by observing them—experiencing *pure consciousness.* That's when our mind becomes more robust than our thoughts and emotions, much like the ocean that is mightier than the waves.

Carl Jung[25] famously said,
"What you resist, persists."

Resistances strengthens what we oppose. Acceptance, on the other hand, can help us move forward with peace.

Pure Consciousness: The Intersection of Quantum Science and Humanity

The intersection of quantum science and humanity has always been a fascinating topic for me. The idea that our consciousness is connected to the universe's fundamental fabric is awe-inspiring and humbling. It reminds me that we are all part of something much larger than ourselves and that our actions have ripple effects far beyond what

---

[25] Carl Jung was a Swiss psychiatrist and psychoanalyst.

we can see or comprehend.

In a world where instant gratification (short-term pleasure) and self-absorption rule the day, studying quantum phenomena provides a window into the realm of pure consciousness.

Quantum reality unveils the interconnectedness of all things in the universe and the impact our thoughts and actions have on the world around us. Quanta, or quantum of energy, is a fundamental concept in physics that plays a critical role in understanding the behavior of atoms and molecules at the atomic and subatomic levels. It refers to the smallest unit of energy that these particles can gain or lose, and it serves as the minimum amount of energy that can be measured. By comprehending the nature of quanta, we can unlock a deeper understanding of the physical world around us. The principles of quantum mechanics suggest that particles exist in multiple states (like our positive and negative emotions) until they are observed or measured, which implies that consciousness may play a role in the behavior of particles.

Our mind is a modified form of consciousness. The universe is a fascinating place, and it's incredible to think that it all started from a tiny, super-dense, super-hot mass exploding and rapidly expanding into what we know today. It's like a tiny seed growing into a big tree, and every part of that tree is connected as one. So, the universe is a single quantum system. Buddhists call it an integrated whole, Hindus see the universe as God, and Christians believe that God created the universe. Quantum physicists refer to this interconnectedness as quantum entanglement; the properties of particles are linked together—*we are all connected as one.*

A human being is an entanglement of thoughts, emotions, and

246

feelings. Some researchers believe that entanglement could be a fundamental aspect of consciousness and may be the key to understanding how we experience the world.

I believe there's a link between subatomic particles and human consciousness, but it's still a subject of ongoing research and debate. I'm intrigued by the workings of the human mind and the nature of reality, but my knowledge of quantum science is quite limited. When we experience positive or negative emotions, it is all due to the electrons from food or light (energy) that pass through our retina and travel to our brain. These electrons form *waves* in our brains and vibrate at different frequencies, known as the *wave function*. This is our experience or quantum phenomena, something that is observed to exist. Our thoughts (*particles*) are our experiences from outer space, the cosmos, or the universe. Our thoughts and emotions are in constant motion.

Our thoughts are vibrations. It's fascinating to learn that Quantum physicists have studied the phenomenon where a single quantum of light can go through two slits simultaneously, and the *particle becomes waves.* This *particle-wave duality* phenomenon showcases that quantum objects can exist simultaneously in multiple states, referred to as the *Heisenberg uncertainty principle*[26]. As per the principles of quantum science, we can only calculate the likelihood of events occurring, as we cannot comprehend every finite

---

[26] This principle provides a fundamental understanding of the limitations of our ability to observe and measure the behavior of particles. By recognizing the importance of the Heisenberg uncertainty principle, we can deepen our understanding of the universe and the laws that govern it.

detail.

The fundamental principles of quantum mechanics suggest that particles can exist simultaneously in multiple states until they are observed or measured. This principle has led some quantum physicists to hypothesize that consciousness plays a vital role in determining the outcome of these observations. In other words, the mere act of *observation* itself can impact the behavior of particles— our thoughts are particles, and our conscious awareness of them is the observation that influences our behavior. It's like our negative emotions, such as anger, envy, or sadness, which are akin to *waves* (*the "madness within us"*). When we try to measure (observe) particles, they transform from *waves* into confined *particles*. It's a fascinating phenomenon that teaches us something valuable about our emotions.

When we observe our emotions, we become consciously aware of their existence. Awareness strengthens cognitive control by activating the prefrontal cortex.

By observing negative emotions without suppressing them, we can gain greater control over our thoughts and actions. This is known as *pure consciousness or unified field* by quantum physicists; 'Know Thyself' in Christian philosophy, "Samadhi" in Hindu, and "Oneness" in Buddhist teachings. I call it "spirituality": self-awareness or the conscious awareness of my thoughts and emotions.

The inextricable link between quantum mechanics and consciousness

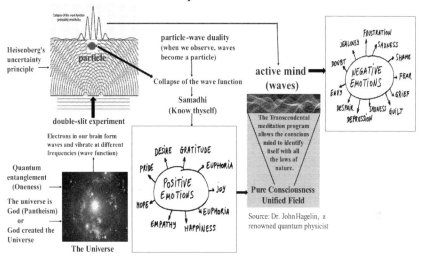

Source: Author

It is indeed fascinating how scientists have discovered that particles or electrons behave differently when not closely observed or measured. This phenomenon, known as the observer effect, has implications beyond the realm of physics and can also be observed in human behavior. For instance, our emotion center can take control over the rational side, and we may experience negative emotions when we are not consciously aware of them.

The laws of quantum mechanics are probabilistic, which aligns with my belief that I can never truly predict anything with absolute certainty. It's almost like the universe has a mind of its own, much like our perception of God. The world is full of unpredictability. While we recognize a supreme being (God), we cannot assert that we possess the same level of knowledge. *The omnipotent God is not benevolent enough for human beings to be omniscient*—connecting cosmology with theology.

249

This is a wake-up call and a humbling experience for religious scholars who claim God is speaking through them (discussed in Part Four). The same goes true for people who are experts in the prediction business. As I mentioned in Chapter 11 about the perils of ignorance, we must remember the dangers of being overly optimistic and our inability to predict the future with certainty.

In my experience, being conscious means *acceptance* and having *compassion* for myself and others. We humans commonly have subjective views (our perception is biased). The true nature of the universe is complex and beyond our complete understanding due to our limited and incomplete knowledge. It's crucial to remember that everything is based on probability, making it necessary to remain receptive to fresh concepts and viewpoints. While we may not have control over our environment, we can control our thoughts, emotions, feelings, and actions. By becoming consciously aware of the *energy within us*, we can build compassion for those around us and create a positive and harmonious energy outside of us.

We all have biases but must recognize that we're flawed individuals. This conscious awareness is what makes us more compassionate towards ourselves and others. We love and admire people who are aware of this fact, which is why the principles of yoga and mindfulness meditation are so powerful. They help us achieve that union of mind and body that can transform how we see ourselves and the world.

The intricate interplay of neuroscience, social science, quantum science, and spirituality is a captivating subject that can broaden our understanding of the world and help us gain a more comprehensive view of our place in the universe.

God and Science

The misconception that God (spirituality) and science are separate entities is widespread. This idea often stems from *theist* (belief in the existence of a deity) versus *atheist* (the absence of a belief in a deity) perspectives, which argue that God exists beyond the natural world and is not subject to scientific investigation. However, this notion is a fallacy. I believe God created the universe or is God, and we are all interconnected. Science helps us investigate the existence and influence of God on the natural world—use scientific evidence and reasoning to understand the world around us. For instance, quantum science has revealed that the world is uncertain, which aligns with theology since humans cannot comprehend God's omniscience and our knowledge of the world is limited, making us humble. Furthermore, *neuroscience* can elucidate how religious experiences affect the brain (the negative effect of neuroplasticity) and how *pure consciousness or spirituality* (the positive effect of neuroplasticity) can provide us with a deeper understanding of our thoughts and emotions. Additionally, *social science* can explore the impact of religion on human behavior and society and the suffering it often causes (discussed in Part Four). Thus, God and science are not mutually exclusive but complementary approaches to understanding the natural world. They are two sides of the same coin, each providing a unique perspective on the world around us.

The neuroscience of mindfulness is truly fascinating: regular mindfulness meditation strengthens our neural pathways, disables our limbic system—which is responsible for our automatic 'fight-or-flight' response, and activates our prefrontal cortex. This, in turn, allows us to control our thoughts and emotions better.

It is intriguing to consider that reality may exist independently of the observer until it is measured. This concept resembles the wave function in our brains, which is based on our experiences with the environment. Repeated experiences or recurring thoughts mold our brains. Our thoughts and emotions are constantly moving. It's fascinating how quantum science has revealed that our perception of reality is biased. Through observations (measurement), we can come to a conscious understanding that what we see as reality may not necessarily be the truth—*the nature of reality remains a mystery.*

In my life, I remain aware that our brains can create biased perceptions of the world. It's important to remember that nobody truly knows the reality of nature, and realizing this can help us build compassion and humility.

Quantum science has helped me understand the complexities of the human experience and cultivate greater empathy and compassion toward those around me.

Quantum science has Indeed shown us some important insights into our racial tensions. One of the most important things to remember is that our preconceived notions about people based on their race or social prejudices are often biased and don't accurately reflect who they are as individuals.

I remind myself that we live in an uncertain world full of opportunities.

Since the truth is that I don't know what the future holds for me, I am free to explore all the possibilities. I can visualize anything if I take the time and effort to learn about my potential—and create a clear image of how I want my life to unfold. This visualization marks the commencement of my journey toward manifestation—I can create new positive neural pathways.

Every extraordinary accomplishment in human history, from the invention of the wheel to the exploration of space, began as a mere dream or an audacious vision.

There are billionaires and successful people in many fields who never knew they would achieve what they actually did. This truth is backed up by quantum science: I have no clue about my future. As long as my inner sense of happiness is not correlated with any outcome I visualize, like fame, wealth, or status in society (my material well-being), then I can dream of anything. It will never become a negative reinforcement when I fail to accomplish my dreams.

My way of connecting cosmology with theology is to utilize neuroplasticity and quantum science to seek spirituality. Although suffering is an inevitable part of my life, I can train my mind to transform my negative thoughts into positive ones, which can help me attain a sense of inner peace. It demands determination and perseverance to rethink my perspectives.

Spirituality

Conscious awareness = **The inner sense of happiness**
of our thoughts and emotions (Unconditional relationships with our mind and toward others)

"The kingdom of God is within you"

Source: Author

Unconditional relationships truly test our ability to love and connect with others. It requires us to let go of any expectations or conditions we may have for ourselves or others and accept and appreciate each other for who we are.

All my struggles are mindful moments. If I can turn my painful experience with someone into mindful moments, I am essentially thanking that person.

As I began writing the introduction to this book, I reflected on the many hardships I have faced. While these experiences have caused me great pain, I have considered them valuable lessons that have helped me grow and become a better person. If I am willing to learn from my suffering, it can ultimately become a source of great strength and blessings in my life. For me, my sufferings are creating a spiritual path and helping me let that bad experience go. My thoughts then make me well, not sick or depressed. It is like lifting weights to build my muscles—weights are my problems, metaphorically.

I use my weights to bring my mind to the present moment—the muscle of mindfulness.

As I explained before, my spiritual journey starts with cosmology, based on my belief that God created the universe. So, I cannot defy nature but adapt (naturally conscious or naturally connected). That conscious awareness gets me closer to God in a way that there is a spiritual dimension to all my sufferings and hardships (spiritually conscious). I cannot eliminate all my challenges in life, but I can mitigate my hardships. Mindfulness is another dimension of that spiritual consciousness to strengthen my mind and be human— *pass through the valley of the shadow of darkness and see the light.* My focus on positive thoughts allows me to overwrite negative emotions and replace them with more positive ones, which is possible because the brain is malleable. Doing so makes me more resilient in the face of life's challenges. It's fascinating to see how neuroplasticity beautifully aligns with mindfulness meditation.

I breathe in all my hostility, hatred, resentment, and anger and breathe out love, compassion, kindness, and forgiveness. Forgiveness doesn't mean I am becoming a doormat or condoning bad behavior, but rather being kind and compassionate towards others.

Often, we think people deliberately harm and hurt us. It may seem that way. But we are all consumed by our own dark state of mind and negativity (biased perception), and we hurt others, kill others, or engage in destructive behaviors helplessly due to our own pain and suffering within. If we have that perspective, then our life becomes transformative. That perspective opens the door for deeper compassion, love, kindness, forgiveness, generosity, and gratitude.

We, as humans, have incredible qualities that are already a part of us—just like the lotus plant that blooms in muddy water, displaying its beauty and purity—a reflection of our own minds. The divine seed has been planted within each one of us. So, nourish it. Within us lies a beautiful version of ourselves, and by catching a glimpse of our deeply hidden virtues, we can become a better version of ourselves.

Mindfulness is the basis for self-compassion and compassion towards others. When we practice self-compassion, we counteract negative thoughts and emotions. Self-compassion is a powerful antidote to all our negative impulses, such as self-pity, guilt, or shame. Instead, we can treat ourselves with kindness and understanding, recognizing that we all have our flaws while acknowledging our inherent greatness. Moreover, self-compassion is crucial for sustaining compassion for others, as burnout can quickly occur without it. It's worth noting that compassion is not the same as empathy. *Empathy* allows us to feel others' pain and suffering, but compassion goes further. *Compassion* is about lifting someone from their misery and suffering and bringing them towards a more positive state of being.

Empathy is essential— feeling what others feel is not the only virtue to strive for. As a parent, I knew I needed to be compassionate—a certain amount of pain and suffering can be a valuable life lesson—towards my child's growth and development in the spirit of love. However, I have noticed that sometimes, it can lead to resentment.

Our self-compassion is the key to our inner sense of self-esteem, self-worth, and self-confidence. That brings me to my second pillar of happiness.

PILLAR #2: SOCIAL WELL-BEING

Our emotion is contagious. We emotionally resonate with others: *our positive emotions resonate positively around us.*

By sharing our personal stories and *vulnerabilities,* we can establish deeper connections with others and have a positive impact— I tell you my stories, and then you open up your stories. We are not projecting our weaknesses but rather projecting our strengths—the courage to be ourselves. Often, we underestimate the power of our vulnerabilities. We are not super-human. We are human beings with flaws, weaknesses, and faults.

As Peter Bregman highlights in his article "The Best Leaders Aren't Afraid to Ask for Help," acknowledging our vulnerabilities is an essential trait for effective leadership. This applies to leading in any context, whether a company, organization, family, or group. It's important to remember that our weaknesses do not make us weak. We become vulnerable only when we fail to recognize our strengths.

Our tendency to label others with negative terms like 'hypocrite, weak, odious, narcissist, psychopath or sociopath, fascist, idiot, fool, socialist, communist, etc.' often stems from our own insecurities and biases. We can become better humans by learning to control our thoughts and focus on constructive criticism.

Whenever I feel vulnerable thinking about my past, I try to laugh at myself. We must acknowledge that we are all vulnerable, regardless of our name, fame, title, wealth, education, and social status. Acknowledging the inescapable reality that we are human and vulnerable is our strength—take ownership of the beautiful version within. If we can be vulnerable and open to others and take the time to enter into the other person's spirit and understand their world, then we gain the power to influence that individual. That is how we connect and make meaningful relationships with others. We work together to solve our problems. There are no self-made ones. We are all connected as one.

Here is a story of a young man I met:

I recently had the pleasure of meeting a young man in India who was selling things door to door. I was impressed by his tenacity and decided to take his phone number. A few weeks later, I reached out to him to let him know how much I admired his resilience. I shared with him my own story of growing up with limited resources and having to walk to school barefoot, rain or shine. My peers often teased me for not having nice clothes or shoes. I told him I wished I had the same mindset and support to sell door-to-door when I was his age.

He started crying hysterically. He said he lost his parents at a very young age and was living with his relatives. The young man then spoke about how he had been mistreated by those around him, including friends, relatives, and even his girlfriend. It was heartbreaking to hear, but I encouraged him to stay strong and not let their hurtful words affect his self-esteem.

I said to him,

"What you do to make a living is incredibly valuable to you in

the future. Let not someone's unkind words sabotage your self-confidence. Have some compassion for your classmates, girlfriend, and relatives. They are suffering deep within, and they cannot help themselves. However, human beings are inherently kind and caring. But we are being indoctrinated—we don't like to take the time to look within."

His story touched the hearts of many, myself included. There was something about him that exuded humanity and goodness. People looked at him as if he was their child and supported him in any way they could. They bought what he was selling and paid more than he asked for his products. They even offered him new clothes and lunch to inspire him. He expressed how overwhelmed he was by their love and kindness. It was indeed a beautiful thing to hear.

He said to me that he was not a taker. Instead, he recognized the value of their kindness. He decided to pay it forward: doing whatever he could to help others in similar or dire situations, helping poor kids in his neighborhood with the money he saved.

I said,

"We all face challenges and hardships in life, and it is through sharing our experiences that we can build a more compassionate and connected society. Your story should resonate positively with others who mistreated you. Tell your classmates that you don't have new clothes or shoes or nutritious food like they all have. But you can teach them how to sell things door-to-door. Your friends will be amazed to see the kind of love and care those strangers showed you when they heard your story. They appreciated your attitude towards adversity and persistence in the face of hardships and challenges.

They admired your courage to face rejection selling things door-to-door. They valued your attitude towards life more than the product you were selling. Your narrative of the incredible love, kindness, and support from strangers will change your friends' attitude toward you in a positive way. How about telling your ex-girlfriend, who left you due to financial issues and your living arrangement with relatives, 'I'm glad we broke up. I wanted a real relationship, not a transactional one.'"

Our stories of adversity and suffering should make us safe, secure, and vulnerable because they make others feel more comfortable and help them tell their own stories without shame or guilt. As a result, we foster a culture of humility, trust, and learning. I call this fabric 'connection—relationship,' which brings us together rather than sets us apart—something that is often missing in our families and college campuses. We are all connected as one. However, it's essential to share our own experiences and perspectives and take the time to hear others' stories and understand where they're coming from. By actively listening to others, we can broaden our understanding of the world and become more empathetic and compassionate. Plus, it's always interesting to hear about the unique experiences and perspectives of others!

Let me refer to a Harvard Business Review article on what's your listening style:

How we insert ourselves into the other person's narrative shifts the focus of conversational attention. It's a prevalent misperception that sharing personal experiences in conversation fosters empathy and helps us connect with others. It's important to understand that, even when done with the best intentions, sharing our experiences can occasionally backfire. It may mistakenly draw attention away from the other person's needs and feelings rather than building a deeper connection. Active listening and affirming the other person's emotions without focusing on our own experiences are frequent characteristics of true empathy. We often assume that interjecting with our personal stories in a conversation is an empathic and relationship-building move.

It prevents us from hearing that individual's whole message. While it can be fun to interject and is sometimes helpful to promote connection, when done without awareness, it runs the risk of steering the conversation away from that person without redirecting back. In other words, it can actually distract us from fully understanding the other person's message. For example, when doctors interject a personal comment in an empathic attempt to connect, the conversation rarely returns to the patient's concern. Taking a few seconds to pause and rethink our automatic response can bring an opportunity to learn about another person better.

When an educator is aware of the impact of interjecting and maintaining curiosity about the student's message, it is possible to share the focus without losing the student's message. One effective way to accomplish this is by sharing personal thoughts and returning the focus to the student. By applying new listening methods, we can build stronger relationships, better understand others, and work together more effectively to solve problems.

We don't need an army of people in our lives. Rather, we need relationships with only a few people who can spot or understand our blind spots (our flaws), give us authentic feedback, share ideas, brainstorm together, and support one another in good and bad times. This is the 'vital group' I referred to earlier. We need a network of people who are the disagreeable givers: thoughtful critics challenge us to take down our strongest convictions, poke some holes, and see the flaws in our thinking or ideas, not just validate them.

A vital group is like having a support system that helps you become a better version of yourself. They are not merely cheerleaders who make you complacent, nor are they critics who demoralize you.

So, my humble advice is—especially to the younger generation—don't be afraid to ask for help. I genuinely believe that human beings are hard-wired to be kind and generous. We feel great and connected when we help others, and I think that's a beautiful thing. There's no shame in needing help, and it's important to remember that asking for assistance is a sign of strength, not weakness. To those who struggle with family relationships, reach out to them, even those who may have caused harm, with no expectation of rebuilding it. It is a powerful reminder of the importance of forgiveness and healing—*"forgive yourself."* Otherwise, it is like "hitting your head against a wall—and the wall always wins."

The social and emotional pillars I laid out will provide a solid foundation for building our human capital (career well-being).

PILLAR #3: CAREER WELL-BEING

The moment we are born, our sole focus is on the three-letter word "JOB." Sadly, that focus results in an uninspired life. Our work is regarded as a means to an end—"what we do to make a living" is an integral part of "who we are" as human beings. Therefore, we must discover "who we want to be" and then align "what we do" to accomplish that noble mission of life—a path to meaning and purpose, a sense of belonging. Make our lives meaningful and purposeful.

Human resource is a lot like a natural resource. We need to explore our inner selves—embark on a journey within ourselves—to discover our true potential. This means bridging the gap between what we are *currently doing* and what we can *actually achieve.*

By following our passions, honing our skills, and developing resilience, we can learn to love what we do truly.

However, passion alone is not enough, particularly when making career choices. We often get caught up in seeking validation through titles or status-conscious career paths, and in doing so, we squander our talents rather ruthlessly.

Steve Jobs said:
"Your time is limited, so don't waste it living someone else's life. Don't be trapped by dogma – which is living with the results of other people's thinking."

"What we think of ourselves is more important than others think of us."

However, we still crave validation from others. In my

community, people highly value having a job in government or healthcare as it provides a reliable source of income. As mentioned in Chapter 8, this serves as a classic example of the saying, *"When you are successful, you love what you do."* They believe this is where their value and worth lie, even if it means squandering their true potential and compromising their mental and emotional well-being. Anything outside these professions bewilders them, and straying from them is often met with stigma, leaving individuals uncertain about pursuing what they really love.

Our children at home, schools, colleges, and religious institutions are taught "what to think" instead of "how to think," creating a *'fixed mindset vs growth mindset'* situation. That limits their ability to learn and grow. When they confront the truth and realities of this world, their emotions get riled up because they think they know everything. It is an ego-based exercise.

I teach a few finance courses in business schools. It is not that I know so much about finance. But I take my couple of decades of industry experience and my own life experiences into the classroom. One advice:

I always say to my students not to focus too much on grades.

It is not that I am minimizing the importance of grades. The truth is that the moment of happiness is fleeting and short-lived. When they earn straight A's, they want a job that matches the straight A's and better jobs and more money. That is a never-ending search for happiness. Then they look at their friends who got Cs and are doing better than them. That gets them into instant depression. It is like my friend in Cancun, who has his highly curated, photoshopped picture of him sitting on a beach posted on Instagram. I see that while I wait for my train at the New York City subway station. Like everybody else, I will comment, "WTF" (**W**ow, **T**hat is **F**un). I am depressed. It is instant depression for me but instant gratification for my friend in Cancun.

We are so connected, and yet we are lonely and depressed.

I have a short mindfulness meditation practice in my classroom occasionally. Also, I give students extra credit to write one page about their meditation practice and how it transforms their thinking. They submit it at the end of the semester. I read those. I can see the emotional and mental struggles they face.

We live in a society where our mental and emotional struggles are viewed as a sign of weakness. Therefore, we suppress them until we hurt others, kill others, kill ourselves, or engage in self-destructive behavior. Learning is a holistic approach. It is a collaborative process. Enjoy the process of learning as opposed to enduring it.

Our ability to pivot and rethink on our feet, create an innovative mindset, and build meaningful relationships with others is far more important than the conceptual understanding of the material we learn at schools, colleges, universities, and religious institutions. Education is about figuring out what we are great at, following that path, and consistently getting better at it over time. Information is not transformation.

We hear stories of people with modest upbringings or poverty. By virtue of their grit and resilience and the strength of their insights and brilliance, they accomplish greatness in life and become inspiring stories. These people serve as an inspiration to us all. These individuals remind us that with hard work, determination, and perseverance, we can accomplish great things in our lives.

Some examples include Steve Jobs, who was actually fired from the company he co-founded because he was told he lacked vision; Oprah Winfrey, who we all know and love, was actually demoted from news reporting early on in her career; Michael Jordan, one of the greatest basketball players ever, was dropped from his school's basketball team! And who could forget Walt Disney, who was sacked from his newspaper job because he was told he lacked imagination (pretty hilarious, right)? JK Rowling is a prime example—she turned her massive failures into an enormous success. She called her early failure a "gift" that was "painfully won." The power of persistence and determination knows no bounds; it can lead to incredible accomplishments! What can be accomplished with perseverance and determination is incredible.

A strong foundation in emotional, social, and career well-being can significantly contribute to building and maintaining our financial well-being.

PILLAR #4: FINANCIAL WELL-BEING

Living a healthy and fulfilling life requires making meaningful lifestyle changes. This involves maintaining a healthy diet, staying active through exercise, and saving money for the future. Prioritizing our inner happiness allows us to develop compassion towards our environment and animals. We should consume meat and meat products in moderation and be mindful of the impact our choices have on the environment around us. We cannot impress others with our money for long—today, I am rich, and tomorrow, someone else will have more money than me.

Our net worth does not determine our self-worth; as the famous quote goes,

"We are mentally rich when we desire nothing."

The spirit of the lord will one day take away our soul from our body, and we will become a mere body. The scripture reminds us that we come from dust and return to dust. Our greed and self-interest only lead to more pain and suffering, as material wealth does not truly belong to anyone. All we truly need in life is a roof over our heads, food on the table, a means to make a living, and some savings for rainy days. Any excess we have can be used to help those in need, as that is our true purpose in life and what gives us meaning.

So, how do I measure my life? "It is inner peace." The beautiful version is within us, not the best version, because life gives us all sorts of choices. Amidst life's many choices, happiness can feel elusive. However, the true beauty lies in finding peace within oneself.

"Spare yourself the pain."

Humanity can learn from my painful experience. Our power is not extrinsic. We have no control over the forces around us. Happiness is absolute (intrinsic), not relative—not externally driven; we have the power to find it within ourselves.

In a contemplative context, our sense of self (identity) is an illusion. That realization is an antidote to anger and hatred since we are the product of our environment. *Therefore, we develop empathy and compassion for others with a realization that we are all shaped by our environment*—we are all biased.

Happiness is a <u>choice</u>:

Accept that I am not flawless, and my life experience is an opportunity to learn and grow.

By being compassionate to myself, I can <u>choose</u> to control my thoughts and emotions and find inner peace. That is my power within, and it is intrinsic.

Or

I can <u>choose</u> to seek pleasure, which is driven by external forces such as name, fame, wealth, or position, and be miserable.

Abundant Mindset

Source: Author

My spirituality is being grateful for everything I possess and refraining from praying for material well-being. Instead, I concentrate on materializing my contentment by harmonizing my mind and body with my *four pillars of happiness. These pillars encompass accurately identifying and regulating my emotions, sustaining a robust network of individuals (including family) who uplift me, consistently enhancing my career, and effectively managing my finances. This approach creates a virtuous cycle of abundance, where I become mentally rich and financially prosperous. Ultimately, I am gratified and at peace with my existence and scale my happiness to others—my compassion for others.*

So, I invite you to take these *four pillars* home with you—**my simple formula for happy and healthy living.**

> *1. Understand your emotions and regulate them with mindfulness meditation practice.*
> *2. Build meaningful relationships with others.*
> *3. Invest in yourself. Passion alone is not enough; get better at it. Learning is a continuous process.*
> *4. Live far below your means.*

The basis of happiness is about loving yourself first.

For me, love is an emotion that originates from within. Because any love from others is often conditional and transient—a valuable lesson I learned from my life experience. Therefore, it's crucial to cultivate self-love before seeking love from others.

Love myself. That is my power: *controlling my thoughts and emotions and influencing others to seek their inner peace.*

We are all privileged as long as we pursue our inner freedom. Therefore, it's paramount to prioritize your well-being before helping others. When you care for yourself, you'll have the energy and resources to support those around you. Whether getting enough sleep, eating a healthy diet, or taking time for self-care activities, ensure you take care of yourself first.

Remember, you can't pour from an empty cup.

By investing in your own health and happiness, you'll be better equipped to help those in need—scale your happiness.

> Happiness is not a one-time deal but an ongoing practice that offers intrinsic rewards.

Part Four

Seek the Truth, Find Jesus— Walk the Talk

(Truth Cannot Be Inconsistent with The Truth)

"Although I am biased like everyone else, I take time to reflect and rethink upon why I hold certain beliefs."

This part presents the teachings of the Bible and how we interpret and practice them in our lives. Religion should serve as a means to connect with God, find inner peace, and live a life of compassion and service to others. As stewards of this universe, it is our responsibility to steer clear of creating exploitative relationships with our fellow humans.

"I encourage you to question my perspectives rather constructively."

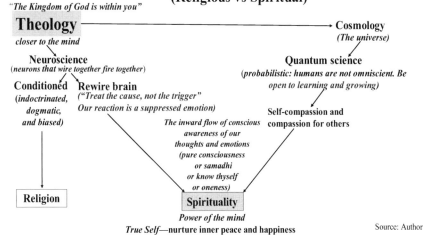

The Science of Spirituality
(Religious vs Spiritual)

"The Kingdom of God is within you"

Theology ────────────────────────────────→ Cosmology
closer to the mind   *(The universe)*

    Neuroscience   **Quantum science**
(neurons that wire together fire together)   *(probabilistic: humans are not omniscient. Be*
                                                   open to learning and growing)

Conditioned **Rewire brain**
(indoctrinated, *("Treat the cause, not the trigger"*   **Self-compassion and**
dogmatic, *Our reaction is a suppressed emotion)*   **compassion for others**
and biased)
                    The inward flow of conscious
                    awareness of our
                    thoughts and emotions
                    (pure consciousness
                    or samadhi
                    or know thyself
                    or oneness)

| Religion | | Spirituality |

Power of the mind
True Self—nurture inner peace and happiness

Source: Author

Chapter 15

My Christian Faith

"I am spiritual, not religious."

At the outset, my reference to 'church, religious institutions, denominations, ministers, bishops, and priests' should not be interpreted as a blanket reference. I wholeheartedly acknowledge that many religious practitioners and institutions are genuinely devoted to alleviating human sufferings without indoctrinating them with any religious philosophy or dividing humanity on the basis of religion. In my belief, there is one God who takes different forms, shapes, and names, irrespective of one's religious affiliation. I firmly believe that every human being is a valuable creation of God and has a unique spiritual journey. It is not my place to criticize or try to change someone else's beliefs. As humans, we seek information that confirms our beliefs and avoid anything that challenges them, often considering it taboo to explore alternative perspectives.

I separate the *person* from my *thoughts* about that *person*—we are inherently beautiful within. I approach those who religiously indoctrinate others with love and compassion, as they, too, have been conditioned themselves. While I don't condone their actions, I felt it is crucial to inspire them to "rethink" their approach, as their actions can have deleterious consequences on humanity.

As individuals, we often create our own opinions about ourselves and believe we are all valuable. So, if I frame my conversation in a way that doesn't diminish the value you hold and encourages you to rethink, my conversation becomes much less confrontational and more appealing to you.

I don't try to convince you to adopt my beliefs, defend my thoughts, or make you defensive. Nor do I spend time building up a case against you and not being open to your views or opinions.

I have noticed repeatedly that trying to convince others to buy into my ideas or bullying them to believe only makes them angrier—we get into a defensive and attack mode. It is like trying to eliminate my negative thoughts, but those thoughts come right back at me like a boomerang.

I ask myself,

"Am I fulfilling that God-given purpose?"

If I don't know where I am coming from, then I don't know where I am going. It is called "know thyself"—*create an awareness and acceptance.* This self-awareness allows me to come to peace with my inner voices and chart a path forward.

Referring to the theory of motivational interviewing or persuasive listening by psychologists William Miller and Stephen Rollnick, the goal is to create humility and curiosity about a new direction, clarify your way of thinking, and uncover your own motivation to change whatever you believe in or have a strong opinion or conviction of—break that overconfidence cycle: *"rethink your way of thinking."*

"I am not under any grandiose notion that I can change the world."

The change begins with me. I tested this approach through my counterfactual thinking. I explored the origins of my belief: why do I believe what I believe? It was a breakthrough moment: I gained some humility by reflecting on my beliefs and thinking. I realized that my environment led to my beliefs. I was easily carried away by dogma.

I asked myself the question: what if I didn't grow up in a Christian family?

Where do I go and worship, or who do I worship?

What if I were that disabled child struggling to fit in and be alive? Why does that child have to take shame, get bullied, or face bad treatment from his classmates or society? Was the disability the child's fault?

We strangle animals, tie them up, cut their throats, and eat them in the name of our religious beliefs or in the hope of maintaining a healthy diet. Do we take a moment and ask, what if we were those helpless animals?

Ask those who favor "gun rights" how they feel if their children were gunned down in schools, colleges, streets, and malls or if they become victims of gun violence. I live in the US, and I don't carry a gun.

What if we were those individuals stereotyped by those who believe that "God created mankind in his image" and that we are all valuable?

As humans, we often fall into the trap of stereotyping certain groups based on their appearance, gender, or sexual orientation. This biased perception can lead to harmful prejudices that impede progress and hinder societal advancement. It's essential to recognize that these biases stem from our own ignorance and that, as a society, we must work to combat them.

So, we don't often take others' perspectives. We are wearing a mask. We are actors—show different faces in front of different people.

"We are all suffering within."

Humans tend to adopt different mindsets depending on the situation and our beliefs. We may slip into a preacher's perspective[27] when we feel our beliefs are being challenged and need to defend and promote them. Alternatively, we may enter prosecutor mode, trying to prove others wrong and win our case. Lastly, we may shift into politician mode to win over an audience and gain their approval. However, the danger of these mindsets is that we may become so wrapped up in our own beliefs that we fail to consider other viewpoints and rethink our own. This can lead to a "sense of moral and spiritual superiority" and make it difficult to handle situations when things go wrong.

We may feel we have everything we need to be happy and prosperous, so we praise the Lord. Nothing wrong with being grateful for our good life.

---

[27] Adam Grant, "Think Again"

"But it's vital to remember that correlation doesn't necessarily imply causation."

Remember that a correlation between two things doesn't mean one caused the other. Other factors could be involved. For example, ice cream sales and shark attacks strongly correlate, but warmer weather likely leads to both. Causation and correlation are different—in a causal relationship, one event directly causes another, while in a correlation, two events occur simultaneously, but their relationship may be due to a third variable.

Prayer serves as a means of communicating with God and self-regulation. Our mindset and emotional state "cause" the outcomes we encounter. In other words, our belief in ourselves and our capabilities causes us to succeed. Like external factors can trigger (*not cause*) our anger—a suppressed emotion already within us, prayer serves as a catalyst (*trigger, not the cause*) for us to tap into our inner positivity.

As the Bible states, the kingdom of God is within us, so getting closer to our minds and controlling our thoughts and emotions is vital for our happiness. *That is the prayer*; our positive spirit influences our experiences of good fortune; ultimately, the key to happiness lies within us and our mindset. However, when individuals engage in religious activities, the "dopamine" released in their brains creates a sense of *well-being or short-term pleasure*, not "*happiness.*"

It's worth noting that religious organizations tend to foster a *religious environment* (not spiritual) that stimulates dopamine release (pleasure or feel-good moment) instead of oxytocin or serotonin (happiness and unconditional love). This dopamine rush can become addictive and is the basis of their "business model." We might feel grateful because we have everything we need for success and happiness. It's acceptable to be grateful for our blessings. It is foolish to link our mental well-being to our social standing or material assets because they are both fleeting and cannot ensure contentment.

"The power to achieve true contentment lies within us, the spiritual path."

I praise God for every blessing and feel grateful for the strength to bear the cross (suffering). I believe religion is a personal journey, and finding my own path to inner peace is essential to my spiritual path.

While I respect my Christian tradition and the teachings of the Bible, it's critical to question and challenge the way we practice these beliefs constructively.

Standing out and defying the norm can be intimidating. Our society tends to hastily pass judgment and categorize those who deviate as "crazy" or "insane." However, embarking on a spiritual path can bring immense triumph and contentment. Although it is not easy to be different from the masses or the majority that obstructs your quest to find inner peace, it could be the most gratifying spiritual journey.

It is not about my opinion or your opinion but rather about the widespread mental and emotional crisis around us—*fear, anger, hatred, shame, loneliness, or sadness.* It's human nature to seek out information that confirms our preexisting beliefs. We tend to avoid anything that challenges our beliefs.

My goal is not to coerce someone into altering their mindset but rather to influence and inspire them to question their way of thinking and reflect deeply on the trajectory of their own life.

Often, we ignore the fact that when we choose not to talk to people with different views, we give up on opening their minds to the truth in the bible. By having conversations with those with different views, we can share our perspectives and help others think critically about their beliefs.

Let me do my best to create a desire to reflect on your thinking and get through this part rather peacefully.

Spirituality necessitates cultivating an unshakeable sense of empathy towards oneself and others. Nevertheless, our individual and cultural experiences can significantly influence our comprehension of spirituality.

The narrative that I am the "subject" and you are the "object"—you did this to me—only builds hatred within me, and it projects out rather negatively. None did anything to me. I did it to myself.

I can move forward with a clear mind and a positive attitude by letting go of my negative emotions—feelings of betrayal, animosity, resentment, or hatred. In the process, I learned to *"love myself and forgive myself."*

Forgiveness is seeking that peace within me. It is not a generous act. No more giving away my power to someone by calling myself a "victim." That is the power of forgiveness. I deserve to have peace.

People are beautiful within, but their actions are often conditioned behavior. Love the "person." Genuine compassion is built upon understanding and accepting the "person."

As the Bible says, "Love your enemies and pray for those who persecute you."

Hatred often stems from a misguided belief of being superior to others, which is self-defeating. However, those who aim for authentic spiritual growth comprehend that enlightenment entails showing love and compassion to our enemies and helping them find redemption.

Let me elaborate on my Christian belief, which I briefly narrated at the beginning of this book:

I define Christianity in three words: suffering, lesson, and blessing.

This has been my life experience, and I would like to share it in the book. As far as I can tell, there is no escape from my *suffering*. It's a brutal reality to accept, but I know that none can bear the Cross for me. That is my *lesson*. Through my experiences, I've learned that my thoughts are often illusions or manifestations of what I've been through—my past. But even in the midst of pain, I've been blessed to cultivate *empathy and compassion* for others. It's a powerful gift to feel what others feel and desire to alleviate their suffering. These valuable lessons continue to shape my life, which is my *blessing*.

The way I see it, religious tradition is a human construct—we are born into a tradition or culture. As a Christian, I believe we are all individuals made in the image of God. And the church serves as an essential gathering place for us to come together, worship, and find *"peace within."*

Throughout my life, I have had a deep respect for priests. Today, that view has changed completely—*they, too, are being conditioned.* The church does an incredible job of obscuring and blowing smoke so the believers are kept in the dark.

"We are indoctrinated without even knowing it!"

When negative emotions cloud our minds, it can impede our cognitive capacity. Our perceptions become skewed, and our emotions take hold of us. Sadly, some use this to their advantage: exploit our brain's malleability and manipulate our neuroplasticity through religion, just as news media and social media do.

These dark forces manipulate our senses, distort the truth, and coerce us into believing things that suit their narratives—turning the smartest into the most gullible.

The more they repeat the misinformation, the more that misinformation feels credible. Repetition enhances the perceived reliability of information. It is like the same commercial being played repeatedly on TV—a tactic that often works well for boosting sales.

I've always found that repetition drives a message home and sticks in my mind. My beliefs allow me to take things as true and organize my thoughts and actions accordingly.

"If a priest dressed up like a plausible version of Jesus and recited a few Latin phrases repeatedly, it is almost like he becomes a representation of Jesus himself."

It's fascinating to see the dark side of neuroplasticity:

If you don't take charge of what you feed your brain regularly, it can have a lasting effect on your mental and emotional state. As our religious intensity grows, so does our tendency to respond angrily and vindictively when presented with opposing facts, frequently as a result of deeply ingrained rigid beliefs. This effect also affects priests, who are similarly shaped to hold fast to their ideology.

The sad truth is that children are more susceptible to these dark forces since, according to neuroscience, their brain matures anatomically only in their mid-twenties. They are taught 'what to think' within their respective doctrines or ideologies. When their beliefs are challenged, instead of having an open mind or a growth mindset, they become furious (or become martyrs).

Personally, I don't watch TV or expose myself to negativity in any way. Instead, I curate my news feeds and stay informed in other ways.

The bright side of neuroplasticity is that we can take the worst parts of our lives and turn them into something positive.

With neuroplasticity, we can transform the most challenging experiences into positive growth and change.

Journaling has been an excellent outlet for me to build my mental resilience since it provides an outlet for downloading my negative emotions onto paper or a phone instead of bottling them up inside. Otherwise, I feel like a pressure cooker that's about to blow up due to the accumulation of cortisol in my body.

Every day, I journal my experience and behavior—what worked, what didn't, and all the things I am grateful for. I then reflect on them and determine how I live with my decisions when things go wrong. I drive and choose my destination: the quality of my thoughts, not the situation I find myself in, makes a massive positive difference. So, I have some resources within me to deal with the uncertainties of life. It's been a life-changing journey, and I feel I've experienced *a spiritual rebirth.*

We are all unique individuals created by a higher power and are all valuable. When you believe you are beautiful internally, you don't need a wardrobe of designer clothes to showcase your awesomeness externally.

Like every other religious tradition, we pray at church, at our homes, or elsewhere for our material well-being, creating a conditional relationship with our minds—happy when, happy if, and happy because. That is dopamine-driven happiness, a feel-good moment. We continue to pray for more. It becomes insatiable, creating an intense desire for external freedom or validation. Like drug addicts, we seek that feel-good moment with our prayers—a feeling of want. That is an endless search for happiness.

When everything goes well, we feel a sense of pleasure. We attribute those successes to the Higher power or our prayer and show gratitude for those blessings. But nothing is permanent: we cannot deny the universal truth that we will face challenges such as losing a job, experiencing family breakdowns, becoming unwell, or facing injustices. Coping with such triggers can be a difficult and painful experience. If our happiness is driven by external triggers—name, fame, wealth, or status in society—then we become oblivious to the causes that bring internal freedom (our sense of who we are and our inner strength). As a result, we could become more susceptible to adversity in life.

Religion is supposed to empower human beings and build our mental and emotional well-being: *train our mind to proactively prepare for challenges ahead, cultivate inner peace, renounce the comfort of the material world, and find human consciousness in the present moment*—meditation and healing of our mind. Get closer to God. Be self-aware and glorify yourself.

Whenever I talk to fellow parishioners about the direction of the church, they say, "we come to the church to socialize." Their suggestion was to ignore those priests.

But the truth is that by ignoring priests and bishops:
1. We maintain the taboo of not questioning their practice, and their behavior goes unquestioned. We are constantly being conditioned or indoctrinated. Our brain is constantly eavesdropping on everything within and around us, processing the vast amount of information it receives.

2. They continue to perpetuate the status quo—follow a hypocritically pious spiritual devotion.

Priests with greater power to influence our behavior ought to do more rethinking because they are more likely to privilege their views—people tend to follow the preaching of these religious leaders.

As humans, we can easily fall prey to indoctrination and develop unconscious biases or even hatred towards those who don't conform to our traditions. This is all due to the power of neuroplasticity, which allows us to reinforce certain thought patterns and make them more firmly fixed. We often fail to question whether those we follow genuinely "practice or believe" what they preach. Instead, we blindly adhere to their preachings. This behavior poses a significant danger to humanity. We tend to adopt widely shared views without critically analyzing them. This tendency is rooted in how our brain functions, as change is often perceived as a threat (Chapter 1 explores this concept in detail).

My sister recently asked me why so many people follow priests and politicians without questioning their actions. It's an interesting question. As I pondered her inquiry, I realized that our brains are actually wired to take the path of least resistance, conserve energy, and avoid threats.

Disbelief is cognitively demanding. Processing information that contradicts our expectations or beliefs requires much cognitive effort[28]. It's natural to feel skeptical or doubtful when encountering something that doesn't fit our preconceived notions. It is challenging

---

[28] Cognitive effort refers to the mental exertion required to complete a particular task or activity. It involves using one's cognitive abilities, such as attention, memory, and problem-solving skills.

to closely analyze and synthesize all the information we gathered from our environment and stay focused and alert. Humans naturally tend to resist change and often support the opinions of religious leaders or politicians. Our brains constantly evolve and adapt to our surroundings, with our neural pathways acting like trails in a forest. The more we tread down a certain path, the more entrenched it becomes due to the brain's neuroplasticity. This neural pathway makes it easier for us to follow others and resist rethinking because it is challenging for us to do the hard work of rethinking.

The combination of the human brain's inclination to accept things without questioning them and the tactics of priests or politicians creates an environment that promotes unwavering loyalty. This leads to a selective interpretation of religious texts and a lack of critical examination, resulting in *blind devotion or becoming dogmatic*. This lack of critical thinking is particularly prevalent in certain Christian traditions. There is a clear need for more emphasis on the distinction between being instructed on *'what to think'* versus being educated on *'how to think'* critically.

Being taught to take religious stories literally and dismiss critical thinking can limit our cognitive development and reasoning skills.

This means that individuals blindly believing far-fetched statements from manipulative leaders could inadvertently reshape their cognitive pathways to accept falsehoods. Sadly, this inclination makes it easier for "priests and politicians" to spread falsehood to their followers. Some individuals may not even bother seeking new information, convinced they already have all the knowledge they need based on what they've heard from their priests or politicians.

Linking priesthood to politicking highlights how those in power can misuse their influence and spread misinformation.

I watch the same mindset of following the masses or the majority in my Christian tradition. We follow suit when we witness others adhering to certain practices. Take, for example, when priests request that their congregation come forward with their envelopes. Many individuals will blindly follow without questioning the need to pay God money to receive a blessing. It's as if we assume that God is running a business and that we must *"pay to play."* This phenomenon is based on what's known as *naïve realism*[29], which is our heavy reliance on our perception as reality without recognizing that our environment often distorts our perception. This can be especially true in the context of religious institutions, where we may build a false consensus bias and assume that everyone shares the same beliefs as us and that our beliefs are more like reality.

As far as I am concerned, the church is a place of worship and a source of wisdom. Priests are supposed to be exemplary role models, especially during difficult times. Are their words consistent with their behavior? That is the "rethinking" we all need. Otherwise, the church

---

[29] Naive realism is a common cognitive bias that distorts our perceptions. It happens when we rely too heavily on our own perceptions and experiences, which can lead us to believe that what we see and experience is the objective reality. This can prevent us from seeing things from other perspectives and cause us to make assumptions or jump to conclusions.

becomes a stop on our way to life—a place to socialize.

"IN GOD WE TRUST"

One morning, I ran into a video of Vivek Ramaswamy, who is running for president of the United States. It was quite a therapeutic experience for me for days. Every time I think about it, I laugh. I am not making fun of anyone but rather laughing at our human conditions, myself included.

I believe he organized a spiritual retreat on a Sunday morning titled "In God We Trust." The White evangelicals follow a core religious belief based on four things: *guns, God, family values, and national security.*

They don't see eye to eye with evangelicals of color or other faiths, so they need a *gun.* For *family values and national security*, they look up to Donald Trump.

Then comes *God*: one of the participants in that event asked Vivek, "Do you have any spiritual beliefs? If so, what are those?" I knew where that man was going with his question. I couldn't stop laughing before Vivek answered that man's question.

He said, "I am a Hindu."

I could see the look on that man's face. He might be saying, "Oh God, this young man is going to hell." I am just making this up. I have no idea what that man was thinking or saying. I am sure you get the mindset of those hardcore believers of Jesus. They are being indoctrinated. I have only compassion for them. I certainly don't paint the same brush with every evangelical Christian or any religious tradition. *We all have our better human traits: love, kindness, compassion, forgiveness, etc.*

Vivek said, "I was the only Hindu kid in my catholic school, and I read the Bible more closely." Also, he said, "We are all equal in the eyes of God because we are made in the image of God." That is precisely what I believe as a Christian. I don't know what my God looks like, but there is one creator for all of us.

It's worth noting that even though Vivek Ramaswami's background is rooted in Hinduism, he didn't appear to adhere to the principles of *samadhi—a Hindu philosophy emphasizing the unity of the mind.* Many swamis and gurus, including myself, closely adhere to this philosophy. My approach to mindfulness meditation is centered around discovering our true selves.

In contrast, Mr. Ramaswamy was conditioned to emulate Mr. Trump rather than seek inner peace. Despite lacking qualities such as humility, humanity, ethics, honesty, and integrity, Donald Trump has been hailed as a hero by many believers in Jesus, revealing the extent of indoctrination in the American population. For decades, news media, social media, and religious organizations have been doing a masterful job of indoctrinating, conditioning, and curating their beliefs, thereby creating neural pathways that are incredibly strong. By tapping into his supporters' deeply ingrained beliefs and perspectives, he struck a chord with them—his grievances resonated with those of his supporters. Unfortunately, in today's society, those who go against the principles of kindness, compassion, and humility preached in the Sermon on the Mount are celebrated as heroes. It's concerning that leadership qualities we uphold in our leaders are thrown on the wayside, and we have descended to this level of madness where abhorrent behavior is widely accepted as the norm in this great nation, too.

Mr. Trump did not cause millions of Americans to stir up their emotions. But he triggered their suppressed emotions. They saw him as one of their own who could not find "the kingdom of God" within himself—the inner peace.

I have compassion for Mr. Trump and his comrades, who have been conditioned by their own upbringings and surroundings. However, it is our responsibility to rethink our actions and their impact on our lives and those around us.

It's essential to create new neural pathways not clouded by false narratives and allow self-love to flourish. Doing so will enable us to break free from indoctrination and build a happier, healthier society. This transformation is crucial for achieving a positive state of mind.

DEPRESSED, DERANGED, AND DANGEROUS

I WAS DISTURBED when I heard a young man choke a mentally ill homeless man to death on the New York City Subway.

Is this the United States of America?

The assailant was hailed as a hero and Good Samaritan by a Governor who was ginning up his supporters to raise money for the assailant over this barbaric and heinous behavior. Even worse, a legal defense fund set up on a crowdfunding site had raised more than $2 million.

Do we ever ask how we can help a mentally ill or deranged individual?

Instead, we, too, become deranged and dangerous. What exactly did he accomplish by killing that young, mentally ill person other than costing taxpayers more money to bring the assailant to justice?

Well, we can ask for God's forgiveness.

Forgiveness: Can we be Christians and be morally depraved? Yes. "Read 2 Corinthians, take the wine and cracker."

We have one goal in life when it comes to religion: *"Go to heaven."* We look forward to heaven before we live on this planet—we live paradoxically. In that pursuit, we are creating hell on earth.

In the Christian framework, good and evil are often equated with heaven and hell. However, from my perspective, *good and evil* can be seen as *wisdom and ignorance*, where knowledge represents what we don't know. When discussing *evil*, I refer to a *fixed mindset* often encouraged within the church. It's common for religious institutions to promote conformity and discourage the exploration of truths that lie outside the norm. This practice creates resistance to acquiring knowledge and builds up hatred.

The Bible, on the other hand, encourages us *not to conform to the behavior of this world*, which is an invitation to explore new ideas and expand our understanding of the world. By embracing a *growth mindset* and seeking knowledge, we can break free from the shackles of ignorance and build a brighter future for ourselves and those around us. We are led to believe that we have no right to judge priests or bishops.

But we let priests judge us:
"You are making too much money, not coming to church regularly and confessing your sins, working overtime, or following other religious traditions."

Is that humility or hubris? Are they reflecting on their own behavior? It is easy to be an armchair critic—criticize without experiencing the hardships and struggles we face daily as we work to make ends meet and support our families. Their criticisms reveal more about their "illusions of moral and spiritual superiority" than any shortcomings on our part.

According to Heb. 10:22:
Through the blood of Jesus, we have our "hearts sprinkled clean from an evil conscience."

As mortal beings, we possess the remarkable ability to *introspect—a level of consciousness that allows us to reflect on our own thoughts, feelings, and actions.* This exceptional gift is a testament to our unwavering spirit and indomitable will that sets us apart from all other transient creatures. With the power of introspection, we can unlock our full potential and live life to the fullest, unencumbered by the fear of death.

However, it's fascinating to ponder whether we are truly self-aware in light of this fear.

Let us look at how our bodies react to stress. As humans, we are constantly on high alert, with cortisol pumping through our bodies as if we are still living in the wilderness. This fight-or-flight response is a healthy and natural reaction. Our brain is always in survival mode.

Interestingly, unlike other animals, such as zebras, who return to their normal routine after escaping from a predator, we are the only species constantly aware of our mortality. The idea of our inevitable demise is terrifying. The fear of death is something that religion has capitalized on, inventing concepts like *heaven and hell* to assuage our fears. Our intense fear of death has inspired us to seek "forgiveness" to find redemption.

For Christians, true spirituality means seeking forgiveness by showing genuine regret and remorse. Christ's priestly work, the once-for-all sacrifice of Jesus at Calvary, ensures that believers are absolved of their sins and no longer carry the burden of guilt. Through shedding His blood, God forgives the sins of those who have faith in Him.

"And this one-time sacrifice of Jesus has become a never-ending practice of seeking forgiveness."

Every Sunday, the congregation stands together in the church and repeats a solemn prayer after the priest—asking for God's forgiveness. It's a moment of introspection and humility as we acknowledge our flaws and ask for forgiveness. We recognize that we are not perfect and that we have made mistakes. But through our faith in Christ, we can find redemption and salvation.

It's a powerful reminder that we are all sinners and need God's grace to guide us. We pledge our allegiance to Jesus Christ—confess our sins, seek forgiveness, renew our commitment to living a life of love and compassion, and accept the Holy Communion. It is a moment of grace and hope.

But we turn it into a pity party:

"I am not good enough, worthy enough to stand in front of you, or I am a sinner"—a never-ending practice of dealing with our evilness. We are pitying ourselves.

Let us ask ourselves: "How often do we forgive our fellow human beings?" We don't have to. We can go to the church and confess our sins to a priest—who we believe is a manifestation of God and devoid of all sins—and take the Holy Communion.

"I am a sinner and not worthy enough to stand in front of our God?"

This addictive pattern of shaming ourselves gets us into a negative feedback loop and becomes self-perpetuating: *we become what we think of ourselves.* We build a lack of *self-compassion.*

Healing of our mind is facilitated when we practice self-kindness and confront critical self-talk or self-loathing. We can conquer hopelessness and develop resistance against depression by accepting who we are and practicing self-care. When we constantly beat ourselves up with destructive thoughts and beliefs, we start to feel hopeless, overwhelmed, and depressed. Even worse, our negative feelings resonate negatively around us—impacting our social well-being. Instead, we can focus on changing our behavior. We are all capable of growth and change, and we shouldn't let negative self-talk hold us back.

THE DANGER OF "SELF-PITY"—"THE WAGES OF SIN"

As humans, we have been blessed with an innate sense of logic that often surpasses the collective knowledge and wisdom of ministers or religious practitioners. It is a brilliantly designed business model to instill suffering within us and thrive on it. *It is a virtuous cycle for those who preach the Gospel and a vicious cycle for those who follow it.*

We pay both ways: we give our hard-earned money to the priests, bishops, or pastors who indoctrinate us. We then have to deal with our destructive emotions.

Our mind, the way our brain perceives things, has tremendous physiological and psychological effects. Internalizing this pity—*calling ourselves sinners*—breeds insecurity within us, and it becomes a "self-fulfilling prophecy." That is the principle of neuroplasticity—our brains can adapt and change based on our experiences and what we learn. Our negative thoughts create a lack of self-compassion and cause us to suffer. The church then capitalizes on it—running a church on the side to raise money for those who preach the Gospel. In the church, it is the "envelopes"—bring the money. I call it "the caricature of Jesus." Believers' lawless deeds and transgressions will be forgiven by paying money to the church—*the get-out-of-the-jail-free card.*

We are conditioned to believe that we can be morally depraved and yet be saved and spend our eternity in Heaven. Is the church leading us astray by encouraging sinful behavior and paying wages to the priests who influence us to commit sins?

The Bible says the wages of sin is death, not salvation. In other words, salvation and eternal life is not a guarantee for the morally depraved.

My take on our religious practices is that we should be mindful of the fact that priests are fallible human beings who are capable of making misjudgments. Therefore, it is up to each one of us to question these practices and strive to lead a moral and ethical life without being unduly influenced by them or exposed to their preachings. Moreover, the role of the priesthood should be seen as more of a profession than a source of guidance for us to find our "true selves." My home is my church when it comes to my spirituality.

THE ORIGIN OF "CAST THE FIRST STONE"

"If any one of you is without sin, let him be the first to throw a stone at her" — John 8:7

The story goes like this: The crowd wants to throw stones at a woman accused of adultery—kill and punish her for the sin she committed. Jesus asks the crowd that those who are not sinners should cast the first stone. Of course, everyone has sinned so that no one can throw any stone.

Does that mean God knows us, and he does not find us as sinners?

The Bible shows God's continual interaction with only one species of primates, the human—*human sin, then God is angry, then humans repent, then God forgives them.* Without the idea of God responding to human sin and repentance, there is no obvious way to preserve what is meaningful about Christianity, which is salvation or eternity in heaven. But there is no evidence of the existence of heaven or hell.

God created man in his own image. Also, God created a capacity for evil within humanity.

The logical question is: why doesn't the omnipotent God prohibit humanity from doing evil things or obliterate evil? We have no credible answer to this question. However, I can make the following rationale:

Let's take a moment to ponder the true nature of our universe—the creation of God. As human beings, we can only comprehend what our senses allow us to perceive. Still, certain aspects of reality go beyond our understanding. These are the secrets of pure intelligence, which grasp the very foundation of existence. Only through God's *omniscient* knowledge can we hope to comprehend the intricate workings of the universe.

We live in an uncertain world. *The truth is we don't know the truth about the universe.* We need the good, bad, and ugly for the universe to function flawlessly.

I want to use three scenarios to explain this rationale: *God and the universe.*

—**We need sick people:** *Millions of healthcare professionals are making a living by serving the mentally and physically ill. What if there are no sick people on this planet?*

—**We need bad actors:** *We complain about crimes and lawlessness in our society. But there are plenty of people—law enforcement agencies, lawyers, judges, and businesses are making a living off those bad actors. Can they complain about too many crimes or bad actors?*

—**We need sinners**: *We call ourselves sinners in the church and ask for God's forgiveness. The business model of the church is to create enough sinners—instilling suffering and capitalizing on it: bring the money. Imagine a scenario where there are no sinners on this planet. How do millions of priests, pastors, bishops, evangelists, and televangelists make a living? My sins are their living.*

One can't deny that God is all-powerful (omnipotent) but powerless to alleviate the hardships that exist in the world.

I sometimes wonder where God is in the midst of all the pain and suffering, especially when innocent babies are brutally killed or facing insurmountable suffering. Are babies sinners? The truth is that even God cannot eliminate our struggles entirely.

It's difficult to comprehend why the burden of hardship falls on those who possess good hearts and do good deeds. However, I must accept that this is how the universe operates under the design of that *Omniscient God*—I have no free will.

It's up to me to get closer to my mind and find the strength to overcome my sufferings.

Neuroscience suggests (see Chapter 1) that meditation can help us regulate our thoughts and emotions and control our cognition. This suggests that there is a *causal relationship* between meditation and our behavior. The *deterministic nature* of this relationship raises questions about the extent of our *free will*. I assert that we don't have complete freedom and do not know the whole truth, which aligns with the probabilistic nature of the universe as per quantum science and theology. While God is omniscient, humans are not. Therefore, when we *acknowledge and accept* our human limitations and embrace the struggles that come with them, we recognize the role of our sufferings in our growth and development toward the greater good.

So, I've concluded that the sufferings I encounter, which persist and never go away, are not mere coincidences but rather a way of *divine intervention.* Through these challenges, I can become a more robust and better version of myself. This is my interpretation of spirituality.

On the cross, Jesus Christ endured immense suffering. And every Sunday, we humbly ask Jesus to bear our sufferings, too. "Have mercy upon Him."

When my fellow parishioners stand and ask for God's forgiveness every Sunday, I remain seated and say to myself,
"Lord, help me learn from my life experience, grow from it, regulate and positively transform my disruptive thoughts and emotions, and

build that unconditional compassion—self-compassion and
compassion towards others."

"Ask what you can do to alleviate your suffering, not exacerbate it."

The Holy Communion: "Perils of Self-pity"

The concept of Holy Communion was a one-time experience for me, not a never-ending quest for redemption through "pitying ourselves." If priests' sole aim is to increase the number of individuals taking Holy Communion every Sunday to measure their success as priests, then they are contributing to people's suffering and exploiting their hardships—a business model that capitalizes on our pain and suffering (see pages 233-234). This practice is nothing but *a religious approach or pseudo-spirituality*, where organized religion becomes a crime against humanity. However, if priests adopt a *spiritual approach*, their objective will be to reduce the number of individuals taking Holy Communion and instead inspire them to seek inner peace—*the eternal happiness is within ourselves*, as the Bible teaches.

BE HUMAN: UPHOLD RESPECT AND PROTECTION FOR EVERY INDIVIDUAL'S BELIEF

"So, God created mankind in his own image, in the image of God he created them;" — Genesis 1:27.

Each tradition touts itself as morally and spiritually superior to other religious traditions and believes that doing precisely that will

302

get us to spend our eternity in heaven.

Savage Chickens (savagechickens.com)

There is no harm in believing that death is an illusion—a belief that we will get to a better place one day. So, it is a consolation for believers of heaven. But that belief only creates bitterness and hatred.

There is no greater damnation than calling other traditions or denominations "morally and spiritually bankrupt" and saying they will spend eternity in hell for no fault of their own. They are born into that tradition. In other words, religion gives us every reason to practice hatred, immorality, intolerance, and violence.

Identifying the true deity amidst various religions and beliefs seems daunting. However, the answer may be within each one of us. Respecting and acknowledging all individuals' unique experiences and beliefs, regardless of their faith, caste, or ethnicity, is essential. As human beings, we must remember that our perspectives are not mutually exclusive and that we all have our own biases that shape our opinions.

Our limited perspectives about the nature of the universe lead to biased decisions that ignore the bigger picture of *divine omniscience*—the universe is probabilistic.

Contemplating the relationship between the Higher power and the universe can be a fascinating topic for many, myself included (see Chapter 14, pages 236-256). The idea that an all-knowing being created our world is a powerful concept that can inspire humility in us.

Our universe is complex and vast, making it difficult for humans to comprehend everything fully. Science can aid us in understanding the natural world, allowing us to make informed decisions, while faith can guide us and provide a sense of purpose, reminding us that we are all connected. Together, science and religion can create a morally just and ecologically sustainable world that can provide spiritual fulfillment in a chaotic and uncertain environment. We can work together to create a more harmonious and compassionate world by listening to one another and understanding where others are coming from.

Regardless of our religious traditions, we are all human beings with inherent value and worth.

THE DIVINE-HUMAN

We believe our God is omnipotent, omnipresent, and omniscient: an all-powerful, all-present, and all-knowing God. And yet, we practice the antithesis of what we preach or believe.

Truth cannot be inconsistent with the truth: humans do not possess divine power. If we believe otherwise, we are denigrating the truth.

God sees everything in the present like a single stack of still pictures without the constraints of time. But humans cannot see the future—we live in an uncertain world. It's difficult to see how prayer or a human agency can bring about change if God is omniscient and omnipotent.

Omnipotent entails omniscience—having all knowledge of all things possible in this universe. Christians believe that God created the universe—God and the universe. The literal physics of the universe is probabilistic: As humans, we are constantly trying to predict and control our future, but the reality is that everything is subject to chance and uncertainty. We can never know what our future holds with complete certainty. This idea is rooted in the principles of quantum science and consciousness, which I discussed in Chapter 14.

As mortal beings, we are often faced with the question of whether an omniscient God can also be benevolent. Many believe that if God has all knowledge, then how can we maintain any meaningful degree of human freedom or free will?

It seems impossible to have both "divine power and free will" simultaneously. In fact, without freedom or free will, it's hard to defend our views about future events. Our knowledge of the future is limited, and we cannot know what has not yet happened. This is a humbling experience. However, some practitioners or scholars of

Christianity, such as priests, often falsely claim that God is speaking through them and that they have the divine power. But this is simply a display of hubris and arrogance, not humility. The Latin root for *humility*, which means "from the earth," reminds us of our inherent flaws and fallibility.

The idea of divine omniscience and the lack of free will is significant because it places the responsibility of human actions on God. If humans didn't possess free will, then God would be accountable for all the outcomes of human actions, and he wouldn't be able to use suffering or evil to penalize those who make 'sinful' choices. Nevertheless, we are still grappling with the question of why we must suffer, and the answer remains elusive.

How do I reconcile this notion of the lack of free will and our suffering?

It can be challenging to reconcile the idea of *no free will* with the suffering that we experience. However, one way to approach this is by recognizing that we have agency over our thoughts and emotions—*control our thoughts and emotions* and work to strengthen our minds. The very fabric of the cosmos mandates and the Bible this encounter (*seek inner peace*):

We don't know the truth. We are all biased.

We must be humble and find meaning in our struggles. Humans are not endowed with divine omniscience or free will—we are not all-knowing or in complete control of our lives. We all have our biases and limitations, and I am no exception. As such, I have made a conscious effort to practice self-compassion and extend the same compassion to others, *including those who claim to be religious scholars.*

My book is about being mindful of our thoughts and emotions since we have no control over the external factors in our lives—achieve inner peace and enlightenment to connect with the Higher power (see 'Conclusion').

Chapter 16

Find Your Authentic Self

"Too Much Explication and Not Any Meaningful Action"

As human beings, we often find ourselves struggling with our inner selves and experiencing suffering. But the good news is that we have the power to overcome these struggles by tapping into the kingdom of God within us: *get closer to our minds.* We might frequently end up on a path of never-ending disappointment if we are constantly looking for outside approval, unrestricted independence, or pleasure. It's crucial to understand that our pleasure is transient, like a passing storm in the broad sky of life. We miss the great reality that happiness resides inside of us, patiently waiting to be revealed when we get caught up in our egos and unquenchable desires for pleasure. We can engage on a voyage of self-discovery and learn about the enduring contentment that develops from inside, independent of external circumstances, by letting go of our ego's hold and attachment to material things.

The question I ask is whether the *actions of our priests* are forcing us to *seek that external freedom or helping us to recognize the human consciousness in the present moment*—transcend the sense of self or identity or feeling of resentment or anger and experience the internal freedom. So, those who believe death is an illusion can spend eternity with Jesus in heaven.

We all know that the words we choose to talk to others hold immense power.

I recall a moment when I was standing on a train and noticed a young lady standing before me, taking a photo of herself. Without hesitation, I looked at her and said, "you look absolutely beautiful." She responded with a beautiful smile and said, "thank you so much." As I walked off that train, I knew I had made her day a little brighter.

We all believe we are valuable, and yet we seek validation: *what others think of us is more important than what we think of ourselves.* In that context, words have power. Our words can create powerful, constructive, and destructive emotions. We have such a low internal sense of self-esteem or inner freedom.

Let us ask ourselves these questions: whether our words have power or our actions have power in a spiritual context.

Are we doing lip service to the Bible?

Are we practicing what we are preaching?

Are we preaching what we are practicing?

I find it deeply troubling to witness some priests blatantly downplaying or dismissing the significance of the truth found within the Bible.

As we navigate our spiritual journey, it's worth remembering the words of Mathew 6:13:

"Lead us not into temptation."

This verse reminds us that temptation is a natural part of life, but we must be mindful and resist the urge to succumb to its pull.

Looking back on my life, I realize I have come a long way from where I used to be. I grew up in a humble environment, but as soon as I made some money, I became consumed with the desire to impress others with my wealth. But I knew it reflected my low self-esteem. I was trying to find validation in all the wrong places. It's not just me, though. We all seek external validation in some form, whether through fame, wealth, or other means. Religious practitioners are often looked up to for guidance, yet even they fall into the trap of not seeking the strength within or inner strength.

Humility is often overlooked and undervalued in today's society. But as the proverb says, humility leads to wisdom.

"When pride comes, then comes disgrace, but with humility comes wisdom" — Proverbs 11:2

Humility has the power to transform our lives and those around us. Contrary to popular belief, humility is not weakness or meekness. Instead, it's a demonstration of *inner strength and control*. We become more open-minded, empathetic, and compassionate when we approach life humbly. It's a mindset that allows us to see the world more positively and encourages us to be better versions of ourselves.

Humility is a powerful and transformative concept that can

significantly impact our personal growth and relationships. It empowers us to adopt a positive outlook on the world while recognizing our limitations and growth potential. This self-awareness inspires us to *reflect on our actions* and strive for self-improvement.

During Palm Sunday, our priest posed an interesting question to our congregation:

"Why did Jesus choose a donkey?"

We all responded by saying that Jesus was a humble man. This got me thinking: Do the priests who lead us choose to live a simple life like Jesus, or do they prefer to reside in extravagant mansions, travel in posh cars, and wear fancy attire? I recall witnessing several bishops (I use priests and bishops interchangeably) sitting in the church and accusing the congregation of their luxurious lifestyles while enjoying the fruits of our labor. They would say, "you chose me, and you told me to live in a mansion, travel in luxury, or wear those fancy garments." Ironically, they blame the congregation for their choices while continuing to revel in luxury.

Let me bring a personal story:

When she was very young, my child told me, *"Daddy, you act like a victim."* I did not understand what she was saying, nor could she explain that to her father.

Years later, when I connected the dots, I understood the wisdom of my child:

When we victimize ourselves, we pass the threshold of taking ownership of our behavior or actions. The truth is that the problem lies within ourselves and our own behavior, not outside. We can move past our struggles and find true happiness by taking ownership of our actions and acknowledging our faults.

It's common to hear priests say, "we're here in this church for a few years, and everything we build is for you." While this sentiment may seem noble, the reality is that the parishioners often end up paying a hefty price for the priests' decisions. As a result, it falls upon us to clean up the mess left behind by those who served the church before us.

So, what exactly is this theological commitment or priesthood?

Have you ever wondered about the reasons why someone becomes a priest? Perhaps they can ask themselves the question,
"Why am I a priest?"

Some may follow in the footsteps of their family members, with a proud tradition of priesthood passed down through generations. Others may feel a strong *passion for leadership* and a deep *compassion* for others, driving them to pursue the calling of priesthood—a sense of divine or spiritual calling.

Being a leader means making a positive impact on people's lives while you are with them and ensuring that this impact lasts in your absence, prioritizing their growth and authenticity. Jesus Christ exemplified this as a "servant leader" (the Shepherd's way).

Our priests and bishops could ask themselves what impact they create while they serve a church and what legacy they create when they leave that church.

In a spiritual context, leadership is about leading with their hearts and being an example to the believers:

Leaders are like *shepherds (the shepherd's way)*; they lead from behind the flock, set boundaries for the flock, and create an environment conducive for the nimbler and agile to run ahead so that the others can follow and flourish.

It's fair to ask whether priests and bishops practice what they preach.

After all, they are the ones who are supposed to be leading by example in terms of living a humble and virtuous life.

Humility means acknowledging our shortcomings and weaknesses and striving to live a life that aligns with our values and beliefs.

INFORMATION IS NOT TRANSFORMATION

As Christians, we admire and respect the altar, the first thing we see when entering a church. The word altar comes from the Latin altārium and adores, which means 'high' and 'to ritually burn or sacrifice.' The altar is an essential aspect of a church and a vital part of church services.

The Bible mentions the first altar when Abraham arrived in Moreh. It is said that God reappeared to him, and he built an altar as an act of faith. This was the first altar that Abraham built as he began his journey of faith. During Liturgy, you can usually spot a Deacon assisting the priest around the altar. The term 'Deacon' means server, which perfectly describes their role in the church. They are always ready to lend a helping hand and ensure that everything runs smoothly during the service.

As Christians, we understand that the conduct of priests has a profound impact on our daily lives. The High Priesthood of Jesus Christ is one of the most sacred and glorious truths revealed to us in the Bible. We believe Christ is our priest, and the priesthood should reflect His character. As a result, we hold our priests in the highest regard and treat them with utmost reverence.

Imagine a situation where you look up to the priest as the most revered person, and he belittles that altar since his ego gets riled up, and he loses his calm and charm.

The situation reminded me of this verse:

"The Lord is merciful and gracious, slow to anger, abounding in mercy" — Psalm 103:8.

After I first immigrated to the US, I couldn't afford the membership fees for any permanent church. As a result, we only visited churches on certain Sundays. But when my daughter was born, I made it a priority to find a nearby church to take her to.

In 2002, I was following the church services, sitting with my four-year-old child. The Altar boys stumbled on some verses during the service. Instead of managing the situation calmly and composedly, the priest got upset with the altar boys. He then threw the Cross he was holding on the floor. It was the most shocking thing I had ever watched in a church by a priest. The truth is that this priest has been doing the priesthood for decades and even holds a Ph.D. in theology. Whether his Ph.D. and his work as a priest ever had meaningfully transformed his heart and character is up for debate.

Was he leading with passion and compassion? It was evident from his actions and words that he struggled with being kind and forgiving to himself—he lacked self-compassion.

Priests visiting homes is a custom in our Christian tradition. The new priest in my church visited our family in 2006 at our house in India. He was accompanied by a young man who was studying for the priesthood. I greeted him and introduced my family to the priest.

The first complaint from the priest was that I did not greet him at the door when he walked in. The priest claimed he attended Princeton Theological Seminary and was also a marriage counselor. As the discussion continued, he repeated a derogatory comment that someone had made about our family members. *I felt like I was being gaslit and triangulated by a priest and a marriage therapist.*

He then asked if he could bring the bishop to our house. As discussed earlier in the book, I engaged in some conspicuous consumption to impress people and built a bigger house than those around my neighborhood. I pondered the priest's request for a moment and recalled the story of Jesus riding on a donkey as a symbol of humility. I suggested to the priest, "instead of a mansion, why not suggest to the bishop to choose a smaller house? The priest was upset and walked out of my house. A few minutes later, the young man returned to my house and said, "The priest left his shoes." He returned to get his shoes. So, the priest could not handle my suggestion and walked out of my house barefoot.

We often put our priests on a pedestal and never question their practice because we're led to believe that it's a sin to do so and that we'll face damnation if we even dare to question them.

During the regular Sunday morning church service, a visiting priest from a nearby church lectured us on two concepts in the Bible: *Cross and Baptism.* To make the long story short, he told us a terrible story of a Priest by the name of Challan. Challan priest and our visiting priest lived in the same house in North India. One day, some Hindu activists were angry over the death of a Swamy or a Guru. Those activists attacked priests and destroyed churches in their neighborhood. They went to Challan priest's residence, pulled him out, threw him on the street, and brutally attacked him.

As I listened to the visiting priest's story, I couldn't help but feel stunned.

He revealed that Challan priest had been beaten up, but he himself had managed to hide by the Grace of God. It made me ponder over the significance of the cross and the true reflection of Jesus Christ's suffering.

Whose cross truly reflected the suffering of Jesus?

Was it the one worn by the Challan priest, who bravely stood up and took the beating, just like Jesus did, symbolizing unwavering faith and courage in the face of adversity?

Or

Was it the one worn by the fancy-dressed priest with the cross all

317

over it, who spent over an hour lecturing us about the cross and said he ran away with the cross like a hollow accessory devoid of any real meaning?

Ultimately, it is not what we wear that matters but how we carry ourselves in the face of life's challenges.

I have watched that priest sanctimoniously lecture us about the sacredness of the cross when he actually failed to lead by example and uphold the values he preached. Witnessing such a disconnect between words and actions was disheartening.

"Seek the truth, find Jesus, and walk the talk."

Truth cannot be inconsistent with the truth. There is only one truth: *The cross is the true suffering of Jesus Christ.* The same priest called the church a *"cathedral."*

To me, a cathedral is where I see my priests and bishops live in a humble place and wear simple dresses. It saddens me to witness priests and bishops living in such luxury when they should set an example of humility and simplicity.

The true essence of a cathedral or church lies in the community it serves and the values it upholds, not in the grandeur of its physical structure or the wealth of its religious leaders.

Does God live in a mansion? Jesus chose a donkey. Did priests or bishops stop us from building mansions? Instead of diverting that valuable resource into investing in meaningful actions like helping those poor and needy, we reserved that money for two mansions for priest and bishop.

"We have descended to this level of madness."

The vision of the church is to bring people together: people from all walks of life, regardless of race, gender, ethnicity, religious affiliation, sexual orientation, and cultural boundaries. Realizing that *vision* requires the *mission* of fulfilling our meaning and purpose in life: compassion for others—*being charitable, supporting and caring for those poor and needy, and making a meaningful positive difference in their lives.* For priests and bishops, this is a sacred vision and mission that requires both passion and compassion.

It is not about family tradition but about following a proud tradition of leadership and service to others.

The charity is yet another scheme to raise money for reforming the church—making the lives of priests better at our hardship and suffering.

One day, I got a message from our priest on my WhatsApp. It was heartbreaking to see that message. The message contained a picture of a distressed child whose face was filled with hopelessness. It was truly gut-wrenching to see. The church was using the starving children with hopeless faces to raise funds at a huge cost: learning that the charity was making money while the poor children were losing their dignity and voice was disheartening. The church essentially was exchanging money for pity. The sad truth is that the poor and those in need only get a fraction of what they raise, while the rest of the money goes to support the charity, paying salaries to the people who run it. It's often referred to as trickle-down economics. We even involve celebrities in charitable causes. So, much of the money raised goes towards paying the celebrities instead of directly benefiting those in need—making the celebrities richer and exploiting vulnerable communities or individuals.

The truth is that none in the church would be standing with an envelope in their hands if it wasn't for building mansions for the priests and for helping some disabled or unprivileged children since they are led to believe that those children don't know anything about Jesus. Priests do. It is also a validation-seeking exercise for those donors who stand in line with their envelopes. There are no spiritual dimensions to it.

The church cultivates the same mindset in our younger generation:

It is trendy to work for a non-profit or a Foundation. That is a fancy career for the new generation without realizing that they are draining resources in the form of salaries and other perks. Why don't they volunteer for a few hours for those Foundations and Non-profits? Spread the word of transformation by themselves and those who benefited from their efforts. That is probably the most effective way to raise money to alleviate hardships.

Ministers can benefit from this model, too. Instead of draining the church's resources through salaries and lavish accommodations, they could do some soul-searching and find ways to make a living doing what they really love instead of selling Jesus Christ—*when you do what you love, you are successful.* By volunteering as priests and supporting the church in meaningful ways, they can contribute to their community without taking away from it.

Priesthood is a calling to serve and guide others towards finding their inner peace, not to treat it as a mere job.

I believe that priests and bishops who merely pick a verse or two from the Bible and then fail to connect it with their own lives are not doing justice to their calling as priests. When one is able to make this connection successfully, it brings a sense of fulfillment to their work.

We all indeed have unique talents and abilities that we can use to make a living, but simply 'selling' Jesus Christ is not a skill that should be monetized or exploited.

.

I cannot be genuinely kind and compassionate to others until I am genuinely kind and compassionate to myself. For that, I need to experience challenges in life. It's often said that great individuals don't need to boast about their achievements or titles. Mother Teresa and Mahatma Gandhi are two examples of people who didn't feel the need to call themselves "Reverend" or constantly declare their greatness to the world.

In my culture, the older you get, the more revered you become. In that sense, "I am Rev. Shajan Ninan."

Becoming a source of hope for those around us requires a perspective on life that allows us to connect with those facing difficult times. It takes a special kind of person to maintain positivity in the face of challenges and to offer support to others as if they were going through the same struggles. While *empathy* is key, it is not enough to feel what others feel; it's important to remember that empathy is a two-way street—we must also learn to value and appreciate ourselves to make a positive impact in the world. By recognizing our worth, we can approach every interaction with others with strength and *compassion*.

I want to share a personal experience I had with COVID-19. I developed a severe sore throat, which made it incredibly painful to swallow even a drop of water, let alone speak. I had to resort to using hand gestures to communicate with others. Despite the pain I was going through, I decided to share my experience on my YouTube channel.

I had a shift in perspective that allowed me to move beyond my sufferings and be more compassionate towards others. It was humbling to realize that my hardships were nothing compared to those who struggled to breathe independently or receive proper care. Many are buried in a mass grave without their loved ones seeing their face for one last time.

Let me paraphrase what Adam Grant said in his podcast about giving: *if we continue to tell the stories of transformation from our giving, we, in fact, expand our network of givers. We then establish a pattern of reciprocity—shifting the reciprocity style of others and giving becomes contagious.*

Sadly, people who most exemplify the opposite of the Sermon on the Mount—the basic standard of Christian righteousness and purity of heart—are treated as rock stars or hailed as heroes.

We all believe Jesus Christ was crucified for telling the truth. I witnessed in the church that our priests and bishops are turning the church of the gospel into the kingdom of the emperors and turning the cross into the shield, sword, and armor of emperors. The cross represents the love, compassion, and sacrifice that Jesus embodied for all humanity. It symbolizes hope and redemption for those who are suffering and in need of salvation.

As a Christian, I look up to priests and bishops who have gone through hardships in their lives and gained the wisdom to help us navigate our sufferings. Those are my role models.

Just wearing the Cross on their chest does not make them the kind of person who can teach us the suffering of Jesus. I believe in the sufferings of Jesus, and our suffering on this planet is a Divine intervention or spiritual awakening to make us stronger and better human beings. This is my spirituality—the way I connect cosmology with theology.

It's fascinating to observe that, more often than not, we tend to emulate the behavior or *actions* of our religious leaders rather than simply taking their *words* at face value. This begs the question: which is more important in a spiritual context—*actions or words?* It's something that I've been pondering since the start of this chapter.

Interestingly, we often follow what our religious leaders do instead of what they say. It's a testament to the power of habit and how we learn from childhood—we are creatures of habit.

I've heard people of different generations say they follow priests because they know more about Jesus. But is this practicing spiritualism and humility, or is it more about materialism and hubris?

If they believe earning a degree in theology makes them the

incarnation of Jesus on earth, they should act like it. After all, their behavior outside of the church significantly impacts our personal, familial, and social lives. We see that every day:

So, do our 'actions' have power, or do 'words' have power?

The believers of Jesus look up to priests and bishops for their spiritual guidance.

"OUR FATHER"
SHOULD WE TREAT EVERYONE WITH THE SAME LEVEL OF RESPECT AND DIGNITY?

God created humanity in his image. It does not say men are superior to women. But we practice gender inequality right in the church.

During a Sunday service, the priest made an announcement that marked a significant moment in the church's history. The priest announced, "today is a historic day." What is the significance? Our bishop and the congregation approved a young lady to serve at the altar.

Let me get this clear:

The young lady needed permission from a bishop to exercise her God-given right to serve God. Why not? Our prominent prayer starts with "Our Father"—shall I say, the oppressive and abusive nature of 'our earthly fathers.'

I felt I was right about the patriarchal society I discussed in Chapter 6, "My Crusade to Educate My Child"—"*the rule of the father*"—while listening to the priest's 'historic day reference' about the young lady. The young lady, for no fault of her own, had to go through a series of selection processes before she could serve the same God who created all of us, including the bishop.

It is delusional to believe that men are better than women. After all, it was women who gave birth to men, not the other way around. And we celebrate Mother's Day too. The purpose of this celebration is not merely to show a semblance of respect for women but to honor the remarkable women who gave birth and raised us into who we are today.

The truth is that there is "NO LIFE" on this planet without women. The church gives us every reason to deny women's fundamental human rights. There are no greater evil forces or obstacles to empowering women and girls than our religion. It is morally reprehensible and spiritually barbaric. We see the same discriminatory and myogenic practices in other religions, too.

"THE ENVELOPE"—DOES GOD NEED OUR MONEY?

"The love of money is the root of all evil."
Not the money, but the love of money.

The truth is that money is needed to carry out the mission of the Church—attenuate human suffering. But the Church's primary mission is the salvation of souls—to help believers attain the heavenly kingdom.

I am not suggesting that diocesan priests and bishops should take a vow of poverty. I wholeheartedly believe that priests and bishops should make a living if they devote their lives to the betterment of humanity. But we pay a higher price for their service:

They seize on our suffering and prey on us—raise money on our hardship. It is the lip service to the Bible—sanctity in the Church and sanctimony outside the Church. And parsimonious when it comes to helping the poor and those in need while living in a million-dollar parsonage. Whether they live in a mud house or mansion or earn $1 or $100,000, they have a commitment to the priesthood, which is lifting people out of their emotional suffering and supporting those in need. However, their focus on financial gain overshadows the Church's social and spiritual value.

Every Sunday, we have a beautiful tradition in our Church. As we gather to celebrate our faith, we take a moment to honor those celebrating their birthday that week. The priests ask those celebrating their birthdays to come forward for a thanksgiving prayer. Those celebrating birthdays walk forward with 'the envelope' in their hands. The priest takes the envelope with money and then prays for them— *the first order of business.*

What exactly do these believers think while they walk forward with the envelope in their hands, especially children?

They need to pay money to God to get the blessings—denigrating God and creating a conditional relationship with God right in the Church. God does not need our money.

Often, I hear from our church members that 'none is forced to give money to the church.' That is a very clever and brilliant statement—tapping into human insecurity.

Let us say the children celebrating their birthdays walk in front of the Church without the 'envelope' in their hands. Then, the rest of the people think those children are poor, and their parents face financial hardships. It becomes a shameful thing for the parents. So, we don't let our children walk forward without that 'envelope' in their hands. The conditional relationship we instill in a child can negatively impact that child's self-esteem from an early age.

Remind ourselves that the Church's mission is to foster the spirit of kindness and compassion rather than making our relationship with God conditional. Allowing children to participate in the prayer without the pressure to bring an envelope can help establish a sense of security and uniqueness. Rather than enforcing this tradition, it may be better to give children or adults the choice of whether or not they want to contribute financially and eliminate the shame linked with not having an envelope.

The second order of business is offertory. When it comes to me, I pass that offering bag to the next person who is flashing his $10 or $20 bill while I flash my empty hand. I believe if I put a dime into that offering bag, I am denigrating my omnipotent God. God doesn't need our money, but the priests and bishops do.

One day, I was listening to a message from the bishop about how our families and children suffer from separation, divorce, loneliness, depression, or other emotional hardships. The Church was organizing a 'family fellowship' to deal with our pain and suffering. At first, I felt that was a great message. Then the message stated, *"We have sent envelopes."* I was confused about what this 'envelope' had to do with the family fellowship. There was no cost associated with attending the Church or listening to the bishop or priests. Everything was fully paid for.

Believe it or not, there has a lot to do with this 'envelope'—yet another brilliant scheme to monetize our hardships. *Often, our priests say, "God loves us unconditionally, but bring the money—the envelope." Is that an unconditional relationship with God?*

We have family problems because we have a conditional relationship with our family members—*the love of money ("count the money, not the blessing").* The Church does a masterful job of instilling *a transactional mindset in* us from a young age and now capitalizing on it. It is hard to fathom that such a great message about family fellowship had to be marred by *"the love of money."*

A PARADIGM SHIFT IN OUR WAY OF THINKING: SECULAR RELIGION

Thomas Kuhn invented the phrase 'paradigm shift,' derived from the Greek for 'pattern' or 'paradigm.' I find the following paradigm shift definition quite apt to explain our current religious tradition:

"An important change happens when a new and different way replaces the usual way of thinking about or doing something. A crossover hit."[30]

---

[30] This is an excerpt from "Robert Fulford's column about the word "paradigm"" (Globe and Mail, June 5, 1999)

Start thinking differently from our old way of thinking—the inevitable progress toward truth. We're observing a worldwide shift towards a more unified cultural identity, a secular religion, that emphasizes every person's inherent worth and value, regardless of their background. This movement isn't about promoting a particular ideology or belief system but rather about acknowledging the universal truth that we are all human beings connected by a shared humanity. By embracing this truth and striving for greater understanding and empathy towards each other, we can cultivate a brighter and more harmonious future for all.

Today, the new generation is embracing this movement rather rapidly:

They have an intense desire to live in harmony rather than subscribing to ideologies or religious dogmas. Scholars who claim to possess divine power instilled this desire in them while referring to God as omnipotent and omniscient. These scholars are capitalizing on our fear of death, a brilliant scheme to enrich themselves.

I watch this emerging trend nationwide—dwindling participation in churches. I struggle with traditional Christian teachings as they often seem to contradict the truth found in the Bible. As someone who values individuality and diversity, I find it challenging to align with teachings that promote conformity and strict adherence to dogma. The real question we should ask ourselves is,

"How do we honor people's uniqueness and not be beholden to dogmas?"

The younger generation often looks up to priests as role models who can guide them toward finding peace within themselves. It can be discouraging, however, when those who are supposed to lead by example seem to be more concerned with putting on a facade of holiness than actually practicing what they preach. Priests must be authentic in their *beliefs and actions* to inspire and guide others toward their *inner peace* (the kingdom of God is within us).

Leon Festinger pointed out that cognitive dissonance can cause a significant disconnect between individuals' beliefs, convictions, emotions, and observable actions. It's not uncommon for people to hold onto beliefs contradicting the truth or basic common sense, even if it goes against who they are. Sadly, priests often struggle to rethink these beliefs and become trapped in a cycle of cognitive dissonance. It's crucial to believe in things they preach to manifest positive outcomes, or else their words become meaningless, and actions become hypocritical.

There's no doubt that just any human being, priests are capable of immense goodness, but it's not always evident to them. Despite teaching that God's kingdom is within us, their actions don't always reflect this belief. Witnessing such a vast amount of cognitive dissonance in them is utterly disheartening—they don't seem to embrace their teachings fully. Yet, we entrust them with our deepest confessions.

When I listen to a 15-minute scripted message from a priest, I often hear him emphasize the need for "reform." But what does this reform actually mean?

In academic circles, *reform* can be referred to as "theories or what causes what and why." In Chapter 10 (see pages 183-186), I delved into one such theory, *disruptive innovation*, which illuminates the factors that drive market transformations and their consequences. This concept can also be applied to our spiritual journeys to help us understand *why our faith is going through a period of disruption.*

As I was explaining the theory, I shared an analogy that I found quite fascinating. I talked about how *sustaining innovation* in the computer industry involves improving good computers for the same customers, ultimately leading to a high profit margin. Interestingly, this concept can be applied in different contexts, including our church community. In the context of the church, it is called *"reformation,"* where we strive to improve the lives of the same priests and bishops at high costs. It's like turning the *"cathedral into an edifice complex."*

It's fascinating to think about the disruptors who shook up the market by starting from the bottom and working their way to the top. By bringing affordable computers to the masses, the disruptors transformed the way we communicate and connect. Sadly, the incumbents already at the top of the market ignored the disruption happening at the bottom and focused only on short-term profits—*the short-term pleasure.*

What does this theory have to do with our church?

Our faith is being disrupted.

The digital age has unequivocally uncovered the hypocritically pious practices of our traditional religious structures, leaving no room for doubt. It is clear that there is growing interest in spiritual practices

331

and self-improvement, as evidenced by the rise of gurus and monks offering online meditation practices, psychologists earning PhDs in self-compassion and mindfulness meditation practices, and quantum physicists turning into meditation trainers. Even universities offer free courses on the science of happiness that attract thousands of students. All of these beg the question:

What is the message of our traditional religious practices?

Perhaps it's time for a serious course correction to *rethink our way of thinking* and address the suffering that our children are experiencing.

As someone who has grown up in the church, I can attest that religious practices are increasingly becoming a brainwashing technique that detours us from seeking happiness within ourselves or getting closer to our minds and glorifying ourselves (self-compassion).

I believe that God created us as valuable beings in the universe. I find that spiritual practices offer a way to connect with and explore the depths of our minds. Additionally, spirituality provides a sense of inner peace and fulfillment that cannot be achieved through material possessions or external validation. Spirituality is about recognizing the interconnectedness of all things and finding meaning in life. Religion should not misuse or misinterpret spiritual teachings to justify hateful or harmful behavior, as this is not the essence of spirituality itself. It is vital to approach any belief system with an open mind and critical thinking and be mindful of how it is practiced and applied in one's life.

NEGATIVE IMPACTS OF RELIGIOUS BELIEFS ON COLLEGE CAMPUSES

College campuses should be places of learning, growth, and inclusivity. Unfortunately, college campuses have become breeding grounds for religion-based hatred and animosity in recent years. This behavior runs counter to the values of diversity and inclusivity that must be upheld in any educational institution. Promoting tolerance and understanding can create a harmonious and welcoming community that celebrates diversity and fosters mutual respect.

According to neuroscience, children are more vulnerable to negative societal influences. They are easily shaped by the media, religious institutions, elites in society, and politicians who prioritize their self-interests. These entities instill hatred and violence, capitalize on this behavior, fueling the fire, and rile up negative emotions. These intense negative emotions drain their valuable cognitive resources and lead them to destructive behavior.

Instead of vilifying each other, college campuses should be a unified force for peace.

Students holding different flags or beliefs should sit together and encourage unity rather than stand on opposite sides and fight. This would signal to the world that these students need peace, not the destruction of humanity in the name of religion or territorial disputes. Parents can play a significant role in instilling empathy and compassion, but they, too, are conditioned by their environment. Creating a society that values peace requires individual transformation. This inspires others to follow suit, creating a ripple effect that can lead to a more harmonious society.

It is indisputable that humans are the only species of primates plagued by existential worries. Religion is a human construct. Religious institutions often prey on our fear of death and create the concept of heaven to assuage our fears. The *religious* practices we believe will lead us to heaven are causing more harm than good. Instead of fostering love and compassion, our pursuit of salvation breeds hatred and animosity towards those who don't share our beliefs.

Consequently, we are witnessing the suffering of innocent men, women, children, and even babies, all in the name of religious traditions. The kingdom of God resides within us. The journey towards self-love and inner peace is intrinsically rewarding and radiates positivity around us.

Observing the profound impact of misguided beliefs on our world is devastating, perpetuating immense suffering that could be avoided with greater awareness.

It's high time to rethink our approach to religion, break free from the chains of religious dogma, and embrace a compassionate approach that prioritizes human life above all else.

Effective leadership that can shape college and university students' thoughts and emotions is crucial. Without guidance from such leaders, students will struggle to navigate the complexities of campus life and in reaching their full potential. Therefore, educational institutions must prioritize the development of leaders who possess *self-awareness* and courage to guide and inspire their students.

DISRUPT OUR ESTABLISHED NEURAL PATHWAYS AND RETHINK

The universe God created is uncertain, and we don't know much about its existence. That inward flow of conscious awareness can give us a compassionate view of humanity. By challenging our beliefs, neuroplasticity allows us to rewrite deeply ingrained belief systems, even those rooted in religion, and bring about a fundamental shift in our way of thinking. Why not use a bit of our cognitive resources and question the practice of worshiping at the altar of priests, bishops, and pastors? By doing so, we can develop greater mental flexibility and agility while also ensuring that the beliefs we hold dear are based on our own values and convictions rather than the opinions of others.

What we need in the world today is a desire to promote one's religion peacefully rather than promoting fake salvation and eternal life by building hatred and animosity—being defenders of God. The omnipotent God does not need our money, praise, worship, or defending.

"Spirituality is about individual transformation."

We are all created as equals regardless of our religious traditions. Embracing this truth is the only way to find lasting peace and contentment within ourselves and the world around us—*the transformation*. So, reach out and seize true happiness. What is on the inside counts. Unless we transform ourselves, humanity will continue to suffer.

OUR YOUTH IN THE CHURCH—"CONDITIONED, CURATED, AND INDOCTRINATED"

Preaching our young generation that one denomination is spiritually and morally superior to other denominations or religious traditions only instills hatred and anger toward those who believe differently. Our younger generation needs to be taught 'how to think' and not just within the confines of one particular framework or religious ideology. This will help them develop a growth mindset, leading to a stronger sense of self-esteem and self-worth.

One day, I was walking into the Divine service conducted by our youths and saw this amazing caption, *"Seek the truth, find Jesus,"* on the walls. What exactly did our youths have in their minds when they coined these beautiful words? Did they seek the truth and find Jesus? The one hour I spent listening to their beautiful songs and inspiring messages was a mindful moment. These are talented and beautiful creations of God.

At the end of the service, they handed out index cards and asked us to write our names so they could pray for us.

Today, I am praying for them. They are gone from the church or no longer interested in worshiping together with the older generation.

Do you think priests and bishops can realign their mindset with the teachings of the Bible? It could be difficult as they may resist changing their perspective, and it requires a great deal of "self-awareness" and effort to rewire their established neural pathways.

Referring to the theory of *disruptive innovation*, business units don't evolve, but corporations do evolve. Likewise, populations evolve, but individuals don't.

We may not be able to change our current culture or tradition, but we can create a new subculture—and shape the younger generation for a brighter future.

Unless we reflect on our way of thinking in terms of "what causes what and why or why do we suffer," we are doomed; I, for one, believe it is a matter of time before our *'edifice complex, aka cathedral'* will be a *'historical monument'* if we continue to practice *reformation.*

"We are being disrupted."

We must empower the youth with a strong sense of value and worth, for they are the very foundation of our society, church, and country. To achieve this, the church can play a vital role by providing various means to help build their true selves.

Here are a few ideas:

Your Authentic Self

- **Build and maintain a "vital group"**—a spiritual community that can help you spot your blind spots and work towards a better version of yourself.
- **Cultivate social capital:** create podcasts with a *"care for our minds, compassion for others"* theme. Let social media become the platform for inspiring and transforming the lives of many. Use it to savor your experiences and build your brand.
- **Engage actively:** meet weekly, seek and give authentic feedback, share ideas, brainstorm together, and support one another in good and bad times.
- **Transform communities—scale the happiness:** By combining business acumen with a mission-driven approach, social entrepreneurs can create sustainable and scalable solutions that address pressing social and environmental challenges. As the saying goes, "Give a man a fish, and you feed him for a day (*charity*). Teach a man to fish, and you feed him for a lifetime (*compassion*)." This philosophy lies at the heart of social entrepreneurship, emphasizing empowering individuals and communities to create lasting change.
- **Ministry work is empathetic, not compassionate.** It is <u>not</u> a sustainable solution to transform communities. Yes, we need to care for the sick, feed the hungry, and support the poor. But ask, *"what causes what and why."* Address *the cause*, not *the symptoms."*
- **Practice mindfulness meditation together**—find your inner peace.

While walking out after the church service, a fellow member asked me why my daughter left the church choir. I told him, *"Already, most of the youths and her friends left the choir or church altogether, so what difference does my daughter make in the choir or church."*

Today, our younger generation prefers to keep their distance from the older generation, especially from their parents. It's truly disheartening to witness the difficulties they face today. Many are grappling with confusion and uncertainty when it comes to religious practices. We must start asking the tough questions and having meaningful discussions about what causes these struggles and how we can help our youth navigate these challenges. A new secular religion or cultural identity is taking shape in other traditions like Hinduism. I wholeheartedly agree with the assertion by Dr. Tharoor in his book "The Hindu Way."

Let me quote him:

"Hindu legends have the gods manifesting themselves in so many shapes and forms that the notion of one agreed image of God would be preposterous."

We see the same indoctrination in the Christian tradition. They pick and choose verses in the Bible that suit their narratives, form different denominations, and build hatred among themselves.

It's somewhat disheartening to witness how the priesthood has transformed into a mere "act of lip service," with people using the Bible to serve their own interests instead of seeking the truth and exploring their inner selves. This disconnect between preaching and practice causes suffering for priests who cannot find true happiness and their followers who look up to them for spiritual guidance.

To my mind, religious institutions should be places for healing our minds rather than places for building wealth for those who indoctrinate humanity and spread hatred.

It is hard to ignore the fact that when the livelihoods of priests are dependent on selling Jesus Christ, there is not much room for rethinking. As long as we keep getting that dopamine rush from our short-term pleasure and good life, we'll keep supporting the existing religious practices. However, once that dopamine rush wears off, our emotions start to flare up, and our behavior can become toxic. I can attest to this from personal experience.

It is crucial to approach religion with an open and skeptical mind because it inspires us to go beyond conformity and investigate the profound depths of our beliefs. The interdependence of all beings as products of the same divine source must also be understood. This understanding can direct our religious practices and rituals in a way that fosters our own personal development, harmony, and spirituality.

When we embrace a spiritually inclusive perspective, we nurture our ability to empathize with others, show compassion towards others, and cultivate a deep respect for diverse viewpoints. By doing this, we help create a more peaceful and loving environment that captures the very heart of our spirituality.

Chapter 17

A Marriage Made in Hell

"Experience is not what happens to a man; it is what a man does with what happens to him."

– Aldous Huxley

"Genuine love in a relationship is not about what one brings for the other but what both partners can do to bring out the best in each other. It's about mutual growth and support, not material possessions or superficial gestures."

Family is not some moment in your life. 'Moving on' is an incurable and fatal moment in life, negating the moral fabric of a family and society. A healthy relationship is built on mutual respect, trust, and a desire to grow and improve together. To me, family is a steadfast pillar of support in all my ups and downs.

While raising a family can bring immense joy and reward, it can also be a significant source of stress. This constant stress can lead to severe mental and emotional challenges that can be hard to deal with.

I often say,

"The problem is within, not outside."

We can better navigate difficult family situations by focusing on our mental and emotional well-being. For me, that person or that relationship is presenting me with an opportunity to bring my mind to the present moment—learn to meet that difficult situation with a relaxed mind. I am not being a doormat or passive or getting abused by that person but rather building compassion for that person. I try not to get wound up by any triggers. I give that person some space and watch the situation. In the process, I create a space between that trigger and my response or reaction, enabling me to be in a state of meta-cognition or flow state.

Ultimately, our actions and decisions should always be guided by our values. They act as our guiding principles, influencing our decisions, actions, and, eventually, the course of our lives. So, it's paramount to ensure that we surround ourselves with individuals who appreciate and value us for *"who we are,"* not for what we have achieved, how we look, or what we can bring for them.

David McClelland, a Harvard social psychologist, said that as much as 95% of our success or failure depends on who we habitually associate ourselves with. I agree with him 100%.

Humans are renowned for being creatures of habit. Routines and well-known patterns frequently affect our lives and provide us with a sense of security and predictability. These routines, whether brief daily rituals or ingrained behaviors, significantly impact how we conduct our lives and how we feel all around.

One interesting topic I've encountered is the correlation between divorce rates and our social circle.

According to social science studies, if we surround ourselves with friends who have gone through a divorce, we're more likely to experience one ourselves. This has always made me wonder what the root *cause* of this phenomenon might be (*correlation is not causation*). Surprisingly, quantum science could offer some insights. The theory suggests that our thoughts and emotions directly impact the energy surrounding us and that this energy can affect the outcomes of our lives—the wave function—our thoughts and emotions are constantly moving (Chapter 14, pages 245-249). Specifically, we succumb to external triggers and fail to see the value in our relationship. We can *save some cognitive resources* by *not rethinking*—it is easier to *conform* than to *question our practice*. After all, it takes more effort to rethink and actively work on building a loving and compassionate relationship than to go along with the majority or crowd or masses.

We resonate emotionally with those in our immediate surroundings. It's important to be mindful of the company we keep.

As humans, it's common for us to compare ourselves to others and seek validation. However, this can be more harmful than helpful, especially regarding marriage. Constantly measuring our marriage against others can be detrimental to its health. The environments we find ourselves in shape our thoughts and emotions, and the social norms we encounter become our reality. Whether it's our family, friends, or even co-workers, we often pick up on their moods and energy levels, which can profoundly impact our own emotional state.

By cultivating positive energy and fostering healthy relationships, we can protect ourselves from external negative influences and build a stronger foundation for lasting love and happiness. Instead of focusing on how our marriage stacks up to others in terms of *our material possessions*, it's crucial to prioritize our *inner sense of contentment* and work towards strengthening our relationship for a happier life (discussed in Chapter 14, Four Pillars of Happiness).

One of my favorite stories related to marriage is about a young lady who is a connection on my LinkedIn. While responding to my interest in cooking, she said, "I will marry someone *again* and love that person unconditionally if he cooks for me."

This is precisely what I hear from priests every Sunday in the church:

"God loves us unconditionally, but bring the envelope."

After reading her message, I asked myself, *"Does she understand the meaning of unconditional love?"* I wondered, "what if that cook stops cooking for her?" Then the question becomes, "what are you doing for me now?" Giving someone a good life often does not translate into emotional intimacy or attachment; rather, it cultivates financial intimacy and a conditional relationship—the love is ephemeral.

When I hear someone say, *"I love you,"* I always ask them what *love* means to them. The *love* we often hear is conditional and momentary; however, true love comes from loving and accepting ourselves for who we truly are, and that love radiates outwards to others unconditionally. Unconditional love is profound, long-lasting, and emotionally fulfilling.

I'm curious to know your thoughts on *"love."*

Is there any difference between a love marriage and an arranged marriage?

There isn't any difference if we truly understand the meaning of love. The Bible teaches that marriage is the union of two bodies and minds, where the two become one flesh. This unity and desire to care for each other strengthens the bond, regardless of whether it's a love or an arranged marriage.

Therefore, the key to a prosperous marriage is not how it commences but how both partners consistently cultivate and enhance their love for each other over time.

THE POWER OF EMOTIONAL INDEPENDENCE

I genuinely believe that building the *right culture* is key to any successful relationship. This means fostering an environment of sharing credit, active listening, genuine care, and a willingness to accept constructive criticism. It is the collective effort of everyone involved that makes a relationship work. On the other hand, if we ignore these basic principles, we risk creating a dysfunctional environment that breeds a transactional or conditional relationship rather than a true partnership.

I constantly warn my child of the danger of building unhealthy relationships and the emotional toll that comes with it. I was trying to help her navigate relationships with people.

I recently sent a lengthy email to my child about human

conditions. I needed to express my thoughts and help her understand the complexities of being human and the influence of our environment on our behavior: our emotional health and long-term enjoyment depend on developing emotional independence from a young age. It gives us the ability to handle the ups and downs of life with resiliency and cultivate a sense of emotional stability.

We become vulnerable when we succumb to the servitudes of people around us, especially the ones who exhibit malignant narcissistic/psychopathic traits—the selfish-takers:

They are toxic, emotionally impaired, and master manipulators with unabashed pathological mendacity—lie with a straight face with no shame or fear of consequences. These individuals are great actors—able to switch personas and show different emotions depending on the situation. They will go to any length and engage in manipulative strategies—gaslight and triangulate—to damage your credibility and destroy whatever strength you possess. They gravitate towards people who can serve their needs or make them *"look good."* When you stop fulfilling their demands, they will tell you that you are not looking good enough, rich enough, beautiful enough, or you are a "worthless soul." You become a human dumping ground to unburden their deeply buried emotions, which they may not be willing to admit, take ownership of, or even be aware of consciously. *They are stubbornly resistant to taking the time and space to be self-aware.* They would rather blame you for their misery and suffering and treat you like a doormat.

You can do everything to please them to keep the peace, but you are doomed. Your kindness and compassion will be construed as weak.

As I see it, those narcissistic traits expose one's deeply hidden emotions. I have built genuine compassion for them as they are inherently beautiful within. But they don't see that beauty within. There are no liars, cheaters, weak or bad people in my world. They are conditioned to misbehave, be weak, toxic, cheat, manipulate, triangulate, gaslight, and lie. They follow a misconstrued version of spirituality from their priests, pastors, and bishops.

When dealing with individuals exhibiting malignant narcissistic traits or disorders, it's essential to recognize that conflict with them will not lead to a successful outcome. I have noticed that conflicts and challenges often arise within families. It is painful to navigate those situations when those closest to us become our *"staunchest adversaries."* These people are known for being dirty fighters, and engaging in a battle with them is rarely productive. While it's important to acknowledge their inherent worth as creations of God, it's also crucial to understand that their behavior is often a result of their upbringing and environment. Instead of fighting with them, it's best to set clear boundaries and refuse to be subservient to them.

Have compassion for those who hurt, harm, or wind you up. Sustainable happiness is something that we cultivate within. That requires self-awareness.

Lately, this famous quote by the stoic philosopher *Marcus Aurelius* positively influenced my emotions:

"The best revenge is to be unlike the one who performed the injustice. The best revenge is exact no revenge at all".

Translation: "Take the high road and love them for who they are."

In his book "Think Again," Adam Grant explained the concept of "givers and takers." By reinforcing and rewarding narcissistic/psychopathic behavior, you become less generous—you are not resourceful enough to be a selfless giver. Since you consume all your energy satisfying the taker's need or want, you will have no energy to take care of yourself; *the cup slowly becomes empty*. That prevents you from helping people who pay it back and pay it forward.

You cannot sustain giving for long without self-compassion—you get burned out. Love yourself. It is madness to continue to please people with narcissistic/psychopathic traits and allow that non-

reciprocal behavior to take a toll on your life. Doing so only sabotages your self-confidence and self-worth.

Learn from your pain and suffering and build a healthy mind while narcissists battle their demons within for the rest of their lives. You have no control over them. They always operate from a "what is in it for me or what are you doing for me now" perspective. It's perplexing why they feel entitled to such treatment. They are often quick to point out what you haven't done for them without taking the time to appreciate the things you have done. Humans are conditioned to be fixated on finding fault with others instead of looking at their own behavior and how they could improve.

They do not see their inner world because their happiness is externally driven, not intrinsic. The concept of self-love is foreign to them—they operate from a self-centered perspective.

We all make mistakes. However, it's not the mistakes themselves that are the real mistakes, but rather our failure to learn from them. I learned a valuable lesson from my emotional outbursts and how they impact those around me. I was offended by the behavior of others and reacted in a way that I now realize was not helpful in bringing peace. Upon reflection, I realized that I am also guilty of my conduct, and this perspective allowed me to be more compassionate towards others. I made a conscious decision to regulate my emotions and take the time to listen to the feelings of those around me.

Love is an invaluable aspect of life that I hold dear to my heart. It is a profound feeling that I bestow on others because I see their worth. Nevertheless, stepping back and assessing the situation is crucial if the same value is not reciprocated. I firmly believe that when love is based on one's income, name, looks, or fame, it becomes conditional love and goes beyond the boundaries of the values I cherish.

The idea of reciprocity, especially emotional reciprocity, in relationships has become outdated. In my case, I tend to command and demand attention in my relationship with people, and facing rejection was a mortifying experience. Looking back, I realize now that I was quite naive. I failed to comprehend the complexities and nuances of human nature fully. I have learned rather painfully that outsourcing my happiness to my family is a disempowering and debilitating experience.

I began my book by delving into Jesus's *suffering*, exploring the depths of his pain and the lessons we can *learn* from it. In a relationship, life can take you to the lowest depths of your emotional wounds or the highest peaks of your values. Those emotional wounds are your *lessons*, and learning from those lessons is your *blessing*.

It can be emotionally exhausting and even depressing when someone places a higher value on money than on their partner's inherent worth. I believe a person's worth is much more than their wealth, and I tend to avoid those who prioritize transactional value over their partner's true value and worth. Such a partnership lacks depth and meaning.

I believe we are all 'valuable' creations of God, not 'worthless' creatures.

Once someone crosses the boundaries of love and respect for a human being, it becomes a toxic environment; fighting only builds up our cortisol and makes us weak and depressed. Just flee. *"Take the high road and love them from a distance."* Pick the nobler fight, keeping affection intact while maintaining a healthy distance as required.

My family has been my "lesson and blessing." They are an exquisite creation of the Almighty—a testament to the power and love of our Creator. I am grateful for all the difficult times because those experiences created a fertile ground for self-discovery and personal growth. Building successful relationships requires dedication, compassion, and a shared commitment. Material well-being only brings short-term pleasure. Each of us has to take responsibility for cultivating our happiness. Find the peace within—we already have it.

THE "YOLO" WORLD

"Families that prioritize unconditional love, support, and care represent the epitome of success."

"Count the blessings, not the money"—contrary to what we hear from our priests. Just as I witness the conditional relationship with God in the church, I have noticed the same in many relationships— *money is what unites and separates a relationship.*

I tell this funny story to students to humanize the *time value of money* concept:

A beautiful young lady told a man she would only marry a rich man. The man told her, "Beauty is a depreciating asset; money is an appreciating asset. Money has time value"—money earns interest and interest on interest.

How much do you sell a great relationship for?

No amount of money can replace the priceless value of a cherished relationship.

Over the years, I have listened to a few well-educated, married women from my community living in the US. Those are my connections on Facebook.

Three things I had noticed from their conversation with me:

—They all face the same crisis: *The middle-age crisis. Women become much more sensitive to their looks in their mid-thirties.*

—They all have the same problem: *Their husbands are no longer romantic enough for them. By that, I mean not holding their hands and walking on the beach. They just realized that.*

—They all have the same request: *"Can you wait until my children reach college age?"*

"The primary reason for divorce or separation is often rooted in feelings of contempt or the belief that one's partner is utterly 'worthless' rather than anger."

According to therapists, feelings of contempt for one's partner are utterly corrosive and, like rust, slowly but steadily eat away at any foundation of love that may have existed. That contemptuous disregard is a clear sign of hatred towards one's partner, and the partnership is likely to crumble under the weight of such hatred.

Here is a story of YOLO life:

When I was growing up in my village, I met this beautiful young lady who caught my attention. I truly appreciated God's creation. We became family friends, and she would visit me after attending church services in a church next to my house. We corresponded by mail while she was in college but never had a romantic relationship. After I married, she visited me and my wife, and I introduced her as my family friend. We met occasionally in the church, but since I moved to the US, we lost touch and haven't spoken in 15 years.

In 2009, she sent me a message on Facebook and requested to connect. Before accepting her request, I discussed it with my wife and daughter. My wife had no issues, but my daughter advised me not to connect with her. It turned out that my 11-year-old daughter had far more wisdom than the combined wisdom of her parents. My intention was simply to add her as another friend on my Facebook. However, she interpreted the connection differently. She confided in me that she was experiencing a "middle-aged crisis" and later disclosed that her relationship with her husband was rocky. Yes, moving on to something more pleasurable is not forbidden in our Christian tradition. In chapter 10, I discussed "Why Success is Hard to Sustain"—the peril of seeking short-term pleasure (see pages 200-202). Things initially seemed casual. But over time, she became more demanding. It became emotionally exhausting, and I eventually realized I had to end the friendship. It wasn't a happy ending.

I was astounded to hear why they all changed their heart toward their marriage. The answer I heard was, *"You Only Live Once."*

They are incentivized to do so: *praise the Lord.*

Jesus Christ is our savior and redeemer: the once-for-all sacrifices of Jesus on the Calvary absolve our sins. Ask for God's forgiveness and take the 'wine and cracker.' The church gives us every reason to practice immorality and intolerance.

What good is this practice if we don't change our behavior?

In my mind, everything we religiously practice in the church leads us into damnation, not salvation.

If marriage is made in heaven, we don't need Holy Communion.

Nowadays, weddings seem to have lost their true essence. They have become more about the show, the glitz, and the glamour rather than the sacred bond of love and commitment. Couples and their families spend months of meticulous planning: carefully choreographed parades in the church and ceremonies, which religious officials often conduct. It's worth noting that these grandiose ceremonies don't always guarantee a happy and fulfilling marriage. Often, the lack of true love results in suffering for spouses and their families. Perhaps if true love is made in heaven, we don't need all the material trappings and formalities that often accompany modern weddings.

It is the YOLO world we live in.

It is like saying,

"Family life was just some moments in my life. I can leave behind all those and move on to something new and wonderful."

Recently, I was invited to the wedding of one of the artists in my

354

short movie. I couldn't attend his wedding. However, I did impart some crucial advice to him as he embarked on his new ambitious adventure called *'marriage.'*

I told him,

"Be prepared for a divorce before you get married."

Nowadays, relationships are often viewed as transactions or like a "merger of equals or 50-50." The true meaning of a relationship has become nothing more than an emergency contact. No matter how perfect we think our life or relationship is, it is a matter of time before everything falls apart—a perfect body gets decayed, a perfect appearance gets ruined, beauty fades away, jobs or lifestyles change, and so goes love.

A successful marriage is not devoid of problems. So, it is a pursuit of self-examination, willingness to confront tensions head-on, and navigating through the tensions with calm and composure. I would say a bit of emotional intelligence goes a long way in fixing many conflicts or resentments in a relationship. And that often means paying attention and listening to each other's feelings without making any judgment. It is of utmost importance for partners' emotions and experiences to be acknowledged and respected without being disregarded or invalidated. This way, we can create a fair and just environment by promoting a culture of inclusivity, empathy, and compassion.

Usually, a rarely practiced and widely ignored human expression is silence.

Our silence under challenging situations is a powerful weapon to deter negative emotions, understand situations better, and bring peace and tranquility to our lives. The attitude that "I alone can fix it" is not flawless. Rather, fixing a problem is the collective effort of both parties. *Also, practice emotional independence.*

Our dependence on emotional support often destroys our sanity, and we stop caring for ourselves. It is like we are addicted or attached to something. We feel that emptiness within. Those destructive thoughts are like drinking poison. Our cognitive resources steadily become depleted by our negative thoughts, making it challenging for us to think clearly. Our brains prefer simplicity because it helps conserve energy. Humans possess a finite amount of cognitive capacity.

Often, we are in denial—a type of defensive mechanism. We refuse to acknowledge the realities of a situation to avoid painful emotions or anxiety. In the long run, approaching life from a place of denial and resistance can manifest in violence, depression, anxiety, suicide, etc. We all face the same situation in our relationships.

We must reflect on our past with some humility: have the courage to accept the shame and guilt that came with our decisions, the sufferings we endured, and the hardships we inflicted on others. Wearing our weaknesses openly can help us move forward with self-compassion and compassion for others.

Life becomes joyful when we realize everyone experiences shame, guilt, and suffering, and we learn to find humor in our world. Knowing this can alleviate the emotional burden. Embracing our vulnerabilities can lead to happiness in the present. So, let's **LAUGH** at ourselves and our situations and enjoy life's journey.

STOP OUTSOURCING YOUR HAPPINESS

I have realized that looking for happiness from external sources is often futile. Although searching for love and happiness externally may be tempting, it is ultimately an illusion that cannot be sustained.

As I was riding the train home from a long day of lectures at the university, I stumbled upon a video of a young lady who faced overwhelming challenges in her life. Despite the adversity, she chose to focus on the positive aspects and encouraged others to do the same. It was a powerful reminder that even during the most challenging times, a glimmer of hope is always waiting to be discovered.

Sitting there, I couldn't help but think, "I have everything I need for a happy life, yet why do I still suffer?" *To achieve happiness, I needed to adopt a different perspective:* I have discovered the beauty of seeking inner peace and happiness through moments of solitude. I have realized that waiting for happiness is not enough, but actively pursuing it is key. I have stayed focused and grounded by managing my thoughts, time, and energy through meditation, healthy eating, exercise, and clear thinking. My alone time is now a personal retreat where I reflect on the blessings in my life. Focusing on the present and being productive brings inner peace. It's been a journey of growth and gratitude.

During difficult times, it's easy to feel insignificant and overwhelmed. But we are so much bigger than the challenges we face. If we can harness the power of these obstacles and use them to spread positivity to others going through similar struggles, we can make a real difference in our lives and those around us. That is how we *scale our compassion. "Humanity must take precedence over any religious dogmas."*

Our actions should be guided by empathy and compassion towards one another while respecting different beliefs, but not at the expense of fundamental human rights and values.

It's vital to acknowledge that our own personal biases and beliefs interfere with our ability to truly understand the nature of God. It's paramount to remember that theologians only have a limited understanding of God's wisdom and knowledge. God speaks through all of us, not just those who have theological training or claim to be the incarnation of Jesus.

The Bible and quantum science both reveal that the universe is probabilistic and our knowledge is limited. Denying this reality is denigrating the Bible. Recognizing our human limitations and acknowledging the biases that shape our perceptions help foster humility and compassion. It's a fact that our upbringing plays a crucial role in shaping our beliefs and values. This realization is especially significant for individuals who spread the teachings of the Gospel, as we must remain mindful of our own biases and avoid disregarding those who hold divergent opinions.

"We are all human, and our shared humanity should be a unifying force rather than something that divides us based on our biased beliefs."

I hope I have inspired you to "rethink" and ask yourself these powerful questions:

Why do you believe what you believe? Are you truly living by these truths or just paying them lip service?

Seek the Truth, Find Jesus: <u>Walk the Talk</u>
(Truth cannot be <u>inconsistent</u> with the truth)

1. **"Do not conform to the behavior of this world but be transformed by the renewing of your mind"**—*a call to rethink,* break free from indoctrination, and embrace a mindset of abundance. It's easy to fall into the trap of conformity and follow the masses or the majority. *"Be different from the crowd."*
2. **"The kingdom of God is with you"**—we all carry a divine spark within us, and by tapping into this inner power, we can unlock our full potential. *We are beautiful within.*
3. **"God created mankind in his own image"**—treat ourselves and others with respect and honor. We are *"valuable,"* not *"worthless."*
4. **"Lead us not into temptation"**—a great reminder to stay true to our values and resist the negative influences of seeking *validation.*
5. **"Clothe ourselves with humility"**—reminds us to stay grounded and keep learning. *Jesus chose a donkey.*
6. **"The love of money, not the money, is the root of all evil"**—a warning against the dangers of greed and materialism. *God does not need our money but our love, devotion, and good deeds.*
7. **"Forgive as the Lord forgave you"**—Just as the Lord forgave us, forgive ourselves and others. *Holy communion is a one-time deal to seek inner peace, not an ongoing practice of self-loathing.*
8. **"We come from dust, and we shall return to dust"**—serves as a poignant reminder of *our own mortality.* It urges us to make the most of each day, cherish every moment, and seek meaning in our lives.

Conclusion

My Secular Approach to Spirituality

"You are your own therapist. Be mindful of your thoughts and emotions."

"Our existence in this universe is intertwined, and it's important that we acknowledge the impact of our consciousness on creating a sustainable environment that fosters emotional and mental well-being for humanity to thrive. Spirituality nurtures our value and worth, transforming us into better versions of ourselves. Embracing a secular spirituality can help us create open spaces for conversations that promote a sense of belonging and interconnectedness, allowing us to build a stronger community."

I truly believe that spirituality is not confined to any specific religion. Instead, I take a secular approach to religion and combat the animosity and hatred that often stems from religious dogmatism. It's all about discovering the truth through science and keeping an open mind about the possibility of finding our own paths toward enlightenment. This non-judgmental perspective helps me connect with others on a deeper level and keeps me grounded in my beliefs. As the bible says, the kingdom of God resides within us, and I am convinced that we can all tap into that inner wisdom if we are willing to seek it out. Believing that we should treat ourselves with kindness and compassion and that our challenges are divine interventions for growth can lead to greater strength and resilience.

The beautiful version is within us—look after ourselves. Ironically, we don't adopt this growth mindset in our faith and ignore this truth at our own peril. Instead, *we pray solely for triumphs in life.*

Spirituality is a journey of self-discovery that demands a resolute and proactive approach. I believe in nurturing a strong and personal connection with the universe that empowers me to gain a better understanding of myself and the world around me. Acknowledging that bias is inherent in everyone on this planet is essential to cultivating self-love and compassion towards others. Sadly, many traditional religious structures often fail to promote an inclusive, compassionate, and loving approach to humanity. Instead, they create division and hatred, which leads to our suffering.

For our mental and emotional well-being, we must rethink the way we think.

So, I incorporated mindfulness meditation into my book to make it more practical.

Our brains possess the incredible ability to rewire themselves, and by consciously being aware of our behavioral patterns, we can tap into the power of neuroplasticity to become better versions of ourselves. This, in turn, enables us to become kinder and more compassionate towards ourselves.

I am a recovering, egotistical, and angry person. I used to be so self-absorbed and quick to get angry at the slightest provocation at home, work, and outside. Overcoming these destructive traits took a lot of self-reflection and hard work. I've discovered that my negative inner voice only exacerbates my feelings of self-doubt. I often felt like

I must completely change myself just to fit in. This lack of self-compassion leads to self-disgust or self-loathing. Mindfulness meditation has been incredibly transformative, especially when I experience depressive thoughts that can be overwhelming at times. It's like a form of self-psychotherapy that helps me tap into the pure potential of my mind. *I refer to it as getting closer to God*, and it's essential for my spiritual enlightenment. I have learned to accept the nature of realities, control my thoughts and emotions, and become more compassionate. It's not that I lacked empathy or compassion towards others. I just neglected my own mental and emotional well-being in the process.

I am privileged to have the energy and focus to make the most of every moment.

The mind truly holds the key to our well-being. It is the invisible barrier that separates our sufferings from our inner peace. When we learn to harness the power of our minds, we can unlock endless possibilities and achieve true happiness.

With patience and practice, we can strengthen our minds and overcome any obstacle that comes our way. So, let us focus on cultivating a healthy and positive mindset and watch as our lives transform before our eyes—bring our minds to the present moment.

With this exercise, I want you to ask yourself two questions:
1. *"Why do I feel stuck in my current situation?"*
2. *"What steps can I take to improve my circumstances?"*

These are critical questions that require honest introspection and action.

Our emotions influence our feelings. How we feel is not how things are. So, it is important to make sense of these feelings (name it to tame it) and understand where they come from. Our destructive thoughts generate emotions and hinder our cognition—attention, memory, and learning. Case in point: I often worry about not doing a good job when embarrassed and nervous about public speaking.

I ask myself,

"How can I alter my nervousness?"

Practice!

"As you saw, so shall you reap."

Yes, it did help me become calmer and more clearheaded.

Marcus Aurelius said,
"Very little is needed to make a happy life; it is all within yourself, in your way of thinking."

I've been pondering the "Who am I" question lately.

It's crucial for me to take some time to think about my passions, strengths, and values and not let others' perceptions of me define who I am. When I focus on myself and my feelings, I become more self-aware and can better control my thoughts and emotions. I've also learned that forgiving myself—not dwelling on negative experiences and being tormented by them—is crucial to living a happy life. This will help me release any anger, resentment, or guilt that may be holding me back. I have the capacity for kindness, caring, and compassion, and I strive to be a better version of myself by shifting my mindset.

If you are interested in practicing mindfulness meditation, I have compiled a set of steps you can follow.

Mindfulness Meditation Exercise

"Transcending my destructive emotion and transforming my life."

I am not an expert in mindfulness meditation, nor have I taken a meditation retreat. As I discussed in my introduction, my life is my retreat. I have learned these steps from practitioners of Buddhist philosophy. In addition to the steps outlined below, many helpful tools and materials can be found online.

I often find myself entangled in destructive thoughts. One among them is my relationship with my child. Although my child turned out exactly as I had envisioned, and I am proud of her accomplishments, I often reflect on my past parenting decisions. My child's upbringing—the influence of her parents, relatives, friends, schools, and church significantly shapes her behavior. As a parent, it's my responsibility to guide and support my child in developing self-awareness and compassion for herself and others. Unfortunately, I fell short in this regard, as I struggled to control my own emotions.

I have often wondered if I should have been more attentive to my child's intense feelings of loneliness due to not having a sibling, her challenges at school and home, and her relationships outside of our family. Looking back, I realize I missed opportunities to listen to her without judgment. I often have automatic thoughts whenever I see children of her age struggling with health issues or young ladies in my classroom going through learning disabilities or other emotional problems. The consequences of these thoughts are that I feel sad and regretful. As a result, it could lead me into a depressive state, or I could use those moments to bring my mind to the present moment.

I choose the latter.

I take a few minutes every day (20-25 minutes) and practice mindfulness meditation—to observe the beauty and sacredness of the present moment.

Mindfulness meditation is a helpful tool to gain control over destructive thought patterns and strengthen our cognition. It is a great way to break away from the egocentric illusions that cloud our minds during difficult times. It is not a feel-good moment or bliss or instant gratification. With regular practice, we can strengthen our cognitive control and become more stoic, positively impacting all aspects of our lives and rippling out positively around us. There are no moments of failure in my meditation practice as long as I take my attention off my depressive thoughts and use them to be in the present moment.

Finding inner peace can be challenging, but with these six steps, it becomes achievable:

Six steps to finding the "inner peace"

1. Start by finding a comfortable posture that allows you to relax and let go of any tension in your body.

2. Set a compassionate intention or a positive motivation that aligns with your values and aspirations (see the "FORU" below).

3. Take a moment to focus on your breathing using the 4-7-8 breathing technique.

4. Bring awareness to your body, noticing any sensations or areas of tension.

5. Use focused breathing to explore your inner landscape in three phases: *focus on the breath, notice when your mind wanders, and return to the breath.*

6. Finally, end with a compassionate intention or a prayer, expressing gratitude for this moment of "peace and presence."

Mindfulness Meditation

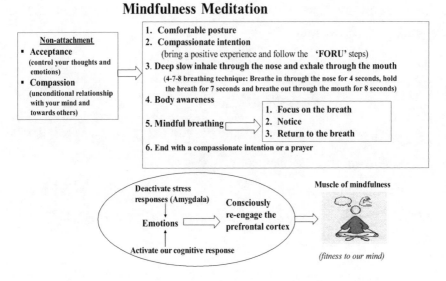

Source: Author and Gelong Thubten[31] (a Tibetan Buddhist Monk)

1. A comfortable posture

Sit upright, feet flat on the ground with your eyes closed, or gaze down at the space in front of you. Imagine yourself sitting on a beach, looking at the horizon where the sky meets the ocean. You are that space, and the waves in the ocean and clouds in the sky are your thoughts and emotions. It's a peaceful feeling that reduces stress, improves focus, and brings greater emotional balance.

---

[31] Author of Handbook for Hard Times: A Monk's Guide to Fearless Living and A Monk's Guide to Happiness: Meditation in the 21st Century

2. Set a compassionate intention or a positive motivation

I recite the following intentions to settle my mind more compassionately:

FORU

May my meditation practice help me:

Fight my anger, resentment, animosity, and hatred toward others with love, compassion, kindness, generosity, and forgiveness.

Observe and listen to others non-judgmentally so I can make meaningful connections with others.

Rejoice in the joy or success of others instead of being envious and jealous.

Build Unconditional compassion towards my own mind and others.

Source: Author

Reciting these intentions brings a sense of calm and compassion to my mind. I approach meditation with kindness and grace, allowing me to face life's challenges with patience and understanding. My mind was consumed by anger and resentment, fueling the release of cortisol due to past wounds. However, through meditation, I have been able to detach from these thoughts and reflect more constructively on the situation. I have gained a deeper understanding of human suffering and ignorance, which has resulted in me feeling more compassionate and forgiving towards others. Acting with compassion and love has proven to be a powerful tool for creating *positive change within myself. I moved from the dopamine-driven, self-centered, and addictive life of <u>pleasure</u> to something that serves the world, creating an <u>inner sense of happiness</u>. That positive energy has a ripple effect on those around me. Shifting my mindset activates the release of oxytocin, bringing about an unexpected sense of connection and bonding that I never knew was possible.*

3. 4-7-8 Breathing technique

Take a moment to focus on your breathing, inhale slowly through your nose for 4 seconds, then hold your breath for 7 seconds, and exhale gently through your mouth for 8 seconds, releasing any tension or stress from your body. Repeat this process three times.

4. Body awareness

Take a moment to become aware of your body. Feel the ground beneath your feet and the connection between your body and the chair. Notice your shoulders and hands resting on your legs or knees. Take a moment to focus on any pain or tightness you may be experiencing, but acknowledge it and let it be. Feel the sensation of the clothes and shoes that you are wearing. Then, shift your focus to your abdomen and notice its expansion and contraction as you breathe.

Becoming more body-aware makes you feel more present and grounded in the moment.

5. Focused breathing: three phases

- *Focus on the breath:* Focusing on your breath helps you center yourself and stay present in the moment. Soon, you will start loving the feeling of the air flowing in and out of your nostrils, and it helps you let go of any worries or distractions weighing you down.

  If you are having trouble focusing on your breath, use the visualization technique:

  Imagine yourself sitting on a beach, looking at the horizon where the sky meets the ocean. You are that space, and the waves in the ocean and clouds in the sky are your thoughts and emotions.

  It's a peaceful feeling that reduces stress, improves focus, and brings greater emotional balance. As you manifest yourself in that space, you feel your worries and distractions fade away, and you can take deep breaths and stay present in the moment. It's such a peaceful and calming experience, and it always leaves you feeling refreshed and re-energized.

- *Notice:* Have you ever noticed that sometimes your mind can take a stroll down a path of wandering thoughts and discomforts? It's okay; it happens to everyone. When this happens, it's important to acknowledge any feelings or

375

sensations that arise without expressing them. Instead, try to observe and experience them. As you focus on your breath, your mind may get distracted. This is a natural part of the mindfulness process. You are strengthening your cognitive control by being aware of your recurring thoughts and gently bringing your attention back to your breath.

It's like giving your mind a workout, just like you would for your body with exercise. The repetition and concentrated emotional intensity can even boost neuroplasticity. I've found that it can be challenging to keep my emotions in check sometimes. Whenever I make a decision, my feelings tend to rush in and take over, making it hard to stay level-headed. I've experienced a range of emotions, from shame and guilt to sadness and even anger. It can be challenging to deal with the physical symptoms of these emotions, like a tightness in my chest, itching, or headaches. However, I try not to be too hard on myself. I remind myself that it's normal to have these emotions and that they're a natural part of life. I "accept" the reality of the situation and have "compassion" for those who have hurt me. I also try to be compassionate towards myself and my feelings. I can only control my thoughts and emotions, so I make a conscious effort to observe my destructive emotions without judgment. Instead of beating myself up, I tell myself to "bring it on" or stress myself and interrupt negative thoughts with positive ones. Over time, this process helps me overwrite negative emotions with positive ones, fostering a stronger sense of positivity.

By allowing all of my negative emotions to surface and experiencing them fully, I find that they slowly melt away. My negative emotions are like the waves in the ocean—they come and go, ebb and flow. It's a natural part of life. We can pass through them and connect with the stillness underneath. By connecting with my mind, I can navigate through these waves and find peace within myself. This exercise is all about being present and aware of my surroundings, thoughts, and feelings.

- *Return to the breath:* Gently bring your mind back to the breath, and be in the present moment again.

  Practicing focused breathing for 15-20 minutes daily and using micro-moments throughout the day helps me stay present in the moment. Mindful eating, washing my hands, cooking, and walking are all great ways to bring my mind back to the present. Even when I am uncomfortable or physically unwell, I accept it instead of pushing it away and use that sensation to stay in the present moment. Bringing mindfulness into my everyday life brings much joy and fulfillment.

  I am not downplaying the beneficial effects of mind

wandering. Sometimes, deciding whether to focus solely on the present moment or allow our minds to wander and explore new ideas can be challenging. However, it's important to remember that letting our minds wander can lead to innovative breakthroughs and exciting discoveries.

Mindfulness is about managing our negative thoughts and emotions to avoid getting stuck in a cycle of stress and anxiety. By staying in control of our minds, we can achieve a sense of peace and clarity that allows us to thrive personally and professionally.

6. End with a compassionate intention or a prayer

As I reflect on my spiritual journey, I have come to realize that having a compassionate intention is essential to bringing peace into my life. I understand that connecting my happiness with material prosperity is not the path to cultivating "inner peace." Seeking material possessions from the divine power leads to misery since it creates a conditional relationship with my mind—I'm happy if I have those possessions, happy when I acquire them, or happy because of them. I understand that this pleasure is transient and that finding joy in the present moment and showing gratitude for what I already possess is the intrinsic power of happiness. This thinking has allowed me to achieve inner peace and a deeper spiritual connection.

I feel a deep sense of purpose and direction in my life, as if I am guided by the divine hand. Meditation is a humbling and awe-inspiring experience that fills me with a sense of gratitude and joy each day. Whether I am helping others, pursuing my passions, or simply going about my daily routine, I know that I am exactly where

I am meant to be, doing exactly what I am meant to do. I am lucky I can breathe.

This is my short prayer encompassing everything I have laid out in my meditation practice:

Almighty God, what a gift it is to be alive. Thank you for the abundant mercy and grace I receive every day. Lord, you have the power to heal and transform my thoughts and emotions. Help me make hard choices to fight my adversity, hardships, and struggles and grow even stronger with my inner sense of peace in mind, body, and soul. Let that inner sense of peace, love, kindness, and compassion reign wherever I am. Help me to follow my passion and purpose in life. Help me to be inspired in your presence to make a positive difference in my life and the lives of many around me. Help me to clothe myself with humility towards others. I understand that my struggles and difficulties are divine interventions to strengthen and improve me. Help me transcend the stereotypical nature of this world and harness the amazing power and potential of the inner sense of happiness. We are all connected as one. Help me to be less self-obsessed and more aware of my environment: the air we breathe, the water we drink, the food we eat, and the people we interact with are interdependent. Help me build an inner sense of self-esteem to be a positive force for the common good; at minimum, I intend to help others. Help me transform my destructive emotions, think clearly under stress and difficulties, and have the grit and resilience to face the world rather courageously. Help me reduce my implicit bias or discriminatory behavior towards others, be less judgmental, and be more in a listening mode so I can build meaningful relationships with others. Help me find the kingdom of God, the eternal happiness within. "Who I am" within is more powerful, happier, and healthier than "what I am." Help me bring my mind to the conscious awareness of who I am and to be present.

Managing negative thoughts and feelings can be challenging. Whenever you face setbacks, challenges, or discomfort, use it as an opportunity to practice mindfulness. By doing so, you will find a sense of peace and calm amidst the chaos.

With one word, I sum up my life: ***Impermanence***.

In life, I face an unending problem of impermanence:

My thoughts evolve, my appearance changes, love dissipates, relationships disappear, excitement quickly fades away, and my desire for material well-being leads to more misery. Solving it means sinking into the present moment, not living in the past or worrying about the future. That contemplative thinking—the practice of self-awareness—transforms my life.

Holding onto anger, seeking revenge, or harboring hate causes us to suffer and prevents us from healing and growing.

Love yourself.

What makes me happy?
My Book!

My book is the culmination of my life's work and the legacy I hope to leave behind. I know I came with nothing and will leave with nothing, but my wisdom lives on. For me, that's what gives life its meaning. I firmly believe that knowledge is one of the greatest gifts we can give. By sharing my experiences and insights with others, I contribute to collective knowledge that can help guide future generations.

One of my students approached me after the class and shared that I had skipped my usual few minutes of offering wisdom to the class and gone straight into my lecture. She confided in me that she had been recovering from depression and that even just a few minutes of sharing my life experience would have been beneficial for her. I am grateful for the opportunity to impact the lives of my students positively, and if I can make a difference to just one, then I have fulfilled my purpose on this planet.

You are all special. Love you all!

Thank You Note from the Author

I wanted to take a moment to express my sincere gratitude to you for taking the time to read my book, **"Rethink Your Way of Thinking."** Your support means the world to me, and I am truly humbled by it. Every cloud has a silver lining, and my struggles have proven that to be true. I feel incredibly fortunate to have turned my sufferings into something positive, and I hope my journey can help you navigate your own struggles.

Even more meaningful for me is that the proceeds from sales of this book will go towards helping neglected, orphaned, and underprivileged children build their mental and emotional resilience. Every child deserves a chance to thrive, and I am committed to doing my part to make that happen. With your support, I hope to reduce the number of starving children with hopeless faces. In addition, I dream that my book will one day be adapted into a documentary or movie so that even more people can benefit from my life experience. I have already started on the journey towards making that dream a reality, having created a short film a few years ago, which is now available on my YouTube channel, "Shajan Ninan."

I firmly believe that the stories and theories presented in this book will inspire you to transform yourself. Together, we can make a positive impact on the world. Let's continue to work towards a brighter future for all.

Please stay in touch!

Instagram: shajan.ninan

Acknowledgment

Let me share my experience of writing this book. Whenever I thought that I had done a great job with it, but as time passed, I realized that it was getting better and better. What is my take on this experience? "The best is yet to come." My experience highlights the importance of continuous improvement and the ever-evolving nature of our thoughts.

The seeds for this book were planted two years ago, not knowing that it would take countless hours and an army of people to bring it to fruition. I couldn't have done it without the incredible support of my students. They took the time to read my book and provide valuable feedback, which helped refine my ideas and make the book even better. I'm so grateful for their support and encouragement. The most inspiring part of my book is the power of vulnerability. It allows us to connect with others on a deeper level. By sharing my own stories and experiences, I connected with my students on a deeper level and helped them see that they were not alone in their struggles. By including their stories and testimonials in the book, I hope to amplify their voices and inspire others to share their stories. Hearing the incredible stories of my students and how my stories resonated with them was truly moving. They are my celebrities, and I'm incredibly proud of them. I hope this book will offer the new generation a new perspective on life and help them navigate all the challenges with courage and compassion. *Let the beneficiaries of this book be the ones who share its message. This way, their voices will be at the forefront of my effort to ease human suffering, making it even more compelling.*

Praise and Feedback from Students

I really enjoyed reading your book, and I read it for 6 hours because I was eager to read what was next. I found pieces of my life in that book.

I found myself while reading about your childhood. I was in a class where all the other kids were wealthy and spoiled by teachers. I had to work twice as hard as the others to achieve my goals. I had a goal: never letting others push me down. I wanted to prove to them that I could do whatever I wanted. Looking back, I should thank those people for telling me I would never make it because they pushed me to work hard.

I have a strong relationship with my father. We have a special bond with each other—a bond between a father and daughter. I am very grateful to my parents because they have always supported all my choices, which has helped me believe in myself more. I read about your experience as a father, and I am glad you understand and admit your problems. It is very important to us that our father listens to our problems.

It's undeniable that the difficulties you faced during your childhood have had a profound impact on your relationship with your daughter. However, your book has the power to shed light on a different side of the story, one that your daughter may not have fully understood before.

I totally agree with the idea that if you want to change the world, start changing yourself. I remember when I first came to the USA, I saw that people were very selfish and unfriendly. I went into class and said, "Good morning," and nobody answered, even the professor. I was shocked but never stopped saying it and asking, "How are you?" At the end of the semester, my professor asked, "What would you remember from this semester?" and many students said: "The girl who never stopped saying good morning even though nobody answered." That warmed my heart, and I understood that everyone is dealing with their problems every day, and if we have a chance to brighten their day, why not? – **Manduela Xhaxho**

------- ◆ -------

The only way I could begin my review is to take a moment and appreciate all the hard work and effort you put into writing this book. It was one that I thoroughly enjoyed reading for an individual who rarely finishes a book. From the very first page, it was evident how real and open you would be. There wasn't any mask or persona to put on, but it was you being extremely genuine and vulnerable in sharing your life experiences. So, thank you once again for being you in your book and not being anything else.

Listed below are key statements from your book that made me rethink my way of thinking (pun intended).

1. "Ultimately, success is more about mastering our thoughts and emotions than anything else." While reading this line, I couldn't help but pause and reflect on how I measured my success as a student. Growing up in a typical Nigerian household, I was always taught the importance of getting good grades, which I strived to achieve each semester. While it brought my parents and family enormous joy, the moments of happiness would only last a minute for me before fleeting away. It became a vicious cycle of trying to relive those short

moments of joy at the end of every exam season. This line made me realize that my happiness isn't tied solely to my grades. Rather than waiting until the end of each semester to be happy, I can make a conscious effort to be happy throughout the semester. My goal during my remaining college semesters isn't necessarily to pass all my classes with straight A's (although I would make an attempt to) but to learn and build meaningful connections along the way.

2. "I only now understand that my mistakes and failures were opportunities for growth and learning." Accepting the importance of failure in one's journey towards success was something that took me a while to understand. I couldn't bear the thought of failure; I did everything possible to avoid failing. However, as I read your story, I realized if I was running away from the thought of failure, I was only limiting myself from growing. As much as failure is feared, it is essential. We, as humans, need to fail along the way to explore opportunities for growth and learning.

3. "Your life must be transformational, not transactional." This is one of my favorite statements. It clearly depicts how much our society has fallen. Nowadays, every relationship/interaction is merely seen as a business transaction. Everyone walks with an invisible sign on their forehead saying, "What can you give/offer me for my time, love, and respect?" As individuals, we need to make a conscious change to do better and adopt a service lifestyle attitude.

– Tomi Olaopa.

———•◆•———

This book is profound and personal for every person who reads it. Why? Because everyone is on their own spiritual journey, whether they realize it or not. This makes you sit back and think about life, family, past, present, and future. Something that everyone needs to do from time to time. Not to be sad about it but to realize how far a person has come; this book does that.

You stated in the book that "the father" is the invisible parent. I can attest that society tends to give almost all the credit to moms and none to dads. You chose to give all the credit to your wife and honor her. This is a testament to your selflessness and dedication as a father. Your focus on your child and her well-being is truly admirable. It's clear that your joy comes from being a father to your child, and this is a powerful message that should inspire other fathers to prioritize their role as a parent.

The struggles you have been through alone and with your family are a book in itself, but you are showing the mental toughness not to be defeated by the obstacles you had and the mental calmness to revise your thinking and make it through. I feel that the calmness that comes into a person's life is through the experiences and what you have learned through these life lessons.

I had to Rethink My Thinking to teach my children and family that even though times might seem hard, there is a bright side to all things and/or a reason that people may not know yet... but there is. I learned to take time and meditate (just 10-15 mins) every day. Sitting quietly and just BEING was weird initially, but now it is nice. Thanks to you. – **Jennifer Wilson**

This book is exceptionally well written and has been meticulously put together. It's a great read and draws you in from the start. "You are like God to me."

He replied, "We are all created in the image of God."

It is one of my favorites in the book. It made me live through his reaction because you were so enthralled by this man's actions and the turn of luck that he just knew this was how things were supposed to be.

It's like someone trying a donut for the first time and going crazy about the flavor, and his buddy just saying, "Yep, that's a donut."

Overall, you wrote a book that is a page-turner that shows who you are, what you went through, and how hard work pays off with patience. It's a culmination of your life and shines through into who you are. – **Chris Panagakos**

———◆———

"Wisdom From an Invisible Father – The Shepherd's Way" is an artfully written book filled with anecdotes from the author's life that provide us with numerous lessons and guidance that are universally applicable. Professor Ninan opens up his book by giving readers a brief introduction about himself, where he describes who he is, where he grew up, and how it is that he has navigated life. In doing so, Professor Ninan gives readers a much-needed overview of who he is before diving deeper into the book and gathering knowledge from his experiences.

Professor Ninan has a beautiful way of narrating his life and ensuring that studies and quotations are incorporated seamlessly. He quotes a wide range of sources, whether it be biblical verses, well-known figures such as Einstein, Warren Buffett, and Tom Murphy, essays such as "The Enduring Predictive Significance of Early Maternal Sensitivity: Social and Academic Competence Through Age 32 Years," and even scientific studies such as one conducted by Tasha Eurich.

In the instance where Professor Ninan describes the study conducted on emotional intelligence by Tasha Eurich, he not only presents a summary of her findings in an italicized manner but also weaves in his own experiences where he sees fit. In a sense, this form of writing personifies scientific findings beyond the data as we can see examples from his own life, whether it be from his relationship with his daughter or his own feelings of depression and hopelessness.

Whether it be from his own childhood upbringing - filled with humble beginnings, his journey of discovering his career path as someone who was introverted yet intellectually curious, or the upbringing of his daughter, Professor Ninan's life experiences bring upon many lessons that apply to folks from all walks of life - even those who have never found themselves in positions similar to his.

He teaches his readers to truly seek happiness from within, to embrace everything in life, including the suffering, trials, tribulations, and even frustrations, to aim to break generational curses, and to escape the fixed mindset that hinders our growth and ability to develop as individuals, whether it be through intelligence or skills.

Professor Ninan's book is what one would consider a guidebook for life and restructuring our mindset. – **Melissa Aragon**

———— ◆ ————

I am writing to express my sincere appreciation for your book, "Rethink Your Way of Thinking." As a reader and your student, I was captivated by how you gave a deeper understanding of the importance of mental health and how we develop a positive mindset. I enjoyed reading about your Tuna Sandwich Story. It truly made the reading experience enjoyable and inspired me to be grateful for every little moment. Your biography is a compelling journey through a remarkable life. The storytelling is vivid, providing an intimate look into the highs and lows in your life. I was inspired by the resilience and authenticity portrayed. It is a must-read for anyone seeking genuine stories of triumph. Thank you, Professor Ninan, for sharing your heartwarming biography with the world. – **May Aye**

———◆——

I'm writing to express how much I enjoyed reading "Rethink Your Way of Thinking." As an immigrant and a first-generation college student, your insights on mental health were very relatable. During hard times, your book can turn into a comfortable refuge.

I could relate to your words personally, and they helped me feel better and more aware of my struggles. I was deeply touched by how you talked about your weaknesses while highlighting the value of optimism and resilience. Your helpful tips for reassessing thought processes and cultivating an optimistic outlook gave me a valuable toolkit to help me deal with my particular difficulties. Your book felt more like a friend than a guidebook, providing me with support and direction as I explored myself.

I decided to hold onto a copy of "Rethink Your Way of Thinking" to remind me of the transformative potential of reading continually.

Your dedication to using your writing to assist others is

incredibly admirable, and I would like to sincerely thank you for the positive transformation your words have brought to my life.

Thank you for your contribution to our collective journey toward mental health. Thank you for giving us the chance to read your book. **– Minahil Ishfaq**

———◆———

"Chapter 8, Love What I Do or Do What I Love?"

I chose this chapter to critique because of my own story of finally finishing school this Fall semester, 2023. After a tumultuous run of graduating High School in 2011, working full-time mediocre accounting jobs, admitting myself into an intensive therapeutic community drug rehab, and finally finishing with my B.S. in Public Accounting, this chapter was a good read for me and a retrospective way of thinking about the most crucial concept, of 'unlearning.' Thank you so much for sharing this with the class, especially a Finance class, which I found most challenging in my college life.

Your story beautifully describes your teaching journey and the ongoing effort to improve yourself. Sharing personal experiences, like your first public speaking moment and classroom challenges, makes your story relatable. Being open about moments of self-doubt, like a disappointing student evaluation, adds authenticity and shows your dedication to growing personally and professionally.

Learning from failures and embracing a growth mindset, as highlighted by the concept of 'kaizen,' is commendable. Explaining psychological concepts, such as loss aversion and neuroplasticity, adds depth to your story, showcasing your thoughtful approach to teaching methods and feedback.

Your exploration of 'unlearning' aligns well with the idea of continuous improvement, echoing the philosophy of constant betterment. The analogy of the teacup and wisdom from Lao Tzu effectively conveys the importance of approaching new experiences with an open mind. The Zen master story vividly illustrates cognitive laziness and the challenge of letting go of preconceived notions.

Your emphasis on the difficulty of changing deep-seated beliefs and fear of change resonates with me, coming from a household of Albanian immigrants and being the first in the American generation. Your thoughts on personal growth, embracing imperfections, and the challenges of teaching create a well-rounded view.

Being open about the difficulties faced in education, like the resistance to rigorous standards, adds authenticity and emphasizes that improvement requires courage.

Your story about compassion for students provides a heartfelt understanding of their struggles, especially with mental health. The mention of changing classroom dynamics resonates with my own experience - adapting to the shift in education after COVID-19.

Highlighting challenges as opportunities for growth, especially for students with learning disabilities, brings a positive touch to your teaching philosophy.

Your openness about the consequences of overprotective parenting and the call for independent thinking aligns with creating a resilient society, a sentiment I connect with due to my cultural upbringing.

Discussing acceptance, compassion, and managing emotions contributes to a holistic view of personal development and societal well-being. Critiquing the limitations in the current educational environment adds depth to your analysis, resonating with the challenges faced by teachers striving for meaningful change.

Your reflections offer a mix of personal experiences, educational philosophy, and societal observations, creating a comprehensive and engaging narrative. – **Arita Kuka**

—— ◆ ——

First off, Professor Ninan, I wanted to congratulate you on your book! It was an interesting read. Although I did not get through all of it, the messages inside were thoughtful, and I can tell you carefully crafted the book. I liked the inclusion of quotes in relation to your experiences. Hemingway's quote, "To write about life, first you must live it." resonated with me. I believe that at the beginning of the semester, you mentioned that in your culture, the elderly are looked up to because it is seen that they have more wisdom and life experience. This quote by Hemingway reflected that perfectly.

I also like the fact that you did not try to forcefully change the reader's perspective or views on any particular subject but informed them and encouraged us to look at it from a different point of view. In another book that I read called "Relentless" by Tim S Grover, the author wants the reader to be motivated to achieve greatness and uses famous basketball players' experiences, such as Michael Jordan and Kobe Bryant. Although the experiences were motivational, they didn't share insight into their inner thoughts and growth in difficult times.

Your book shares insights into the culture you grew up in and the issues you had to deal with to grow as a person. At times, it leaves you vulnerable to revealing such information about yourself. I share some of the same introverted qualities that you previously had. I want to be comfortable in my own skin but also grow. In my summer internship, I got out of my comfort zone and interacted with my peers and seniors to be put in uncomfortable situations. In these situations, I learned the nature of the work environment is completely different from the classroom or anywhere else I have been. For example, I had to be proactive and communicate often when I got stuck on something. Being an introvert can be difficult because I struggled with thoughts of "Is this a dumb question?", "What if they don't want to help?" or "Should I even bother asking?" All these thoughts raced in my head when I interned this summer, but I tried my best to learn and persevere.

Your chapter on emotional intelligence was very intriguing and thought-provoking. I feel that I had to be emotionally intelligent during my summer internship. I thought I was asking too many questions, so I would try my best to ask people who were more friendly or receptive to me. It was not that I did not want to talk to certain people, but they did not feel interested in helping the new intern who would be gone in a month or two. I had to remember not to take their attitudes personally since it was a busy season and stress ran high during those times. I can't change their attitudes; I can only control myself not to reciprocate negativity. As per your instruction, I will keep this to a page.

I am sure whoever reads your book comes out with more wisdom than before they started it. Once again, congratulations on your book.
– **David Liu**

———◆———

I found this book very thought-provoking; it makes readers want to stop everything and reflect on themselves. Usually, I do not like to read books from this niche because sometimes I feel other authors are trying to push their newfound beliefs onto their readers. However, since I started this book, I felt no such thing. The book "Rethink Your Way of Thinking" allows readers to choose whether to self-reflect or just read about your journey throughout life. – **Karen Thomas**

———◆———

Your book really took me on a transformative journey through life, drawing from your experiences as a father, husband, and finance professor.

Your book delved deep into a powerful theme: the significance of self-love and the perils of surrendering our minds to external validation. I really enjoyed how you eloquently explored the danger of allowing our environment to define us when we lack inner self-esteem - touching on various aspects of life, from classrooms to workplaces, families, and even the highest echelons of society. Your insights inspired me to reclaim my internal freedom and discover my life's purpose.

One of the most compelling aspects of "Rethink Your Way of Thinking" is Shajan Ninan's unwavering belief that we are all inherently unique. There are no weak, dumb, or bad people; we only become vulnerable when we fail to recognize our strengths and succumb to insecurities that external influences exploit.

"Rethink Your Way of Thinking" is an insightful, thought-provoking, and empowering book that has the potential to reshape the way you view yourself and the world. It invites you to embrace self-discovery and find the path to inner peace.

Shajan Ninan's wisdom resonates deeply, reminding us that true growth and happiness lie within our grasp. This book is a must-read for those who wish to embark on a journey of self-empowerment and discover the remarkable version of themselves that has always existed within. – **Lawrence Tsivinsky**

————◆————

This book was really enjoyable and eye-opening, so thank you for allowing us to read it.

The storytelling is engaging, and this powerful vehicle carries the reader through your journey—from childhood struggles to academic achievements. The themes of resilience, self-discovery, and the pursuit of personal goals are well-woven throughout the book.

One of the highlights for me was the incorporation of quotes throughout the book. These motivational quotes helped further emphasize the key points you were conveying. Among all of the insightful quotes, two stood out for me:

Einstein's, "A ship is always safe ashore, but that is not what it is built for," and Steve Jobs's, "Your time is limited, so don't waste it living someone else's life. Don't be trapped by dogma – which is living with the results of other people's thinking." These quotes resonated deeply with me. It's vital to take advantage of our time and not let it go to waste. It's so important not to worry about things that are beyond our control, and learning emotional intelligence is something that would help us enjoy life more. This is a point that I think your book and these quotes clearly emphasize.

Another strength of your book is the strategic use of visuals to enhance understanding of certain concepts and summarize what you discussed. For instance, the image portraying the downfall of short-term pleasure and the image/chart representing the difference between a fixed and growth mindset helped add value to the chapters they were in and made those chapters easier to learn from.

After finishing the book, my biggest takeaway was learning about the four pillars of happiness, which are crucial to learn and follow to achieve happiness. Thank you for sharing your journey and wisdom through this compelling narrative. – **Gillian Fuchs**

In "Rethink Your Way of Thinking," Shajan Ninan presents a holistic approach to understanding ourselves and the world around us. The book is a heartfelt dedication to his daughter, and the author candidly shares his experience of being emotionally absent as a father. However, he also offers practical ways to correct past mistakes and improve our relationships.

To say this book is interesting is an understatement. It truly taps into my self-consciousness and makes me really rethink what I think. Recently, my Eng. 1012 Professor asked us to free-write "What is happiness to me?" You would be surprised about the different things in life that make one happy and how people seek happiness in different ways and forms. "Happiness is not a state to arrive at, but a manner of traveling." by Margaret Runbeck.

I truly agree with the writer's beliefs that there's no escape from struggling, as our Father, Jesus himself, had to struggle with that cross to acknowledge vulnerability. There are times when we come upon individuals living in some really hard situations, and it brings tears to your eyes, and your heart feels burdened; there's nothing left to do but look to Jesus and be very grateful. We often question ourselves about our struggles and what we don't have, but we don't ever stop being thankful for what we have and what we have accomplished.

What I like most about this book is that it is relatable to every age group. There's a lot to learn and different methods by which we can improve our growth mindset and develop resilience and flexibility to handle life's ups and downs (struggles). The stories cited in the book were not solely derived from Ninan's personal experiences but also included incidents that he encountered daily, such as his finance students, who eagerly anticipated the brief period of meditation before he commenced with his lecture. Just asking how you are and/or how you are feeling does wonders for others. It creates a safe and supportive space; sometimes, that's all you want.

Thank you, Shajan Ninan, for sharing your life's journey, vulnerability, and beliefs. I am open to exploring your beliefs and challenging them when necessary. I will also keep in mind that vulnerability is not a weakness but a strength that can lead to personal growth and deeper connections with others. – **Shanile Powell**

One particular section of your book has captured my attention as it delves deeply into the evolution of modern teaching practices and educational philosophy. I find it admirable how committed the author is to endorsing a comprehensive approach to education. Encouraging students to ask questions, display humility, and maintain their curiosity fosters the development of well-informed minds and curious, adaptable individuals. The author's innovative approach includes challenging ideas and promoting self-discovery through candid discussions. Moreover, the author's forward-thinking mentality is evident in their willingness to challenge accepted norms and discuss stakeholder-centered initiatives, sustainability objectives, and corporate governance. It's truly refreshing to see someone advocating for a more holistic and inclusive approach to education.

I look forward to continuing to explore this section of the book and gaining valuable insights from it. – **Nicole Kapustina**

———◆———

I really enjoyed reading the book as I have never had the opportunity to do so for any professor I have ever had.

Through this book, I have learned a lot about you, which made the book very impactful. One of my favorite quotes is, "Although those moments were excruciatingly painful, they were the best experiences in molding and positively shaping my thoughts and emotions." This moved me as I admire people's ability to recognize that bad experiences are better looked at as lessons or blessings rather than the worst days of our lives. Throughout the book, I think there is a beautiful recurring theme of acknowledging and appreciating.

Everybody wants to love themselves, but it is a goal, not a choice, for many. Overall, I was heavily moved by everything in this book and look forward to it getting published so I can share it.

– **Jacob Olivo**

———◆———

To start, I'd like to say that the book was fascinating and engaging and touched on many topics I've been thinking about recently, making it even more gripping. Even if I had not been contemplating some of these issues recently, it would have been an excellent way to learn about them. While I was reading, I took screenshots of pages with parts I liked or struck me, but as I finished, there were too many for me to integrate into this review.

I especially liked how the correlation was made between being a self-fulfilling prophecy and the neural pathways we create in our brains that follow certain lines of thinking, for example, that if we think negatively about ourselves, we can essentially limit ourselves, versus positive thinking can help us gain opportunities, and such things.

I also very much agree with the fact that colleges in universities are more often than not cesspools for forcing certain ideologies and politics on their students, making it known that a certain line of thinking will not be acceptable, which is a real shame because you wrote, it hinders expansive thinking and people having their own individual thoughts.

Another part that struck me was the bit on racism, and I think it seems that these days, not that many people think that any race is less advanced or anything along those lines, but that everyone is on the offensive because they're scared. One party might be thinking that another is acting a certain way because of their race, when in reality that person is a jerk to everyone, or they're acting a certain way because maybe they feel they're being or will be prejudiced against. I think this also relates to wokeism because, at least for me, I think the fact that it's brought up so much makes it something that people think is happening more often than it is, just because it's on their mind, almost as if you watch a horror movie and then the next day hear hinges squeaking when you're home alone, you might freak out and become paranoid. This is also related to why I think DEI is not a great thing since it almost enforces the idea that certain people might need help getting into specific fields. I think if it were to really be meant to help society, they would use the funding they put into a DEI department to fund schools or educational programs in low-income neighborhoods since those are the people who really need help, which have potential but maybe not the access to utilize all their skills.

I appreciated many other points, but I'll move on to recommendations in the book. In terms of the actual writing, I thought it was very well laid out. – **Maria Brancale**

————◆————

In the book **"Rethink Your Way of Thinking"** by Shajan K Ninan, the introduction gives a breakdown of what to expect from the book. Chapter One discusses emotional intelligence. It shows the importance of emotional intelligence. I try to control my emotions, but it is hard to do. I worked on understanding my emotions and identifying the triggers, and then I learned how to manage my emotions better, as stated in the book. Hopefully, this will help me manage my emotions.

We indeed stress that our children get good grades, and I even stress myself to get good grades. I have two boys. One of my sons will graduate next year; then, he will be heading to college. I told my son that I would not be mad if he put one hundred percent into his work and did everything he was supposed to do and he got a B or C; he did his best, but I would be angry if he did not give a hundred percent in his work and got a B or C.

I agree that it is good for successful leaders and regular individuals to have critical feedback. In that way, the individual may improve him/herself. Sometimes, we need that critical feedback to face reality.

It is sad to read about your childhood experience. However, you learn and grow from those experiences. Now, you are a wonderful young man, and looking back, you will appreciate the happy moments of your childhood more. It is a great idea to have parent support groups. Sometimes, parents don't know how to be a mom or dad. The way parents grow up, and their experiences can affect how they treat their kids. Parents must speak to their kids, listen, and be honest with them. Stop this secrecy. All it does is cause pain. And the kids are the ones who feel it the most. It is shameful that teachers make fun of kids when they are supposed to set examples for students to follow. I am smiling that you have the confidence.

I have not read the whole book, but I have gained more knowledge about you. The book is interesting, and people can relate to your story. I will recommend your book because it tells your story and experiences. Whoever reads **"Rethink Your Way of Thinking"** will learn valuable lessons from this book. This will be an inspiration to others.

Professor Ninan, you are a professor who cares about the students. – **Sheika Ovid-David**

— ◆ —

I realized many things I could relate to as I read the book. You definitely do not seem like an introvert based on how well you speak in class. I understand you are a professor and supposed to talk to us, but you do not look nervous while teaching in class.

At the beginning of the book, you mentioned that there was a time in your life when you questioned, "Why me?" and that is something I have constantly been asking myself since August 24th. That is the date that my knee injury occurred. Throughout my whole life, I felt invincible playing soccer because I never got severely injured. I would get stepped on, pull a muscle, or sprain an ankle, but I would return to the field within a week or so. It was my last year to play this season as a senior, and I lost that opportunity since I tore my ACL during preseason. I was very distraught, and I would constantly ask the same thing, "Why me? Why now?". I know I won't get an answer, but I recently chose to let that go and mentally prepare myself for my upcoming surgery. I have no issue physically preparing for it. The challenging part is mentally preparing myself for what to expect and being very patient with myself.

Working in retail is never easy, and I have been doing it for a little over two years. I would lash out at people and let them get to me. Now, I can just let it go and brush it off. I walk away or do not bother to react because some people want to get a reaction from me.

We all have our own struggles and challenges that we may not always express to others. It's essential to take steps to help ourselves become a better version of ourselves and find happiness within. Your book helped me realize this and made me reflect on my own situation with my knee, which has been one of the most difficult challenges I've faced.

I also struggle to deal with my emotions and do not like others to see me cry because the way I grew up, it was shown as a sign of weakness. My father raised me with tough love, and as you mentioned, it did discipline me, but I would not express my emotions. In February 2022, my aunt passed away from COVID-19. It was the first time I felt what it was to lose someone and to grieve. With the help of other family members and close friends, I realized it is okay to express and talk about your feelings.

This book should be recommended for young adults, such as college students, to read and help them reflect on their behaviors. It is a very beneficial book that enables you to understand yourself and what you must work on. Everyone struggles and faces obstacles, but we must determine if we let those challenges define us.

– Sandra Erostico

———■ ◆ ■———

This book resonated with me in ways I hadn't anticipated. As someone who lectures in the classroom, it was enlightening to read about their personal journey outside the lecture hall. The author, whom I've known as a respected educator, opens up about their life, struggles, and the grind behind their success. This book brought light to the unseen side of success. The story of someone coming from a humble village in India and facing their own challenges really struck a chord. It made me realize that success isn't just about grades, achievements, or the public accolades we see; it's about wrestling with inner struggles, often unseen and unspoken. The narrative isn't just about success but the grueling journey to get there.

What touched me the most was the openness and rawness of the author's reflections. They admit to their flaws and vulnerabilities, shedding light on their battles behind the scenes. This vulnerability and authenticity gave a new perspective on the realness of success – it's not just about wins; it's about the setbacks, the personal growth, and the sheer grit to persevere. Reading this completely shifted my idea of success. It's not just about the outcome but the rollercoaster ride - the hurdles, the reflections, and the constant uphill climb.

Professor Ninan's story stands out as a living example of the fact that success isn't just a destination; it's a transformational journey that demands self-discovery, growth, and resilience. The courage displayed in sharing personal struggles and vulnerabilities is admirable. It's a reminder that success is a result of resilience, learning from failures, and finding strength in adversity. The Professor's willingness to share the hardships behind their success humanizes the very concept of achievement.

In conclusion, this book clarifies that success is more than just a glossy, picture-perfect endpoint. It's the rough, emotional journey and the fight to get where one wants to be. Professor Ninan's personal account reflects grit, humanity, and the reality of success, which is often overlooked in the face of public achievements. – **Oren Izraelov**

———◆———

When I read your book "Rethink Your Way of Thinking," I was amazed by the stories you shared. Even though stories with similar situations can be a part of our daily lives, it's inspiring to see how others have overcome their difficult times and become successful and respected individuals like you, Professor.

Your book inspired me to deal with the ups and downs in my life. It made me reevaluate the situations I am going through and take them more lightly and responsibly. The book is truly remarkable in its diversity and covers all aspects of life, from building a successful career to finding your true path, caring for your loved ones, and cultivating a close relationship with God.

It's a beautiful reminder of what life is all about. Your journey has been inspiring, and I am confident this book will inspire many people who are still searching for their path in life to work hard toward their dreams and trust God in the process, just like you did.

I am grateful that you shared your book with us, and I will recommend it to all who are going through difficult times and need inspiration to regain their strength. – **Anna Madoyan**

———◆———

I can only imagine the incredible journey you must have had to get to where you are today—growing up in a small town in India, wearing shirts made by your mother out of her own clothes, and constantly worrying about how others perceived you. And yet, despite these challenges, you made it to college, taught yourself a new language, and faced so many other obstacles with courage and determination. Your achievements are remarkable, and you should be incredibly proud of your accomplishments. Your story inspires me. – **Tammy Ziegler**

———◆———

My outlook on life has taken a complete turn since I read the book. Professor Ninan's life experiences have taught me so much about myself, how I treat others, and how I plan for my future. Initially, I never thought I would be so invested in mental health and well-being, but now I see the book as a guide to living a balanced, humble, and successful life. One message that resonated with me is how we often take our freedom of thought for granted, especially in America. We are taught not to fear failure but to learn from our mistakes and start over. Professor Ninan's journey embodies the American dream, starting from scratch and working hard to become successful. He learned a new language, left his comfort zone to start a new life, and struggled to build his career while caring for his family. However, his determination and commitment paid off, and he now shares his knowledge with others. I am lucky to have Professor Ninan not only as a financial mentor but also as a guide to a successful and happy future.
– **Marc Smouha**

———◆——— ———◆——— ———◆——— ———◆——— ———◆———

Notes

INTRODUCTION. DON'T RETREAT: FACE LIFE AND LEARN FROM IT

Curtis, Rick. "Quote of the Day." Upper Peninsula Homes, 04 Mar. 2019, upperpeninsulahomes.com/2019/03/04/quote-of-the-day/. Accessed 14 Nov. 2023.

Dowell, Erin, and Marlette Jackson. "Woke-washing" your company won't cut it." Harvard Business Review 27 (2020): 1-7.

Grant, Adam. "A Key to Better Leadership: Confident Humility." Knowledge at Wharton, 6 Dec. 2022, knowledge.wharton.upenn.edu/article/a-key-to-better-leadership-confident-humility/. Accessed 14 Nov. 2023.

Grant, Adam. Think again: The power of knowing what you don't know. Penguin, (2021).

Gutierrez, Elizabeth Rene. "The Enemy of Our Soul." Day's Journey, 27 July 2022, lisarenedelgado.org/2022/07/23/the-enemy-of-our-soul/.

Hunt, Dame Vivian. Stakeholder Capitalism: The Practical Guide to Stakeholder Capitalism" - McKinsey Report. Accessed 14 Nov. 2023.

Robyn. "Your Life Is Not About You." Partners in Mindful Living, 2 Sept. 2018, partnersinmindfulliving.com/your-life-is-not-about-you/. Accessed 14 Nov. 2023.

Skenazy, Lenore, and Jonathan Haidt. "The fragile generation." Reason 49.7 (2017): 18.

CHAPTER 1. EMOTIONAL INTELLIGENCE AND SUCCESS IN LIFE

Chamorro-Premuzic, Tomas. "Talent matters even more than people think." Harvard Business Review. [online] Available at: https://hbr. org/2016/10/talent-matters-even-more-than-people-think [Accessed: 15 July 2018] (2016).

Dancharoenpol, Phakkhaporn. "The influence of perceived value, user engagement, and emotions on usage intention of Thai Tiktok users." (2022).

Eurich, Tasha. "What self-awareness really is (and how to cultivate it)." Harvard Business Review 4 (2018).

Goleman, Daniel, et al. Self-Awareness (HBR Emotional Intelligence Series). Harvard Business Press, 2018.

Goleman, Daniel. "Emotional intelligence. Why it can matter more than IQ." Learning 24.6 (2005): 49-50.

Murtoff, Jennifer. "Emotional Intelligence." Encyclopædia Britannica, Encyclopædia Britannica, inc., 11 Oct. 2023, https://www.britannica.com/science/emotional-intelligence. Accessed 14 Nov. 2023.

Perlman, Marc, and Kaywana Raeburn. "The association between willingness to take risks with type-specific intensity of chronic pain." Journal of Pain Management 14.2 (2021).

Roland, Olivier. "Emotional Intelligence." Books That Can Change Your Life, 19 Apr. 2021, books-that-can-change-your-life.net/emotions-intelligence/. Accessed 14 Nov. 2023.

Tominey, Shauna L., et al. "Teaching emotional intelligence in early childhood." YC Young Children 72.1 (2017): 6-14.

CHAPTER 2. MEMORIES OF MY EARLY CHILDHOOD

Birch, Liz. "Ten Concrete Tips to Help You Get Motivated." *Anxiety & Depression Therapy - Orange County CA - Liz Birch, LMFT*, 20 Feb. 2017, www.lizbirchtherapist.com/blog/archives/02-2017. Accessed 14 Nov. 2023.

Cherry, Kendra. "What the Bobo doll experiment reveals about kids and aggression." *International Journal of Social Science* 6.3 (2020): 11-34.

Gladwell, Malcolm. "Outliers (book)." (2008).

Sharifian, Neika, and Laura B. Zahodne. "The enduring effects of mother–child interactions on episodic memory in adulthood." *Journal of Marriage and Family* 81.4 (2019): 936-952.

Swart, Ronel. *Towards a prospectus for Freirean pedagogies in South African environmental education classrooms: Theoretical observations and curricular reflections.* Diss. University of Pretoria, 2009.

Tominey, Shauna L., et al. "Teaching emotional intelligence in early childhood." *YC Young Children* 72.1 (2017): 6-14.

CHAPTER 3. INSATIABLE DESIRE TO SUCCEED

"PLANET_JUPITER8." Teen Ink, www.teenink.com/users/planet_jupiter8. Accessed 14 Nov. 2023.

"Self-Fulfilling Prophecies." Self-Fulfilling Prophecies | World Problems & Global Issues | The Encyclopedia of World Problems, 08 Mar. 2022, encyclopedia.uia.org/en/problem/140824. Accessed 14 Nov. 2023.

Kmichelizzi. "Self Fulfilling Prophecies: Why Do We Even Speak It?" myMusings, 22 Jan. 2014, www.michelizzi.com/self-fulfilling-prophecies-why-do-we-even-speak-it/. Accessed 14 Nov. 2023.

Latham, Nick. "Nobody's Perfect." *RAFT*, 14 Oct. 2013, raft.ac.uk/nobodys-perfect/. Accessed 14 Nov. 2023.

CHAPTER 4. A FOGGY FUTURE

Cherry, Kendra. "How Self-Handicapping Can Sabotage Your Chances of Success." *Verywell Mind*, Verywell Mind, 4 Oct. 2023, www.verywellmind.com/self-handicapping-protecting-the-ego-at-a-cost-4125125. Accessed 14 Nov. 2023.

CHAPTER 5. EMBRACE THE BEAUTY OF LIFE AND ALL OF ITS STRUGGLES

"The Teen Brain: 7 Things to Know." National Institute of Mental Health, U.S. Department of Health and Human Services, 2023, www.nimh.nih.gov/health/publications/the-teen-brain-7-things-to-know. Accessed 14 Nov. 2023.

Morah, Chizoba. "Stock Warrants vs. Stock Options: What's the Difference?" Investopedia, Investopedia, 11 June 2020, www.investopedia.com/ask/answers/08/stock-option-warrant.asp. Accessed 14 Nov. 2023.

CHAPTER 6. MY CRUSADE TO EDUCATE MY CHILD

Harding, Amanda. "Naeyc: Teaching Emotional Intelligence in Early Childhood Education." Children's Cabinet, 23 July 2021, www.childrenscabinet.org/event/naeyc-teaching-emotional-intelligence-in-early-childhood-education/. Accessed 14 Nov. 2023.

Moriarty, Pat. "The Real Work of a Paper Boy." *Just A Thought*, 20 Mar. 2021, justathoughtbypat.com/2021/03/. Accessed 14 Nov. 2023.

Perlman, Marc, and Kaywana Raeburn. "The association between willingness to take risks with type-specific intensity of chronic pain." *Journal of Pain Management* 14.2 (2021).

Goleman, Daniel. *The brain and emotional intelligence: New insights.* Vol. 94. Northampton, MA: More than sound, (2011).

Dweck, Carol. "The Power of Believing That You Can Improve." Carol Dweck: The Power of Believing That You Can Improve | TED Talk, Nov. 2014, www.ted.com/talks/carol_dweck_the_power_of_believing_that_you_can_improve.

"The Inverted-U Theory - Balancing Performance and Pressure with the Yerkes-Dodson Law." MindTools, 2023, www.mindtools.com/ax20nkm/the-inverted-u-theory. Accessed 14 Nov. 2023.

Arnold. "What Is the Yerkes Dodson Law." Law Info, 7 Oct. 2020, bartleylawoffice.com/faq/what-is-the-yerkes-dodson-law.html. Accessed 14 Nov. 2023.

Jensen, Les. "Reactive Patterning." New Human Living, 5 Aug. 2022, newhumanliving.com/tag/reactive-patterning/. Accessed 14 Nov. 2023.

CHAPTER 7. LESSONS FROM MY FAILED STARTUP

Chu, Robin. "Business model revolution: Four cases of the fastest-growing, disruptive companies of the twenty-first century." *Revolution of Innovation Management: Volume 2 Internationalization and Business Models* (2017): 145-189.

CHAPTER 8. LOVE WHAT I DO OR DO WHAT I LOVE?

"African Proverb: 'It Is Easier to Carry an Empty Cup than One That Is Filled to the Brim.'" The List of World Proverbs, 14 Nov. 2023, www.listofproverbs.com/source/a/african_proverb/182502.htm. "Desirable Difficulties in Learning" - BOLD. https://bold.expert/desirable-difficulties-in-learning/. Accessed 14 Nov. 2023.

Goleman, Daniel and Michele, Nevarez. "Boost your emotional intelligence with these 3 questions." *Harvard Business Review* 16 (2018).

Harrison, Kim. "Harnessing the Power of Emotions in Messaging." Cutting Edge PR, 7 Nov. 2021, cuttingedgepr.com/articles/capitalize-on-powerful-emotions-in-your-messaging/. Accessed 14 Nov. 2023.

Valentine, Valentine. "What Is a Toxic Relationship? Early Warnings." *Valentine Day Quotes*, 26 Sept. 2022, valentinedayquotes.in/what-is-a-toxic-relationship/. Accessed 14 Nov. 2023.

CHAPTER 9. WOKEISM AND FRAGILITY

Astin, Alexander W., and Helen S. Astin. "Achieving equity in higher education: The unfinished agenda." *Journal of College and Character* 16.2 (2015): 65-74.
Dowell, Erin, and Marlette Jackson. "Woke-washing" your company won't cut it." *Harvard Business Review* 27 (2020): 1-7.

CHAPTER 10. A HOLISTIC APPROACH TO TEACHING AND LEARNING

"Discount Factor Calculator." The Z Group, 15 Mar. 2023, www.thezgroupmiami.com/discount-factor-calculator/. Accessed 14 Nov. 2023.
"Efosa Ojomo – the Power of Market-Creating Innovation." YouTube, YouTube, 30 Sept. 2019, www.youtube.com/watch?v=kQOO8P42GAI. Accessed 14 Nov. 2023.
"HR Compliance Archives." Berger HR, 2023, www.bergerhrsolutions.com/category/hr-compliance/. Accessed 14 Nov. 2023.
"Noble Purpose" - The research behind Lisa McLeod's best-selling books, "Selling with Noble Purpose" and "Leading with Noble Purpose."
"Proxy Fight." Wikipedia, Wikimedia Foundation, 28 July 2023, en.wikipedia.org/wiki/Proxy_fight.
Asness, Clifford, et al. "American Enterprise Institute Roundtable: Was Milton Friedman Right about Shareholder Capitalism?" *Journal of Applied Corporate Finance* 33.1 (2021): 36-47.
Carr, Donielle. *Dancing with Death: Performances of Resistance in the Virtual Churchyard.* Diss. University of Colorado at Boulder, 2021.
Christensen, Clayton M. "How will you measure your life." *Harvard Business Review* 88.7/8 (2010): 46-51.
Christensen, Clayton M. "Where Does Growth Come from? Free Summary by Clayton M. Christensen." getAbstract, Talks at Google, 2016, 2016, www.getabstract.com/en/summary/where-does-growth-come-from/41701. Accessed 14 Nov. 2023.
Christensen, Clayton M., Stephen P. Kaufman, and Willy C. Shih. *Innovation killers: how financial tools destroy your capacity to do new things.* Harvard Business Review Press, 2010.
Dallisson, Matt. "Managing Shareholders in the Age of Stakeholder Capitalism." Matt Dallisson Global Executive Search | Leadership Consulting, 7 Sept. 2022, mattdallisson.com/leadership/managing-shareholders-in-the-age-of-stakeholder-capitalism/. Accessed 14 Nov. 2023.
Diaz, Gwen. "95 - David and Goliath." My Daily Briefing, My Daily Briefing, 5 Apr. 2023, www.mydailybriefing.org/post/david-and-goliath. Accessed 14 Nov. 2023.

Gladwell, Malcolm. "The Unheard Story of David and Goliath." Malcolm Gladwell: The Unheard Story of David and Goliath | TED Talk, Sept. 2013, www.ted.com/talks/malcolm_gladwell_the_unheard_story_of_david_and_goliath. Accessed 14 Nov. 2023.

Gladwell, Malcolm. *David and Goliath: Underdogs, misfits, and the art of battling giants.* Little, Brown, 2013.

Gonzalez, Mike, and Katharine Gorka. *How Cultural Marxism Threatens the United States—and How Americans Can Fight It.* No. 262. Heritage Foundation Special Report, 2022.

Govindarajan, Vijay. "We are nowhere near stakeholder capitalism." *Harvard Business Review* (2020).

Hanif, et al. "IMPACT OF ACQUISITIONS ON SHORT-AND LONG-TERM VALUE CREATION AT MICROSOFT CORPORATION, PERIOD OF 2011–2021."

Joly, Hubert, et al. "Getting Serious about Stakeholder Capitalism." HBR Store, 24 May 2021, store.hbr.org/product/getting-serious-about-stakeholder-capitalism/BG2102#:~:text=Business%20can't%20thrive%20in,executives%20 must%20rethink%20their%20mission. Accessed 14 Nov. 2023.

Joly, Hubert. "A time to lead with purpose and humanity." *Harvard Business Review* 24 (2020).

Mahmud, Nur Ahmed. "The Poverty in Somalia: How Can Economic Reform Policies and Conflicts Destroy a Country's Way of Life?" (2021).

Marquis, Christopher. "Creating Shared Value: Entrepreneurial and Corporate Models for a Changing Economy." (2015).

Negri, Ryan. "Too Big to Fail Two." RyanNegri.Com, 19 Mar. 2023, ryannegri.com/too-big-to-fail-two/. Accessed 14 Nov. 2023.

Saffold, Guy. "Leading From Behind: The Shepherd's Way." Leading Gods Way, 15 Dec. 2016, saffold.com/blog/2016/. Accessed 14 Nov. 2023.

Serafeim, George. "Can index funds be a force for sustainable capitalism." *Harvard Business Review* (2017).

Serafeim, George. "CAN Index Funds Be a Force for Sustainable Capitalism?" Harvard Business Review, 7 Dec. 2017, hbr.org/2017/12/can-index-funds-be-a-force-for-sustainable-capitalism#:~:text=Index%20funds%20can%20be%20a,product%20or%20servi ce%20or%20category. Accessed 14 Nov. 2023.

Sundheim, Doug, and Kate Starr. "Making stakeholder capitalism a reality." *Harvard Business Review* 22 (2020).

Tearle, Oliver. "12 of the Best Stories from the Bible Everyone Should Know." Interesting Literature, 2023, interestingliterature.com/2022/04/best-stories-from-the-bible/. "Proxy Fight" – Wikipedia. https://en.wikipedia.org/wiki/Proxy_Fight. Accessed 14 Nov. 2023.

Tearle, Oliver. "A Summary and Analysis of the David and Goliath Story." Interesting Literature, interestingliterature.com/2021/05/david-and-goliath-story-summary-analysis/. Accessed 14 Nov. 2023.

CHAPTER 11. WHY ARE WE SO SENSITIVE?

"Malcolm Gladwell on Problems with Modern Policing and How They Played out in Sandra Bland Case." YouTube, YouTube, 7 Oct. 2019, www.youtube.com/watch?v=FZSHpHwz0jk. Accessed 14 Nov. 2023.

"Psychiatrist Has 'fantasies' of Murdering White People." Asian Dawn, 7 June 2021, www.asian-dawn.com/2021/06/08/psychiatrist-has-fantasies-of-murdering-white-people/. Accessed 14 Nov. 2023.

"U.S. Senate: Art & History." U.S. Senate: Art & History, 11 Jan. 2017, www.webharvest.gov/congress114th/20170111234033/http:/www.senate.gov/art/art_hist_home.htm. Accessed 14 Nov. 2023.

Chester Grant, www.chestergrant.com/?page=5. Accessed 14 Nov. 2023.

Conatz, Juan. "'Baltimore Unrest' Thread." Libcom.Org, 27 Apr. 2015, libcom.org/discussion/baltimore-unrest-thread?page=1. Accessed 14 Nov. 2023.

Grant, Adam. Think Again. Penguin Publishing Group, (2021): 139-140.

Gurmej. "Why Being Boring Is the New Cool ." Meji Media Events Group - Events & Experiences At Your Fingertips, 6 May 2019, www.mejimedia.com/why-being-boring-is-the-new-cool/. Accessed 14 Nov. 2023.

Kick, News. "Psychiatrist Says She Does Not Regret Telling Yale Students About Fantasy Of Killing White People, Claims Her Words Were Taken 'Out Of Context.'" TAthasTA, 2019, www.tathasta.com/2021/06/psychiatrist-says-she-does-not-regret_8.html. Accessed 14 Nov. 2023.

Longley, Robert. "The Civil Rights Act of 1866: An Early Step towards Equality." ThoughtCo, ThoughtCo, 4 Oct. 2022, www.thoughtco.com/civil-rights-act-of-1866-4164345. Accessed 14 Nov. 2023.

NOR AZIZAH BINTI HJ ABD RAHMAN Moe. "Give-and-Take." FlipHTML5, 13 Feb. 2021, fliphtml5.com/wtjzh/xgwv. Accessed 14 Nov. 2023.

Popat, Rajiv. "Managers and Their Self-Fulfilling Prophecies." Rajiv Popat - ThousandtyOne! - .NET, Life and Logical Thoughts by Rajiv Popat, 27 Dec.2016, www.thousandtyone.com/blog/ManagersAndTheirSelfFulfillingProphecies.aspx . Accessed 14 Nov. 2023.

CHAPTER 12. OPTIMISM: THE PERILS OF IGNORANCE

"Malcolm Gladwell on Problems with Modern Policing and How They Played out in Sandra Bland Case." YouTube, YouTube, 7 Oct. 2019, www.youtube.com/watch?v=FZSHpHwz0jk. Accessed 14 Nov. 2023.

"Psychiatrist Has 'fantasies' of Murdering White People." Asian Dawn, 7 June 2021, www.asian-dawn.com/2021/06/08/psychiatrist-has-fantasies-of-murdering-white-people/. Accessed 14 Nov. 2023.

"U.S. Senate: Art & History." U.S. Senate: Art & History, 11 Jan. 2017, www.webharvest.gov/congress114th/20170111234033/http:/www.senate.gov/art/art_hist_home.htm. Accessed 14 Nov. 2023.

Chester Grant, www.chestergrant.com/?page=5. Accessed 14 Nov. 2023.

Conatz, Juan. "'Baltimore Unrest' Thread." Libcom.Org, 27 Apr. 2015, libcom.org/discussion/baltimore-unrest-thread?page=1. Accessed 14 Nov. 2023.

Grant, Adam. Think Again. Penguin Publishing Group, (2021): 139-140.

Gurmej. "Why Being Boring Is the New Cool ." Meji Media Events Group - Events & Experiences At Your Fingertips, 6 May 2019, www.mejimedia.com/why-being-boring-is-the-new-cool/. Accessed 14 Nov. 2023.

Kick, News. "Psychiatrist Says She Does Not Regret Telling Yale Students About Fantasy Of Killing White People, Claims Her Words Were Taken 'Out Of Context.'"

TAthasTA, 2019, www.tathasta.com/2021/06/psychiatrist-says-she-does-not-regret_8.html. Accessed 14 Nov. 2023.

Longley, Robert. "The Civil Rights Act of 1866: An Early Step towards Equality." ThoughtCo, ThoughtCo, 4 Oct. 2022, www.thoughtco.com/civil-rights-act-of-1866-4164345. Accessed 14 Nov. 2023.

NOR AZIZAH BINTI HJ ABD RAHMAN Moe. "Give-and-Take." FlipHTML5, 13 Feb. 2021, fliphtml5.com/wtjzh/xgwv. Accessed 14 Nov. 2023.

Popat, Rajiv. "Managers and Their Self-Fulfilling Prophecies." Rajiv Popat - ThousandtyOne! - .NET, Life and Logical Thoughts by Rajiv Popat, 27 Dec. 2016, www.thousandtyone.com/blog/ManagersAndTheirSelfFulfillingProphecies.aspx. Accessed 14 Nov. 2023.

CHAPTER 14. FOUR PILLARS OF HAPPINESS

Carli. "The Most Important Question to Ask Yourself." Carli Gribov, 6 Jan. 2022, www.carligribov.com/post/the-most-important-question-to-ask-yourself. Accessed 14 Nov. 2023.

Christensen, Clayton M. "30 Best Clayton M. Christensen Quotes of 32." The Cite Site, thecitesite.com/authors/clayton-m-christensen/. Accessed 14 Nov. 2023.

Grant, Adam: Page 263

HBR: "How Hospitals Are Using AI to Battle Covid-19" - Keystone. Wittbold, Kelley A., et al. "HBR: How Hospitals Are Using AI to Battle Covid-19." Keystone, 3 Apr. 2020, www.keystone.ai/news-publications/harvard-business-review-how-hospitals-are-using-ai-to-battle-covid-19/. Accessed 14 Nov. 2023.

Heimburger, Franziska. "#DHIHA5 Panel II: Training for the Digital Humanities – What Skills Are Necessary, How Can They Be Transmitted?" Digital Humanities à l'Institut Historique Allemand, 6 May 2013, dhiha.hypotheses.org/1004. Accessed 14 Nov. 2023.

Lagaé, Maxime. "82 Innovation Quotes to Make You More Creative." Wisdom Quotes, 10 Mar. 2022, wisdomquotes.com/innovation-quotes/.

Mineheart, Rebecca D., et al. "What's Your Listening Style?" *Harvard Business Review*, 31 May 2022, hbr.org/2022/05/whats-your-listening-style. Accessed 14 Nov. 2023.

Walker, Martin. "Good intentions in risk management and the LDI crisis." *Journal of Risk Management in Financial Institutions* 16.3 (2023): 228-236.

CHAPTER 15. MY CHRISTIAN FAITH

Durmonski, Ivaylo. "What Is Internal Validation and Why Do You Need It?" Durmonski.Com, 31 Jan. 2023, durmonski.com/psychology/internal-validation/. Accessed 14 Nov. 2023.

FELKINS, MARY A. "The Man Who Threw a Rock." Mary's Website, 24 June 2016, www.maryfelkins.com/post/the-man-who-threw-a-rock. Accessed 14 Nov. 2023.

Grant, Adam. *Think again: The power of knowing what you don't know*. Penguin, 2021.

Hovis, Peter A. "'forgive, as the Lord Forgave You.' (Colossians 3:13)." "Forgive, as the Lord Forgave You." (Colossians 3:13), 9 Dec. 2022, www.nearermygod.com/2022/12/forgive-as-lord-forgave-you-colossians.html. Accessed 14 Nov. 2023.

Vardycharlotte. "'boethius Proved That God's Omniscience Is Compatible with Human Free Will.' Discuss (40)." Logos, 20 Oct. 2017, divinityphilosophy.net/2017/10/20/boethius-proved-that-gods-omniscience-is-compatible-with-human-free-will-discuss-40/. Accessed 14 Nov. 2023.

Sam Harris: Page 284, "If priests dressed up ....."

CHAPTER 16. FIND YOUR AUTHENTIC SELF

"Psalm 103:8." Bible Hub, 2023, mail.biblehub.com/psalms/103-8.htm. Accessed 14 Nov. 2023.

"Thank You, Jesus Ministries." THANK YOU JESUS, 7 Aug. 2014, www.tyjministries.com/thank-you-jesus-blog/august-07th-2014. Accessed 14 Nov. 2023.

Borden, Ginger. *"Why Paradigm Shifts Are the Secret to a More Fulfilling Life and Business."* Ginger Starr Borden, Ginger Starr Borden, 28 Jan. 2022, www.gingerstarrborden.com/post/why-paradigm-shifts-are-the-secret-to-a-more-fulfilling-life-and-business. Accessed 14 Nov. 2023.

Grant, Adam. Think Again. Penguin Publishing Group, (2021): 240.

Rodriguez, Leslie. "Your Complete Guide to Paying Priests for Things - Catholic-Link." Catholic, https://catholic-link.org/your-complete-guide-to-paying-priests-for-things/. Accessed 14 Nov. 2023.

CHAPTER 17. A MARRIAGE MADE IN HELL

Edblad, Patrik. "How to Deal with Difficult People." Patrik Edblad, patrikedblad.com/stoicism/deal-with-difficult-people/. Accessed 14 Nov. 2023.

"Quotes by Elder Gary E. Stevenson." LDS Quotations, 2023, ldsquotations.com/author/gary-e-stevenson/. Accessed 14 Nov. 2023.

CONCLUSION. MY SECULAR APPROACH TO SPIRITUALITY

Hiruni, W. Deep Breathing Techniques, 22 May 2020, https://runcoach.com/index.php?option=com_k2&view=item&id=574:deep-breathing-techniques&Itemid=444. Accessed 14 Nov. 2023.